Faces of the Future

— the lessons of science fiction

Faces of the Future

— the lessons of science fiction

BRIAN ASH

Elek/Pemberton London

Published in Great Britain in 1975 by
Elek Books Ltd,
54—58 Caledonian Road, London N1 9RN
in association with Pemberton Publishing Co. Ltd.
88 Islington High Street, London N1 8EN.

ISBN 0 236 31004 6

Printed in Great Britain
by Unwin Brothers Limited
The Gresham Press, Old Woking, Surrey
A member of the Staples Printing Group

Contents

For Edmund — who thinks more science fiction than he writes.

One Moment in Annihilation's Waste,
One Moment, of the Well of Life to taste —
The Stars are setting and the Caravan
Starts for the Dawn of Nothing — Oh,
                    make haste!

Rubáiyát of Omar Khayyám, translated
by Edward Fitzgerald

1 Sense of Wonder

The human mind is lit by an elemental sense of wonder, a probing, restless curiosity that is our primate heritage and that from its beginnings has sought a knowledge, some knowledge, of the future. To satisfy that need as it exists today there has come into being a massive and thoroughly modern creation, science fiction, the literature of extrapolative, industrial man.

William Tenn, introduction to *Of All Possible Worlds*

In essence, all fiction is a dream of life. Throughout history the contemporary author, attempting to record his personal interpretation of human existence in a conventional form, has drawn upon the images and schemes of the world as it appears to him to be. This is the measure of his own experience as he apprehends it — and he colours his literary palette accordingly. He concentrates on accepted realities, making free with them as his particular brand of creativity demands. Alongside him, however, since the beginning, an adjacent space has been filled by another species of writer — one who has sought to extend the framework of his canvas and to set his action against a portrayed reality which patently does not exist. To him we owe the great fantasies and allegorical flights of imagination which range in time from Homer's *Odyssey* to Orwell's *Animal Farm*; and to him also we can attribute the particular form of literary endeavour which, with some diffidence, can be described as 'science fiction'.

In his *Profiles of the Future* Arthur C. Clarke, whose ability as a visionary has earned him a respected place in the factual world of science, announced in 1962 that *only* readers or writers of science fiction were really competent to discuss the possibilities of the future! The italics are his own — and, admittedly, more than a decade has passed since he made that sweeping claim. But Clarke was hardly suggesting that serious studies of scientific and socio-economic possibilities, although of necessity they must take a short-term view, are not being conducted elsewhere. He was simply claiming that a full consideration of future prospects requires the kind of speculative imagination — together with what Coleridge poetically called 'willing suspension of disbelief' — which can only be found in the realms of science fiction.

1

What, then, is science fiction? Theodore Sturgeon, a leading practitioner in the genre, once alarmed an audience of devotees by declaring that 90 per cent of science fiction is — worthless. To which he added: but isn't that true of 90 per cent of *everything*? Without necessarily agreeing with either remark, it is not difficult to see what he meant.

A definition of science fiction can be attempted in twenty words and remain unachieved in two thousand. As a type of writing it is much easier to describe than to define. In the course of this study many examples of the genre will be examined which may at first sight strike the rational mind as ridiculous. They could be satire, allegory, fantasy, or simply straightforward speculation — and, as often as not, they may have a macabre humour all of their own. Regardless of labels, they frequently yield meaning and critical observation of human behaviour at more than one level. But it should be emphasized that they are *only* examples, culled from a very extensive field to illustrate various points of view. Those well acquainted with science fiction will undoubtedly argue that there are many others which could have been chosen — and indeed there are.*

There is also a considerable accumulation in the genre of what have become known as 'space operas', and which are really no more than unsubtle reworkings of the kind of adventure themes that have already been ground inexorably into the upper stratum of planet earth. This is not to decry their value as vehicles of entertainment, but to admit — at the risk of eternally offending those enthusiasts who hunger after accounts of mile-long space-ships — that they are irrelevant to our purpose here.

Nevertheless, it should be borne in mind that even the 10 per cent of science fiction which Theodore Sturgeon has described as being of value was originally offered as entertainment; although, in company with other entertainments — particularly those of a speculative nature — much of it provides insight into the curious paradoxes of man. (For many the first paradox of science fiction could still be that it is taken seriously at all. However, the days when the great bulk of it appeared between the garishly illustrated covers of pulp magazines are beginning to recede; and enough reputable publishers have now added science

*Throughout the text, the year of first publication is given wherever it could be identified — it does not always coincide with the copyright date which has later appeared against a reprint of the work concerned in anthologies, collections or foreign editions. On the very few occasions when research proved unprofitable, no precise date is given, but the period in which the work was written is usually made clear.

fiction sections to their lists to suggest, to any but the committed sceptic, that there could be more to the genre than topless space-waitresses struggling in the grips of hairy octopods from Mars. Science fiction also boasts a long and notable ancestry, which we shall examine in due course.)

It is quite possible to class almost the entire serious side of the genre under the divergent headings of 'utopian' and 'anti-utopian' writing, in which the future is seen as more (or less) agreeable than the present day according to the predilections of the author. Before we come to consider definitions, it is worth looking in some detail at an example of the science fiction story at its best. In one of the classic latter-day anti-utopias, *The Space Merchants* by Frederik Pohl and C.M. Kornbluth, many of the features which identify modern science fiction are handled with imagination and a collaborative skill for which the two authors are rightly renowned.

The novel, which originally appeared as a serial entitled *Gravy Planet*, is set in an America of the fairly immediate future. There the growth of giant business empires has hastened the complete decline of democratic government. The corporations nominate their own senators and congressmen to represent them, and the function of the Presidency has been relegated to that of an office boy. The entire society is organized on a relentless production-consumption basis, its morals — what few of them remain — being dictated wholly by the shallow and cynical ethics of the advertising industry. The story relates the fall from grace of one Mitchell Courtenay, a star-class copysmith in the advertising agency of Fowler Schocken Associates who has been assigned the task of handling the exploitation of the planet Venus.

Courtenay's agency is closely allied with the monolithic Starrzelius corporation, which manufactures every conceivable consumer product and is threatened by only one equally power-ful rival. The extent of the Starrzelius operation can be gauged by its success in merging the whole Indian sub-continent into a single manufacturing complex! As the story opens, the board of Fowler Schocken are reviewing the progress of the latest Starr-zelius beverage, 'Coffiest', which is currently being sampled in fifteen key cities. The executive in charge of the account brings his report to a close with a eulogy on the product's unique selling proposition:

'But — and here's what makes this campaign truly great, in my estimation — each sample of Coffiest contains three milligrams of a simple alkaloid. Nothing harmful. But definitely habit-forming. After ten weeks the customer is hooked for life. It would cost him at least five thousand dollars for a cure, so it's simpler for him to go right on drinking Coffiest — three cups with every meal and a pot beside his bed at night, just as it says on the jar.'

It is an interesting reflection on the population density of the time that the Chairman of Fowler Schocken is inordinately proud of a directors' conference room — where this opening meeting is held — which measures exactly ten feet by twelve. He also finds it in keeping with their star-class social status that none of his fellow directors enjoys less than a two-room apartment for a home. As the narrative unfolds, the extent of the plunder of natural resources in the holy name of profit becomes chillingly clear. The supply of unpolluted fresh water is curtailed by drastic rationing; it is available at a price, but sea water is normally tapped for all household and personal chores. Natural wood has become so rare that it is fashioned into jewellery as a commodity more valuable than gold. Synthetic food is the order of the day, unless one is prepared to pay dearly. The petroleum reserves of the earth are so near to exhaustion that private transport — for those who can afford it — has reverted to the same means of propulsion which graced the sedan chair, or to the atavistic use of pedals. As Courtenay recalls: 'Science is *always* a step ahead of the failure of natural resources. After all, when real meat got scarce, we had soyaburgers ready. When oil ran low, technology developed the pedicab.'

The ordinary citizens of this economically expanding society — those below star status — suffer a life of slavish devotion to the social benefits of the free enterprise system. For anyone of even moderate standing to be overheard criticizing the ethical content of an advertisement is to risk downgrading to a production centre which is more a penitentiary than a place of work. However, a rebellious underground does manage to exist. It consists of dedicated conservationists, brutishly referred to as 'Consies', who risk a form of brainwashing which will bequeath them a twenty-year spell of mental agony if they are captured.

With the return of the first successful manned flight to Venus, Starrzelius and the Fowler Schocken agency have for the time being acquired the commercial advantage over their competitors for the development of the new world. Their prime objective is

4

to recruit fifteen hundred potential settlers who will embark on a giant spaceship, already nearing completion, as an initial step in earth's colonization of its nearest planetary neighbour. It is no easy task. The Venusian atmosphere consists of a murky unbreatheable gas; and at ground level violent dust storms rage perpetually, accompanied by sheets of lightning. But it is not the problem of selling an idealized image of Venus which Courtenay finds his major obstacle—advertising possesses a bevy of techniques to take care of that, and his agency has already signed up the one space pilot to return from Venus alive. Courtenay spares a few minutes to explain to him the greater mystique of advertising:

'"Here in this profession we reach into the souls of men and women. We do it by taking talent and — redirecting it. Nobody should play with lives the way we do unless he's motivated by the highest ideals."

"I get you", he said softly. "Don't worry about my motives. I'm not in this thing for money or fame. I'm in it so the human race can have some elbow room and dignity again."

"That's it", I said, putting on Expression Number One. But inwardly I was startled. The 'highest ideal' I had been about to cite was Sales.'

What bother Courtenay are the recurring attempts which are made on his life within a few days of his accepting the Venus assignment. In the normal course of events the assassination of a rival's top executives is part of accepted business procedure — so long as the competing organization files a formal notification that it is engaging in a feud. In the case of the Venus project, however, no such representation has been made; at least so Courtenay's Chairman informs him, at the end of a lecture on his responsibilities:

'He sat down and lit a Starr. After just exactly the right split second of hesitation, he pushed the pack to me. "Mitch, you're a youngster, only star class a short time. But you've got power. Five words from you, and in a matter of weeks or months half a million consumers will find their lives completely changed. That's power, Mitch, absolute power. And you know the old saying. Power ennobles. Absolute power ennobles absolutely."

"Yes, sir", I said. I knew all the old sayings. I also knew that he was going to answer my question eventually.'

5

Courtenay is still in doubt whether the Consies or a competitive agency — or both — are after him, when he is suddenly kidnapped and awakes to find himself precipitated with a false identity into the lowest level of a remorseless production combine. After gruelling months in a situation where he is provided with first-hand evidence of the appalling quality of life at the opposite end of the production-consumption pipeline, he joins the local Consie cell who quickly recognize his talents as a propagandist. However, his alignment with the conservationists is no indication of a change in his basic loyalties; he simply sees it as an opportunity to escape to 'civilization' as a Consie agent and there to denounce the movement in return for his old job. Like most well-laid plans, it meets with complications which he could not have foreseen.

Once back on his home ground he is promptly abducted by the principal rival agency, Taunton's. Only after a series of murderous encounters is he able to confront his own Chairman during an unofficial visit to the moon. Finally reinstated at Fowler Schocken, he surrounds himself with a platoon of armed bodyguards, vainly attempting to persuade his Chairman to follow suit. When that gentleman is discovered garotted in a pedicab, Courtenay acquires supreme control of the agency. But by now he is beginning to entertain real doubts regarding the system he is dedicated to serve:

'The interests of producers and consumers are not identical;
Most of the world is unhappy;
Workmen don't automatically find the job they do best;
Entrepreneurs don't play a hard, fair game by the rules;
The Consies are sane, intelligent, and well organized.
In a dissociated fashion that would have delighted Fowler Schocken and his analyst, I said to myself: "You know, Mitch, you're talking like a Consie".'

A major factor in Courtenay's conversion is the revelation that his wife, with whom he has a trial marriage which she refuses to make permanent, has herself joined the conservationists. It was she who arranged his original kidnapping in an effort to convert him to their views. Thereafter he manipulates the power of Fowler Schocken Associates to ensure that the pioneers recruited for Venus are wholehearted Consies. Following a last-minute denouement in the House of Congress where he is denounced by the head of Taunton's, he is hustled aboard the

Venus spaceship moments before lift-off.

*****

The Space Merchants, with its logical extrapolation of the present-day growth of multi-national corporations, the now current concern for the conservation of natural resources and the problem of population explosion, is an imaginative projection of a future which could well exist for want of adequate controls. Only its major ideas have been touched on in the foregoing outline; but they are sufficient to show the extent of social criticism which the book contains. None of them, when we think about it, is particularly unlikely. The kidnapping of business executives, and their murder, has already become a major hazard in South America and elsewhere. If at present it is confined to the operations of urban guerillas, it is easily conceivable that it could develop from there — once a course of action has been established its aims tend to become diverse.

Massive production complexes which to all intents and purposes own their workers are already in existence in Japan, although their treatment of employees clearly does not presently compare with the conditions described in *The Space Merchants*. It is the callous manipulation of the consumer by the manufacturers and their advertising agents, and their complete disregard for human values, which is one of the most disagreeable aspects of the story. As Courtenay says: 'Increase of population was always good news to us. More people, more sales. Decrease of IQ was always good news to us. Less brains, more sales.' Every aspect of the novel points, in fact, to the perils of a future in which industrial societies have allowed themselves to be persuaded of the necessity for continuous economic growth. Admittedly, there are some enlightened politicians and public commentators, together with the advocates of conservation, who are talking of these dangers today; but so far none has been able to portray them as graphically, and with such dramatic effect, as Kornbluth and Pohl in *The Space Merchants*. What makes it all the more remarkable is that the book is not a recent arrival of the last two or three years. It was first published two decades ago in 1953 — only four years after Orwell's *Nineteen Eighty-four* — when few people were thinking much about conservation. Few people, that is, except the writers of science fiction.

Acquaintance with *The Space Merchants* makes it easier to

appreciate more fully the somewhat terse definition of science fiction in Webster's *Third* and *Seventh New Collegiate* dictionaries: 'fiction dealing principally with the impact of actual or imagined science upon society or individuals'. Frederik Pohl himself has amplified this to better effect in his introduction to *Ninth Galaxy Reader* (1965):

'It isn't really science fiction's business to describe what science is going to find. It is much more science fiction's business to say what the human race will make of it all. In fact, this is the thing — the one thing, maybe the only thing — that science fiction does better than any other tool available ... It gives us a look at consequences. And it does it superbly.'

H. Bruce Franklin added one further qualification in his 1966 collection of early American stories in the genre, *Future Perfect*, by calling science fiction 'the literature which, growing with science, evaluates it and relates it meaningfully to the rest of existence'.

Most speculative writing is basically a response to the opening question 'What would happen if ...?' In the less high-flown variety that question may be confined to a prosaic level, for example: 'What would happen if', let us say, 'a new widespread influenza or similar virus left most of the inhabitants of the British Isles with lifelong chronic catarrh?' (It could be argued that this is an unlikely proposition, but few would maintain that it is completely impossible.) The extrapolation might run:

Striking developments would occur in the pharmaceutical and tissue manufacturing industries;
Culinary arts would turn increasingly to the preparation of more highly-spiced foods to take account of the new, diminished physical sense of taste;
People would have to speak louder, since chronic catarrh usually affects the hearing; telephones and other communication devices would have to be adjusted accordingly; the Noise Abatement Society could find itself out of a job;
The English language would undergo various shifts in pronunciation as a result of universal nasal congestion;
And so on, if necessary, *ad absurdum*.

It is easy to see how, in the hands of an imaginative writer, a possibly comic tale could be set against some such background. The central character, for instance, might be conceived as an

8

individual who had successfully avoided the virus, only to find himself a disadvantaged outsider in a subtly changed society. What would he do — wear ear and nose plugs to make himself socially acceptable?

Such a story could reasonably be categorized as science fiction — because the writer had imagined the outbreak of a virus as a possible future event which would have scientific as well as sociological implications. Of course, if the catarrh had been occasioned instead by automotive emissions resulting from a newly-developed petrol additive, the tale would have that much firmer a science fiction footing. In either case, the ingenuity of people to adapt to, and hopefully to overcome, the impediments of a changed biological condition would almost certainly involve some known or future application of science.

This intentionally lightweight example of a speculative proposition shows that it is unnecessary for a good science fiction story to begin with some startlingly original premise. But, as we shall discover, many of them do. Suppose that opening question were to ask 'What would happen if, at some date in the future, a scientific technique were evolved which would enable a man to travel into the past for the purpose of liquidating his own great-grandmother before she had produced any young?' This seemingly impossible suggestion, if it is followed through, gives rise to a series of paradoxes in both philosophy and physics which has proved irresistible to writers of science fiction. Would the man disappear without trace the very instant after committing the act, since he would presumably have destroyed the historical basis for his own existence? On the other hand, would he have existed at all to make the journey through time if, in the past, his great-grandmother had already died by what might have been regarded in her day as supernatural intervention? These are simply the opening questions in what becomes a progressively more complex argument as it goes along.

The concept of time travel, if we are to understand its resultant paradoxes, demands what in our present state of scientific ignorance we can only call, echoing Coleridge, the 'willing suspension of disbelief'. Should this appear too heady a proposition, it is worth noting that modern nuclear physics requires a similar mental approach of any layman — or scientist for that matter — who has the temerity to invade its inner sanctum. The theory of anti-matter, to take a 'straightforward' example, first propounded by Adrian Dirac at Cambridge in

9

1931 when he discussed the possibilities of the anti-electron, was vindicated a year later at the California Institute of Technology. There the existence of such a particle was discovered by Carl D. Anderson. He named it the 'positron'. Thus it became acceptable to conceive of anti-matter as composed of particles bearing an opposite electrical charge which, when they collided with ordinary matter, induced an explosion of mutual annihilation. Seventeen years later, again at the California Institute, Richard Phillips Feynman argued that positrons were actually no more than electrons briefly *moving backwards in time* before they came to their annihilating conclusion — a theory which the scientific philosopher Hans Reichenbach was at pains to describe as 'the most serious blow the concept of time has ever received in physics'.

When mind-stultifying ideas such as these are already a part of the nuclear physicist's stock-in-trade, 'willing suspension of disbelief' becomes less demanding an imaginative leap than it might once have seemed. Nevertheless, there exists a school of thought, subscribed to by a number of both readers and writers of science fiction, which insists that if a story cannot be explained convincingly in terms of today's knowledge of science, then the writing is science fantasy and not science fiction. If one assumes an obligation to adhere rigidly to definitions, that assertion could be true. But it is debatable whether it matters. In considering one aspect of H.G. Wells's highly entertaining — but also frightening — *The First Men in the Moon*, we are confronted with a spaceflight achieved by means of a gravity shield which the author could not possibly have justified at the time in the light of prevailing science. (We shall encounter far more curious methods of getting man aloft in the next chapter.)

However, when Wells's two explorers arrive on the moon, they literally uncover a Selenite civilization in which intelligent beings are physically altered after birth — often with cruelty — to suit them for the performance of a particular function within a superbly efficient society:

' "I came upon a number of young Selenites confined in jars from which only the fore-limbs protruded, who were being compressed to become machine-minders of a special sort. The extended 'hand' in this highly developed system of technical education is stimulated by irritants and nourished by injection .... Phi-oo ... explained that in the earlier stages these queer little creatures are apt to display signs of suffering in their various cramped situations, but they easily become indurated of their lot; and he took me on to where a number of flexible-limbed messengers were being drawn out and broken in." '

This is the equivalent of the human science of ergonomics deliberately turned inside out — reshaping the worker to fit the job, rather than the reverse. It was certainly possible as an extension of current developments in biology when the story was published in 1901; and Wells was a trained biologist whose *Opus One* was a textbook on the subject. It seems reasonable to suppose that the significant message in *The First Men in the Moon* is a warning of the potential inherent in applied biology for enslaving man irrevocably to the service of the state. If that is the case, how should a footling thing like the implausible overcoming of gravity detract from the book's central theme?

Throughout this study it is inevitable that similar inconsistencies in scientific plausibility will occur. The example of *The First Men in the Moon* demonstrates how little they usually affect the treatment of social ideas which is intrinsically a part of that valuable 10 per cent of science fiction.

Besides the 'willing suspension of disbelief', there is one other prerequisite to a full appreciation of science fiction; anyone who has succeeded in retaining even a memory of the timeless vision of existence enjoyed in childhood will recognize it readily as one of the inimitable experiences of life. It is called, very simply, 'sense of wonder'.

'Sense of wonder', as perceived through the eyes of a child, can be described — at best inadequately — as the innocent appreciation of the novelty of all that delights the unprejudiced human consciousness before loss and the strictures of society begin to obscure the intensity of the view. Through the perception of children, generation after generation, the mystery of that discovery is continually renewed. It is no exaggeration to call 'sense of wonder' the *élan vital* of science fiction. The one thing about which imaginative scientists now agree is that the record-chasing rate of scientific advancement during the past seventy years can be likened to no more than the relatively slow progress of a car moving from first into second gear. The real acceleration has barely begun; and the rate of social and technological change we have experienced thus far in this century is pedestrian by comparison with what we may expect during its last quarter and beyond. Whatever the near future holds for humanity will be so vastly different from the present day that it is possible to envisage a time when 'sense of wonder' might become the first essential of human understanding, as of course — in one sense — it always has been. Science fiction, in this context, is all we have available in the present as a chronicle of future change.

Unfortunately, it has to be recognized that even while, as is happening now, a disquieting atmosphere of flux begins to pervade almost all the structures of modern society, the extent to which a random sample of everyday man appears to appreciate the way the world is going is dispiritingly small. The basic conservatism of the great majority of humanity is an inadequate beacon in the foreshadow of *The Space Merchants* and the many other states of oppression which will be considered in the second half of this book. The speculative writer sees this conservatism as loss of imaginative nerve. He assumes that the future, if it is to belong to us at all, must begin in our imaginings to belong to us now.

There is much in science fiction which can be regarded as criticism of 'progress', and much more besides which is scathing on the subject of human nature. It is an unhappy fact that a large share of the serious work in the genre seems less than optimistic about the future states of man. Anti-utopias, totalitarian tyrannies, mass manipulation and mass privations abound; and if the landscape sometimes glows with the occasional rosier view, its general vista in many stories is predominantly one of gloom. What makes this valuable, if harrowing, for students of the future human condition is that so many different writers, who have let their considerable imaginations play about the ultimate direction of present trends, have come to a similar conclusion: unless man himself improves, his future — for all its technological wonders — will finally be little better than the primordial slime from which he has so painfully climbed. That, of course, is hardly a view unique to the authors of science fiction.

*****

No-one would pretend that even the best science fiction falls into the category of what critics of conventional literature would conspire to earmark as 'great writing'. It is a literature not so much of characterization as of ideas. As Kingsley Amis and

12

Robert Conquest found it necessary to reiterate in the introduction to their 1961 anthology *Spectrum 1*:

'Here we must repeat something that has been said many times before, since experience shows that it has not even yet been properly grasped: science fiction is not ordinary fiction and cannot be judged as if it were, though we agree that it should be judged as rigorously. Many of the particular criteria of literary merit are inapplicable, or work with a modified application, outside their particular field... Notions of 'plausibility' and of 'relevance' are others which have to undergo modifications when applied in the field of science fiction.'

In terms of output, science fiction has enjoyed an unprecedented growth during the past half century. In Donald B. Day's *Index to the Science Fiction Magazines, 1926–1950* ten thousand stories are listed. This excludes the novels of the period, also the stories which appeared in publications other than those devoted entirely to the genre; and it is a figure which covers only the first twenty-five of the fifty years. Applying Sturgeon's guillotine, we are left with a minimum of one thousand works, to which can conservatively be added another one thousand to bring the total up to date. And to this we must also put some five hundred novels. Two-and-a-half thousand *valuable* speculative interpretations of the interaction between science and humanity — all the government 'think tanks' and 'institutes of future studies' in existence have never produced, let alone published, anything comparable.

Science fiction is not, and never has been, primarily concerned with prophecy. Among the multitude of works in the genre it is inevitable that there should have been from time to time some remarkably accurate predictions, particularly in the technology-inspired stories during the early part of the century. We do not after all risk *one* future, but a nearly infinite variety of possible tomorrows, both as individuals and as a race. Science fiction has already provided faces for a great number of these possibilities, some of them more improbable than others. It will continue to do so while there remain speculative writers who are willing, and permitted, to contribute to the genre. It is not without irony that in many of those projected futures their work would almost certainly be proscribed. During 1970, the best-known Russian science fiction authors, Boris and Arkadi Strugatsky, were blacklisted in the Soviet Union; in Spain an entire issue of the magazine *Nueva Dimension* was seized by the political police.

Having evoked the authoritative dictum of Arthur C. Clarke at the beginning of this study, we must necessarily also include his own comment *as a scientist* in *Profiles of the Future* on the reaction to science fiction in one particularly sensitive quarter:

'A critical — the adjective is important — reading of science fiction is essential training for anyone wishing to look more than ten years ahead. The facts of the future can hardly be imagined *ab initio* by those who are unfamiliar with the fantasies of the past.

This claim may produce indignation, especially among those second-rate scientists who sometimes make fun of science fiction (I have never known a first-rate one to do so — and I know several who write it).'

To those 'fantasies of the past' we must first look, before considering their latter-day counterparts.

2 The Forerunners

*Some of the amateur scholars of science fiction are veritable
Hitlers for aggrandizing their field. If they perceive in, say, a
sixteenth century satire some vaguely speculative element
they see it as a trembling and persecuted minority, demand
Anschluss, and proceed to annexe the satire to science fiction.*

C.M. Kornbluth, *The Science Fiction Novel*

As Isaac Asimov has remarked in discussing early speculative
writing, fantasy tends to take a 'cavalier approach to reality'.
It is true that an investigation back through the rich vein of
historical fantasy will reveal the occasional sharp gleam of
scientific foresight, but it is a rare occurrence and even then not
necessarily an example of the true ore of science fiction. Nevertheless, many of the fantasies of the past have employed both
'sense of wonder' and 'willing suspension of disbelief' to create
situations in which social criticism and healthy doses of satire
have been allowed to play on the then contemporary scene. To
that extent they can certainly be described as close relatives, if
not direct forebears, of the genre which finally took definite
shape towards the close of the nineteenth century — and in that
light they merit our attention.

There seems to have been no time during recorded history
when some men, at least, have not wished humanity more
capable and better than it actually appeared. In one sense the
great mythological epics of the ancient world can be seen as
attempts to reconcile man to the 'vagaries of human nature by
highlighting the idiosyncratic behaviour of the original inhabitants of Olympus. But if the gods moved in mysterious ways,
frequently emulating the least desirable characteristics of their
mortal inferiors, humans themselves dreamt of appropriating the
gifts of lesser creatures still. Behind the eyes which in antiquity
observed the flight of birds there already lay the brain that
could imagine, and yearn for, the reality of man in flight.

Perhaps the simplest interpretation of the story of Daedalus
and Icarus, in their attempt to escape from Crete, is the warning
to the adventurer not to aspire too greatly, to set his sights on
less exalted things. But the full meaning of the myth runs
deeper; and the moral turns out to be two-edged. Daedalus

15

after all — within the terms of the tale — proved that human flight was possible; he returned to *terra firma* in one piece. It was left to Icarus to demonstrate by flying too close to the sun the wilfulness and foolhardiness of the young, and to show by his spectacular fall — when the wax which secured the feathers of his wings began to melt — the price which would inevitably have to be paid for extending the frontiers of human achievement. The meaning of the legend, then, is clear; and it hardly matters that the modern science of aerodynamics has proved that a genuine man-sized angel, if his plumage were to be other than purely decorative, would require a wingspan of many yards and chest muscles extending forwards some several feet!

The genius of Daedalus, as the accounts have come down to us, identifies him as probably the greatest of the creative inventors in the service of both gods and men. In addition to providing the world with a preview of robotics in the shape of the man of bronze he built for King Minos of Crete, he was the constructor, for the same monarch, of the labyrinth through which Theseus precariously unwound his ball of thread as he stalked the Minotaur. That Daedalus should have been chosen for this particular task was hardly coincidental, since he, as much as anyone, was responsible for the Minotaur in the first place. Virgil describes with some distaste the lust of Pasiphae, the wife of Minos, for a white bull which emerged Venus-like from the sea; and Ovid relates how she prevailed upon Daedalus to produce a life-size replica cow inside which she could squat to assuage her curious desire. The outcome was the Minotaur — quarter god, as much a burden to himself as to anyone else, and the only hybrid monster in Greek mythology to sport an animal head. His confinement in the labyrinth was to prove no more than a foretaste of the future treatment of deviants recounted in much science fiction.

Further examples of the idiosyncrasies of the gods and demigods, as well as those of humanity, appear in two satirical works by the Greek, Lucian of Samosata; his stories also gain distinction by being among the earliest accounts of journeys to the moon — *Icaromenippos* and *A True History*. Lucian (c AD 125-200), who entertained few illusions concerning his fellow men, echoed Daedalus in the first of these satires by imagining a moonflight achieved with the use of strapped-on wings. When Menippos arrives at his goal he discourses with the natural inhabitants, feasts among the gods in Heaven, and is provided with the opportunity to observe in unedifying detail the earth he has left behind:

'I saw Ptolemaios sleep with his sister ... Alexander in Thessalia being murdered by his wife, Antigones sharing bed with the wife of his son, and Attalos's son give his father poison ... Similar visions met me both among Scythes and Thracians in the royal palaces; everywhere fornication, murder, intrigues, blackmailings, perjuries, terrorism and treachery within the families ... a variegated and diversified picture.'

A True History consists of a string of extraordinary fantasies which Lucian freely admits at the outset could not possibly have occurred; his purpose in writing the work was probably to satirize other so-called 'true' adventure narratives prevalent at the time. The erstwhile heroes of his *True History* are flung into the sky by a waterspout while they are sailing in the vicinity of the Pillars of Hercules, only coming to rest eight days later on the surface of the moon. There they find themselves embroiled in a space-war between the lunar monarch and the King of the Sun over the rights to colonize other planets in the Solar System — an anticipation, by some eighteen hundred years, of the 'space operas' which were to benumb the uncritical pulp-magazine readers of the 1930s.

Lucian of Samosata wrote in an era which saw the curtain inexorably descending on the closing stages of Greek science. As Christianity fastened its grip upon the body of Europe, the notion that the moon was anything other than a God-given light to illumine the heavens for the benefit of man was an idea contrary to Holy Writ — it was to remain so for thirteen hundred years.

*****

In the long night, which overtook and stifled Western man's growing awareness of the universe from the fourth century AD, few stars shone. We may sympathize with one of them, Friar Roger Bacon — the 'Doctor Mirabilis' of the Franciscans, pursuing his work in mathematics and optics, and yearning in the gloom of his cell for the new ways of scientific thinking which he was confident would come, but whose advent he was powerless in the thirteenth century to hasten one wit. His dreams

17

reveal a remarkable exercise in long-range prediction:

> 'Instruments may be made by which the largest ships, with
> only one man guiding them, will be carried with greater
> velocity than if they were full of sailors. Chariots may be
> constructed that will move with incredible rapidity without
> the help of animals. Instruments of flying may be formed in
> which a man, sitting at his ease and meditating in any
> subject, may beat the air with artificial wings after the manner
> of birds ... as also machines which will enable men to walk
> at the bottom of the seas ...'

The notebooks of Leonardo da Vinci record the farsighted
view which he, too, entertained regarding the possibilities for
scientific development and the rationalization of a complete
cosmology; but they were ideas which remained in his notebooks. Not until Nicolaus Copernicus introduced his literally
revolutionary theory of the Solar System in 1543, and Galileo
Galilei turned his telescope on the moon in 1609 and saw
mountains, did the quality of Bacon's enheartening vision begin
to be realized. And if twenty-four years later Galileo yielded un-
willingly to the irresistible persuasion of the Inquisition, the
damage to Holy Writ was already too great to be undone.

Galileo's telescope proved the catalyst for a spate of lunar
voyages and other extraterrestrial excursions which were to
enthral and occasionally horrify whoever was able to read them
throughout the next hundred years. However, the fact that the
heavens stayed forbidden ground to the more cautious speculative writer until the beginning of the seventeenth century did
not preclude the setting of fantasies in unknown lands or on
familiar parts of earth. In 1516, the year which saw the appearance of Sir Thomas More's socially critical *Utopia*, the Italian
poet Ludovico Ariosto produced his epic *Orlando Furioso*, a
swashbuckling forerunner of 'Sword and Sorcery' fantasy
replete with chivalrous knights, blood-drenched battlefields and
— as it happens — an imaginative account of a journey to the
moon. Over a period of more than a quarter of a century
Rabelais poured out his satirical masterpiece *Gargantua and
Pantagruel* (1532—64) in which Pantagruel, the philosophic
giant, travels eternally in a quest for truth, receiving along the
way an admirably humanist education. The Age of Chivalry, and
spiritual pilgrimages after this or that grail, were dealt a sideways,
almost deadly, blow by Cervantes' 'lean and foolish knight' who

rode vainly across the scene only four years before Galileo focussed his 'optick tube' upon the stars.

The beginnings of the scientific awakening saw Francis Bacon's prophetic *The New Atlantis* (1624) unleashing a glittering array of future wonders, from underwater craft to flying machines. Of his utopian 'House of Salomon' he wrote: 'The end of our Foundation is the knowledge of causes, and secret motions of things; and the enlarging of the bounds of the Human Empire, to the effecting of all things possible.' *The New Atlantis* was Bacon's final expression of his belief in the value of scientific research which he had set out comprehensively in 1620 in the manifesto *Novum Organum* to King James the First of England. If any speculative writer wished today to compile an alternative history of the seventeenth and eighteenth centuries, he could do little better than begin with the question: 'What would have happened if Bacon, then Lord Chancellor, had been allowed time to implement his plans instead of losing office in 1621 when the House of Lords hammered him for accepting bribes?'

1627 saw the arrival in Prague of new and more accurate tables of planetary motions, compiled by one of the first magnitude stars in the history of astronomy, Johannes Kepler. The tables, together with Kepler's laws on the revolutions of the planets, were to guide Newton as he prepared his *Principia Mathematica*. It fell also to Kepler to write perhaps the oddest of all the moon ventures to grace the literature of the seventeenth century. His *Somnium*, published in 1634 four years after his death, describes a lunar journey undertaken with the impetus of demonic power summoned by a wise sorceress named Fiolxhilda. It is probable that Fiolxhilda represented an idealized portrait of Kepler's own mother, who was anything but wise and who had, in her time, been arrested and accused of witchcraft. She was only saved from the stake by the timely intervention of the Imperial Mathematician — who just happened to be her son.

Unlike the lunar fantasies which preceded it, *Somnium* includes descriptions of the moon which Kepler knew to have some scientific foundation. His narrative dwells on the immensity of the mountains, the alternately blazing and chilling extremes of temperature, and the ubiquitous profusion of craters. He imagined these last as the entrances to gigantic underground chambers in which the moon's inhabitants sought refuge from the icy nights — an idea which Wells was to expand with considerable effect in *The First Men in the Moon*.

19

That John Wilkins — a former master of colleges at both Oxford and Cambridge, the founding secretary of the Royal Society and also Bishop of Chester before he died — had read *Somnium* is unlikely; but he was certainly aware of Kepler's other writings when he published his speculative *The Discovery of a New World* anonymously in 1638. The work consisted of thirteen 'propositions' regarding the nature of the moon, to which Wilkins added a fourteenth for the publication of the book's third edition in 1640, calling it 'A Discourse Concerning the Possibility of a Passage Thither':

'Yea, but (you will say) there can be no sayling thither ... Wee have not now any Drake, or Columbus to undertake this voyage, or any Daedalus to invent a conveiance through the ayre ... Tis the opinion of Keplar [*sic*], that as soone as the art of flying is found out, some of their nation will make one of the first Colonies, that shall transplant into that other world. I suppose, his appropriating this preheminence to his owne Countrymen, may arise from an overpartiall affection to them.'

What prompted Wilkins to write his fourteenth 'proposition' was his own discovery of Francis Godwin's *The Man in the Moone, or a Discourse of a Voyage Thither by Domingo Gonsales, The Speedy Messenger*. Also a cleric, who was appointed Bishop of Llandaff and later Bishop of Hereford by Elizabeth I, Godwin had already been dead five years when his *Man in the Moone* was published, again anonymously, in 1638. Unlike Wilkins, he was no scientist; and while the former followed through scientific arguments in his work, Godwin contented himself with a satirical fantasy which relied on the conveying of his 'Speedy Messenger' to the moon harnessed to a team of trained swans known as 'gansas'. What he finds on landing is a utopian society the very reverse of seventeenth-century England. Medicine has conquered all ills; famine and warfare have ceased to exist; man is naturally monogamous and lives in harmony with his fellows. The pecking order in this ideal state is determined by an individual's height; and the taller an inhabitant grows, the more intelligent and long-lived he becomes.

If Godwin himself was not a scientist, he undoubtedly enjoyed a thorough knowledge of the scientific ideas of his day. Gonsales refers briefly to some aspects of Copernican theory, but — wisely, in view of his author's vocation — neatly evades expressing the belief that the earth revolves around the sun. (The merest hints at Copernicus in the story were probably enough to warrant its writer's anonymity — even after his death.) Gonsales and his gansas crop up in a variety of later works having a bearing on the moon; and unless an earlier reference can be unearthed, the modern vernacular expression 'speedy Gonsales', must surely be attributed as originating from the pen of the man who in 1601 published a catalogue of the Bishops of England!

During the ten years which followed Galileo's death in 1642, at least two maps of the moon were drawn — those of Johann Hevelius and the Italian priest Riccioli. By present-day standards they were, at best, wildly inaccurate; but it was Riccioli who first adopted the appealing custom of naming the craters after scientists and other historical figures, a practice which later induced Descartes to describe the moon as 'the graveyard of astronomers'. Nearly two hundred years were to elapse before improvements in telescopes enabled Wilhelm Beer and Johann Mädler in Berlin to prepare an authoritative map of the observable side of the moon. Until that time there remained ample scope for speculation and fantasy concerning what might exist in the bright crater of Aristarchus or on the great plain of Ptolemy. No more unlikely a character to employ that distant landscape for the purposes of satire could be envisaged than the renowned duellist and member of the Gaston Guards immortalised in Edmond Rostand's comedy *Cyrano de Bergerac*.

The real-life Cyrano, who was never less than the witty eccentric whom Rostand portrayed, and whose exploits had already assumed legendary status by the time of his death at the age of thirty-five, left behind him a number of manuscripts to be printed posthumously. Among them was *The Comical History of the States and Empires of the World of the Moon* (1656), in which a variety of methods of conquering gravity are expounded, ranging from the ludicrous to the astoundingly precise. In almost the same breath Cyrano turns from the idea of strapping bottles of dew to the body — in the hope, since dew rises in the morning, that they would uplift the bearer — to the concept of multistage rockets! On yet another page he is firmly back in the realms of fantasy with a 'by-your-own-bootstraps' suggestion which would have all but brought to tears the failed inventors of countless perpetual motion machines:

'After the Preparations, I got a very light Machine of Iron made, into which I went, and when I was well seated in my place, I threw this Magnetick Bowl as high as I could up into the air. Now the Iron Machine, which I had purposely made more massive in the middle than at the ends, was presently elevated, and in a just poise; because the middle received the greatest force of Attraction. So then, as I arrived at the place whither my Lode-stone had attracted me, I presently threw up my Bowl in the Air over me.'

In their own fashion, Cyrano's lunar beings reflect their creator's ebullient personality and the rebellious attitude which he flamboyantly maintained towards the French institutions of his age. Currency is exchanged not in money but in verse; and people rise and fall in social grace according to the size of their noses (Cyrano's was every bit as large as Rostand pictured it). Wars are arranged with the combatants so handicapped as to make them equal; the old obey the young and hold them in high esteem. (Here again we are struck by the strange oscillations in Cyrano's writing — he moves swiftly from mere fanciful pre-occupations to uncanny predictions of the world today. We need only consider the current balance of armaments, on a small scale in the Middle East and in more alarming proportions between the super-powers, to recognize his accuracy in envisaging a state of material and psychological warfare where neither side can 'win'. And in modern society the young have not only achieved impressive status in such areas as economic consumption and political protest, but also in certain professional and managerial fields where — whether there is wisdom in it or not — a major qualification for promotion and success is youth.)

Among the unfamiliar devices employed by Cyrano's curious lunar race are predictions of both the electric light bulb and the gramophone. And who else should the narrator accost on the moon but Godwin's Domingo Gonsales, surrounded by a collection of monkeys attired, like him, in ruffs and breeches. Apparently the Queen of the Moon deems Spanish clothes appropriate wear for apes, and finding Gonsales in the same dress she assumes him to be another of their kind.

A comparable work is Cyrano's *The Comical History of the States and Empires of the World of the Sun* (1662), in which he took a further opportunity, in 'high fantastic' style, to give vent to his iconoclasm and speculative view of science. Its appearance marked the beginning of a pause of some sixty years in the out-flow of notable fantasies of this particular type. Scientific speculation, nevertheless, continued in other quarters — and not necessarily those of the natural philosophers. In 1660 Francesco Lama, an Italian Jesuit, concluded that the Almighty would never allow man to build flying machines, since it would be possible to hurl projectiles from them at people below! It could be that Francesco's conclusion smacked a little of 'sour grapes'. He was the author of a theory that airships might be made of vacuum-filled metal containers, clearly taking no account of the effect of atmospheric pressure on an evacuated metal sphere which Otto von Guericke had demonstrated in 1654 — the pulling power of fourteen horses had failed to separate its two halves. In fact, Francesco's opinion was very much akin to that of another cleric who two centuries later let it be known that if God had intended men to fly, he would have given them wings. His name, inappropriately, was Wright — and his sons ended an era in twelve short seconds at Kitty Hawk.

*****

Newton's monumental *Principia Mathematica*, when it was finally published in 1687, brushed aside the remaining irrational objections of the upholders of Holy Writ as so much sticks and straw. The clear sweep of intellectual and scientific reason which the book enshrined revolutionized the thought of Europe and severed the restraining links with the past. Newton laid down the principles of motion for the planets and set out the laws of gravity, which showed, among other things, the limits of earth's atmosphere and the fact that the moon had virtually none at all (it was not, however, to discourage writers from setting further fantasies on the lunar globe). Twelve years earlier another land-mark in the discovery of the nature of the universe had also occurred in England, when King Charles the Second decreed that the revolutions of the moon and the positions of the stars should be 'anew observed, examined and corrected for the use of my seamen'. The result was the Greenwich Observatory, designed by Sir Christopher Wren and built with funds obtained from 'the sale of old and decayed gunpowder'. Characteristically, when the Reverend John Flamsteed, the first Astronomer Royal, took possession of the observatory, he lightheartedly set about casting its horoscope — the act of a scientist 'cocking a snook' at the alchemists of a receding age.

The Greenwich telescope opened up a further expanse of the heavens to the enquiring scrutiny of man; but there was much, even within the confines of our own solar system, which it was not powerful enough to reveal. In a quite extraordinary piece of prediction, Jonathan Swift described in *Gulliver's Travels* (1726) the two miniature moons of Mars, Deimos and Phobos, years before any instrument existed which could have detected them. With that exception, Swift's classic satire, overrun as it is with minute Lilliputians, monstrous Brobdignagians, talking horses and other peculiarities, is a work of pure fantasy. Nevertheless, its relevance as a biting criticism of Swift's own age, and of human nature in general, has secured it a place in literature far in advance of a work with a similar aim which appeared only a year after it.

This was *A Voyage to Cacklogallinia*, written pseudonymously by 'Captain Samuel Brunt' who drew heavily on Godwin's *Man in the Moone*. Brunt is shipwrecked on the uncharted island of the title which is inhabited by giant birds of equal intelligence to man. The Cacklogallinian philosophers are convinced that gold can be mined from the mountains of the moon, and Brunt is inveigled into joining an expedition financed by capital raised through the island's stock market. The book is evidently a satire in part on the practice which joint stock companies had at the time of offering shares in overseas ventures of dubious promise (the 'South Sea Bubble' had burst only seven years earlier). The moon project stimulates heavy speculation on the Cacklogallinian exchange, and Brunt and his feathered partner set off for the moon in a palanquin supported by four more of the birds.

Galileo's *Systema Mundi* is consulted during the journey; but the lunar scene when reached differs spectacularly from the prospectors' expectations. The 'Selenites' they meet are insubstantial wraithlike beings, although distinctly less disconcerting than a succession of what appear to be humans in grotesque dress and attitudes who materialize and vanish in front of the visitors throughout their stay. The explanation, when it comes, is in the best traditions of fantasy:

'While I was speaking, a Man on Horseback ran full speed upon me with a drawn sabre, to cleave me down; but the Selenite waving his Hand, he soon vanished. "You need", said he, "apprehend nothing from these Shades; they are the Souls of the Inhabitants of your World, which being loos'd from the Body by Sleep, resort here, and for the short Space allotted them, indulge the Passions which predominate, or undergo the Misfortunes they fear while they are in your Globe".'

The identity of the Selenites themselves is similarly chastening. They are the souls of earth's dead who have successfully adhered to virtue in their lifetime. As such, they have scant use for gold, which in any case is not in evidence on the moon; and their only interests are the pursuit of philosophy and religion. Predictably, this revelation leads to the rapid collapse of the market in moon shares and to the financial ruin of Cacklogallinia.

Gulliver's Travels and Brunt's *Voyage*, which also enjoyed a wide readership, proved the trigger mechanism for a fresh chain of fantastic voyaging which erupted during the following two decades. 1741 saw the publication of Ludwig Holberg's *The Subterranean Journey of Niels Klim*, a Swiftian exercise in satire conducted underground, followed in 1744 by one of the first attempts to take man farther afield than the moon, and written by the German astronomer, Eberhard Christian Kindermann. The practice of astronomy clearly occupied Kindermann's attention to the exclusion of other branches of science, for he, too, seemed ignorant of von Guericke's metal sphere and described a journey to Mars using the method of propulsion suggested by Francesco Lama. He was, perhaps, also unaware of the desirability of endowing his book with something other than a jaw-breaking title; he called it simply *Die geshwinde Reise auf dem Luft-schiff nach der obern Welt, welche jungsthin funf Personnen angestellet.*

Another underground saga arrived in 1751, in the form of Robert Patlock's *Life and Adventures of Peter Wilkins, a Cornish Man,* together with yet a further moon voyage containing a prediction of sorts which — after an interval of two-hundred-and-eighteen years — came true. In *The Life and Astonishing Transactions of John Daniel,* Ralph Morris depicted a flying machine adorned with wings of calico and constructed by Daniel's son Jacob, a youngster of 'sedentary disposition and amazing ingenuity'. Aboard this contraption father and son eventually land on the moon during the long lunar night. At first they venture out only briefly and return to the refuge of their machine to sleep, much as Armstrong and Aldrin were to do. In both cases — the fictional and the real — the name of the craft was 'Eagle'.

Not to be outdone by the progenitors of extra-terrestrial excursions, Voltaire, in what is now one of his lesser-known works, reversed the tables by bringing giant visitors from outer space to earth in his tale *Micromegas* (1752). Like Swift, he also mentions the dwarf moons of Mars, probably because he was already acquainted with *Gulliver*. He wrote *Micromegas* as a framework in which human society could be viewed from an alien standpoint, and as a satire on the bewildering behaviour of man.

*****

On 21st November, 1783, what was for that age an incredible crowd of half a million — among them the ill-fated Louis XVI of France and his queen, Marie Antoinette, together with Benjamin Franklin, then emissary to the Court — gathered to witness the first tentative step on the long ascent which is still merely beginning for Man. It was the first human flight in a balloon, presaged by the unmanned launchings of the Montgolfier brothers' hot-air balloon and J.A.C. Charles's hydrogen-filled version earlier in the year. The first British manned flight took place in Edinburgh on 24 August, 1784, and before that year was out satirical engravings were appearing extolling the virtues of aerial yachts designed for 'conveying the high Fliers of Fashion over the Channel from Dover to Calais'...

'Che sara sara
Ye Masters of Packets! ye poor silly loons!
Sell your boats and get Blanchard to make you Balloons.
For our fair modern Witches, no longer aquatic,
Will never more cross but in boats Aerostatic.'

It was natural, then, that the first account of a visit to the planet Uranus should employ a balloon as the method of travel. *A Journey lately performed through the Air in an Aerostatic Globe ... To the newly discovered Planet, Georgium Sidus* was published as a pamphlet, also in 1784, with the identity of its author concealed under the pseudonym of 'Vivenair'. The pamphlet was in reality a thinly-veiled attack on George III's determination to strengthen the power of the monarchy by opposing the Cabinet form of government in the British Parliament. Uranus had been discovered by William Herschel in 1781 and named 'Georgium Sidus' (George's Star) in the hope of the astronomer's receiving royal patronage — he duly got it. It proved an ideal setting for Vivenair's satire on the Court and English society in the early years of George's reign, and his dislike of the hypocrisy and growing materialism of the period are clearly indicated in his descriptions of the inhabitants he professed to have found there. The courtiers and ministers surrounding the King of Uranus are discovered to be genuinely two-faced. While the expression on their countenances which are turned towards the King reflect the proper degree of respect and subservience, the faces at the back of their heads reveal their true motivations — avarice, ambition, jealousy and contempt.

Vivenair's pamphlet more or less closes the circle opened sixteen hundred years earlier by Lucian of Samosata's *Icaromenippos*. Both works, and many of those which appeared during the interval, used the medium of fantasy and an extraterrestrial viewpoint to look back at the vagaries of human nature. Very little by way of solution or improvement is offered. If some of the unworldly societies portrayed give hints of utopian vision, they are bereft of any explanation as to how a more rational and equitable order of things might be achieved. Scientific progress by the end of the eighteenth century had kindled the imaginations of but a handful of writers and philosophers who, with Benjamin Franklin, could surmise:

> 'We may perhaps learn to deprive large masses of their gravity, and give them absolute levity, for the sake of easy transport. Agriculture may diminish its labour and double its produce, all diseases may be ... cured ... and our lives lengthened at pleasure ...   O that men would cease to be wolves to one another.'

And if Condorcet, likewise, did provide the world with the promise of reason, human brotherhood and the limitless possibility of improving man, it says much for the times he was addressing that he was obliged to commit suicide in captivity during the bloody recriminations of the Jacobins in the second year of the French Revolution. Nevertheless, his ideas of universal progress had by 1772 already found form in the

27

prophetic and utopian *L'An 2440* of his countryman, Louis S. Mercier; they were to do so again in Jean-Baptiste Cousin de Grainville's *Le dernier homme* in 1805. But by then the century had turned and an era was beginning in which Condorcet's message of progress through science was to fall, somewhat equivocally, on a multitude of receptive minds.

3 Towards El Dorado

*I wish that everything that can, may be mechanized as
quickly as possible, so as to give man more power and liberty
of mind to higher things.*

Jakob Burckhardt, nineteenth-century historian

It is curious that one of the first nineteenth-century novels which
comes near to being classed as science fiction, and which can
certainly be described as science fantasy, should have been
written in an idiom known to aficionados as 'Gothic horror'.
Mary Wollstonecraft Shelley's *Frankenstein* (1818), despite its
implications that scientific possibilities include the ability to
create life in more or less the image of man, is written in a style
which dates back to 1765 when a new literary genre can rightly
be said to have 'wormed' its way into existence. The book
which founded this grisly tradition, as flourishing now as it was
a century and a half ago, rejoiced in the title of *The Castle of
Otranto*. It was offered to the public as the work of one
Onuphrio Muralto, Canon of the Church of St. Nicholas at
Otranto in Italy, and its translator was named as 'William
Marshal, Gent'. The novel, for so it must be described, consists
of a series of horrific episodes centred around a castle where a
terrible curse precipitates the appearance of giant articles of
clothing, statues which bleed, and the rest of the lurid parapher-
nalia which has come to be associated with the genre. The book
was an instant success, so much so that its true perpetrator was
persuaded to reveal his identity. He turned out to be none other
than Horace Walpole, a renowned gentleman of letters who
ought to have known better.

There is probably little to be gained for the purposes of this
study in examining the connections which some commentators
have professed to find between Gothic horror and science
fiction. To be factual, examples of both genres *were* printed in
the same pulp magazine, *Weird Tales*, which began publication
in 1923, although it was more properly the home of horror and
science fantasy than of science fiction. There is, however, one
aspect of Gothic horror which is worth noting, inasmuch as it
bears something in common with anti-utopian writing. In
Walpole's *Otranto*, for all its pervading atmosphere of evil, good

29

eventually prevailed. That was not always to be the case in later works in that genre; and it is not difficult to see the influence of de Sade in G.M. Lewis's *The Monk* (1796) which overflows with murder, devil worship, walking corpses and incestuous rape.

De Sade, in fact, commented on the advent of Gothic horror in his *L'Idée sur les Romans* (1800), suggesting that the French Revolution had shocked Europe into a state of mind in which the writing of romantic fiction had little place. To maintain the reader's interest, the author found it necessary to call upon Hell. De Sade's philosophy of evil for its own sake finds echoes in many twentieth-century anti-utopias; it is implicit in the words of O'Brien, the interrogator of Orwell's *Nineteen Eighty-four*.

Mary Shelley's *Frankenstein* clumsily employed many of the devices of the Gothic horror novel. The account of the doctor's first revelation as he brings his creature to life is a good example:

'How can I describe my emotions at this catastrophe...? His limbs were in proportion, and I had selected his features as beautiful. Beautiful! Great God! His yellow skin scarcely covered the work of muscles and arteries beneath; his hair was of a lustrous black, and flowing; his teeth of a pearly whiteness; but these luxuriances only formed a more horrid contrast with his watery eyes, that seemed almost of the same colour as the dun-white sockets in which they were set, his shrivelled complexion and straight black lips.'

It should not overtax the faculties to imagine the reaction of Percy Bysshe Shelley when effusions of this kind made his wife's work far better known throughout Europe than his own romantic verse.

James Whale's classic film of the story, featuring Boris Karloff, succeeded in 1931 in preserving much of the unexpected tenderness of the original, even if the scenario covered only a part of the book. The irony of the work is that Frankenstein's creation is initially a monster only in appearance. Beneath his grotesque exterior is a completely innocent and gentle being plaintively attempting to communicate with people who are too horrified by his deformity to want to know. Whale's film beautifully captures this aspect in the scene where the creature encounters a small girl playing beside a lake. Together they throw flowers into the water until the creature, enthralled to find that they float, flings the child in after them unaware that she will sink and drown. The film closes with the local villagers in arms and

Frankenstein and his prodigy going to their respective fates. In the original, however, the tale at that point has barely begun. Over the years the creature slowly learns to understand human behaviour and, in need of affection, approaches his creator to demand a mate. Frankenstein refuses, and in desperation the creature finally becomes the monster he outwardly resembles — murdering the doctor's family and friends, and alternately pursuing and being chased by Frankenstein until the tragedy ends in the wilderness of the Arctic Circle.

The other tragedy of *Frankenstein* is that its authoress should have chosen to write it in the blood-curdling vein of the most notorious literature of the time. Disregarding its lack of literary merit, the novel is a powerful plea for tolerance and an imaginative indictment of the human capacity to mistrust and fear others whose physical appearance is unlike our own, and whose ways are equally unfamiliar. There is also a religious significance in the fact that as the story progresses the creature becomes more likeable than his relentless creator, more fallible admittedly — and therefore more to be feared. Mary Shelley went on to write a post-catastrophe novel, *The Last Man* (1826), which, though it related the regression of society into a savage state, proved less effective than her depiction of the inherent savagery in man through the story of *Frankenstein.*

An odd combination of Gothic horror and rudimentary science fiction can also be found in J. Webb's *The Mummy — A Tale of the Twenty-second Century* (1827), in which the now familiar aberration of a mummy coming to life is acted out against the technological backdrop of AD 2130. However, the author who genuinely raised the writing of Gothic horror out of its morass, enveloping it with a wealth of psychological insight until his work bore little relation to the rest of the genre, can also, paradoxically, be called one of the first regular writers of science fiction and the father of the modern detective story — Edgar Allan Poe.

In August 1835, the *Southern Literary Messenger* of Richmond, Virginia, carried the first half of what was intended to be a two-part story by Poe on — once again — a journey to the moon. Entitled *Hans Phaall — A Tale*, it was among the last of the romantic fantasies on the subject to be published; and it included scientific observations which distinguish it from earlier efforts. Although the ascent is undertaken in a common form of balloon, Poe knew enough about atmospheric pressure to seal his voyager in an airtight container. His description of the earth as the balloon rises is extraordinarily reminiscent of those of the first astronauts, and understandably better put:

'At a vast distance to the eastward, although perfectly discernible, extended the islands of Great Britain, the entire Atlantic coast of France and Spain, with a small portion of the northern part of the continent of Africa. Of individual edifices not a trace could be discovered, and the proudest cities of mankind had utterly faded away from the face of the earth.... the dark Mediterranean sea, dotted with islands..., spread itself out to the eastward as far as my vision extended, until its entire mass of waters seemed at length to tumble headlong over the abyss of the horizon...'

Three weeks after the opening part of *Hans Phaall* went to press, an event occurred which caused Poe to destroy the remainder of his tale. On 21 August there ran in the New York *Sun* the first instalment of what is still possibly the most spectacular hoax in the history of journalism. Under the heading 'Celestial Discoveries' a brief article purported to quote from the Edinburgh *Courant* on the recent observations by the astronomer Sir John Herschel at the Cape of Good Hope. Throughout the rest of the month, and on into September, the astonished readers were regaled by an account of discoveries made with Herschel's immense new telescope which, when turned on the moon, had revealed vegetation, animals, humanoid-type beavers, and finally winged men! Whatever the reception to these announcements in scientific quarters, their effect on the circulation of the New York *Sun* surpassed editor Benjamin Day's sublimest expectations. On 28 August he was able to report (truthfully) that the sale of his paper had risen to 19,360 copies, more than 2,000 higher than *The Times* of London and consequently the largest daily circulation on earth.

The author of the hoax was later identified as Richard Adams Locke, a 12-dollar-a-week reporter on the *Sun*'s own staff who had suggested the idea to Day and had himself written the entire story. The outcome of Locke's deception was described by Poe, who could conceivably have been drunk at the time, as 'one of the most important steps ever taken in the pathway of human progress'. He was referring to the popularization of the 'penny press' which the *Sun*'s wayward regard for ethics had achieved. Sir John Herschel was, to his own amusement, the only character in Locke's report who actually did exist. The son of the discoverer of Uranus, he was a leading astronomer in his own right and one-time President of the Royal Astronomical Society. Poe, in fact, had studied John Herschel's 'Treatise on Astronomy' while he was planning *Hans Phaall*. He tore up the second part of his manuscript when the hoax was at its height, believing that his fiction had been overtaken by fact.

Poe's science fiction writings of necessity occupy second place to his singular output of horror stories and his highly original verse; but enough of them survive to indicate his interest in providing convincing scientific backgrounds to some of them at least. They include a vision of a future society in *Mellonta Tauta*, presented in much the same fashion as a science fiction writer might develop the theme today, an unfinished Antarctic voyage entitled *The Narrative of Arthur Gordon Pym's Adventures* (1838), and an uncharacteristically humorous story, 'The Man That Was Used Up', in which the central figure is entirely built of prostheses. His gruesome 'The Facts in the Case of M. Valdemar' (1845) is probably the only horror tale he wrote which can also be classed as science fiction. Remarkably, it was accepted in some quarters as a *factual* account of a man dying in a mesmeric trance which is prolonged beyond the point of death; within a year or two it was quoted as such in the British *Popular Record of Modern Science*. (Such gullibility may seem odd to the present-day observer; but it is as well to remember that Mesmer in his time was obliged to champion the 'scientific' nature of his work in the face of a furious rearguard action which brought together the last remnants of demonology and the religious and medical conservatism of the late eighteenth century. He called his discovery 'animal magnetism', which in retrospect we can see was of much the same order of 'science' as the alchemists' dream of 'phlogiston' — the magical substance they believed to be contained in everything capable of catching fire. Nevertheless, mesmerism was a science of sorts, and it pointed the way to what was eventually to become a crucial factor in science fiction. For this was no mere gadgetry, far less a further astronomical revelation — it was science applied *direct* to man, and to the individual being. In Poe's tale, Valdemar's mind is kept alive, not by supernatural forces but by human intervention. With the growing refinement today of mechanical and chemical life-support systems, the ethical problems of keeping a man alive when he should already be dead no longer belong to fiction.)

The unusual quality of Poe's stories exerted a far-reaching influence, particularly in France where translations of his work by Baudelaire inspired such disparately employed artists as Debussy and Mallarmé. It can be found in the writings of Robert Louis Stevenson and Sir Arthur Conan Doyle, whose Sherlock Holmes owes much to Poe's archetypal detective, Auguste Dupin. It is difficult now to credit that this writer of genius, who endured a love-life of peculiar complexity and whose sporadic bouts of compulsive drinking finally ended in his death at the age of forty, received practically nothing by way of payment for his efforts and frequently had to be content with no more than a handful of free copies of his own published work.

*****

The advance of science in the nineteenth century, and with it the growth of industrial technology, ushered in the machine age on which much of the prosperity of the Victorians was to be based. Improvements in the quality of iron, to take but one example, had already led to the changeover from wooden to metal lathes by 1800. In 1810 Henry Maudslay introduced the engineer's self-acting lathe, merely the first of a series of innovations which were to earn him a niche in the edifice of history as 'the father of modern engineering'.

The precision of Maudslay's inventions and their development by a number of his pupils provided the well-spring of the machine tool industry — a branch of engineering that produced machines which, in their turn, begot further machines, opening the lock-gates to a seemingly incessant flood of ideas whose rise marked the progress of the technological revolution. Its beginnings, of course, lay very much in the age of iron and steam. In 1770 James Watt had developed his separate condensing engine — a vastly more efficient form of motive power than the inventions of Newcomen and Savery which had preceded it. Its performance was measured against the pulling power of horses; and it was made, naturally, of iron. Since 1735 the use of improved cast iron, first produced by Abraham Darby by burning coke in the high furnace, had seen a rapid proliferation of engineering achievements ranging all the way from iron machinery and bridges to ornamental gates. Not until more than a century later, however, with the advent of the Bessemer converter — to be followed shortly by the Siemens regenerative gas furnace —

was the ground laid for the open hearth process which could make *steel* of any desired carbon content. The restraints on the full development of machines, imposed by the limitations of the metals with which they were built, were at last released; and the technological forces which were already changing the pattern of British society raced ahead.

In the middle decades of the century, the enlarging vision of such entrepreneurial figures as Brunel had added further impetus by the creation of large-scale projects which gave rise to subsidiary industries. Brunel's giant steamships, which can still excite admiration today, are only one example of ambitious undertakings that demanded a host of less exalted, but equally innovatory, processes to facilitate their construction. And, as if to spread the growing confidence in technology to every corner of the land, there came the railways. Evolving from the time when Trevithick's engines had dragged coal-trucks from pit-face to mineshaft, they progressed swiftly from Stephenson's 'Rocket' and the introduction of the Stockton-Darlington and Liverpool-Manchester lines to a complex of iron ways which traversed the entire country.

The industrial cornucopia had been tipped exultantly — and the wonders of the machine ran free. One high point in that precipitous flow was the introduction of the Parsons steam turbine, for the generation of electrical power. Hans Christian Oersted had found in 1820 that a wire joined to the two poles of a voltaic cell could, in the right position, influence the line of axis of a compass needle — he had discovered the magnetic lines of force. From this principle it took a mere five years for William Sturgeon to evolve the first electro-magnet. Six years later, in 1831, Faraday showed how current could be made to flow along a wire by rotating a copper disc between the magnetic poles. In that single demonstration he bequeathed the benefits of both the electric motor and the dynamo to man. Within a decade, coal-raised steam was providing the power to drive electrical generators, Joseph Henry had devised the telegraph and his fellow American, Samuel Finley Breese Morse, had refined it and compiled the communications code which bears his name. In 1845 an electric cable was laid between Dover and Calais; within eleven years another had crossed beneath the Atlantic.

It was inevitable that the accelerating rate of innovation in the first half of the nineteenth century should have bestowed on its progenitors an aura almost akin to that of gods on earth.

It may be an oversimplification of the awareness of the times to suggest that man discovered then that he could fundamentally change the physical state of the world; but the intimations that he could ultimately master nature were certainly dawning upon him as he watched his own adaptive genius grow. In the upward sweep of material marvels, it would have been difficult for the more trusting not to believe that Condorcet's great humanist message was, in its own fashion, pointing the way to an El Dorado of mankind's individual making. On that May morning in 1851, when the first World's Fair opened in Hyde Park, encapsulated within Sir Joseph Paxton's palace of crystal and iron, there could have been few who visited it who would not have vouchsafed that progress was immutable, that the prosperity of the era was largely vested in the impersonal beauty of the tireless machine, and that advancement through science would lead, more or less without serious impediment, to a world in which enlightened and rational men could hardly be other than good.

It is almost unnecessary to record that such periods of high optimism have, with few exceptions in human history, brought tribulation in their wake. At the very point in time when the World's Fair of 1851 was resounding with the praises of millennial man, science was unlocking the doors to an alternative philosophy which was to put humanity peremptorily back in its place.

In 1847 Alfred Russel Wallace had expressed his intention of studying some particular family of plants or animals with a view to evolving a theory on the origin of species. Eleven years later he sent an essay reporting his findings from the Malay Archipelago to Charles Darwin, with a request that it be read to the Linnean Society in London. The paper revealed the uncanny coincidence that Wallace had independently arrived at virtually the same conclusions Darwin himself had reached twenty years earlier. Darwin had withheld publication of his theory for two decades, fully aware of the bitter controversy it would arouse. However, on receipt of Wallace's essay, he put his own theory into writing and both papers were read before the Linnean Society on 1 July, 1858. In the following year *On the Origin of Species* was published in book form; and the remorselessness of the Cosmic Process which determines the destiny of all life was laid out for the tempering of progressive man.

As if this biological revelation were not enough, the physicists of the mid-nineteenth century had already delivered a bombshell all of their own. Dating back to Sadi Carnot's *Réflexions sur la*

Puissance Motrice du Feu (1824), the study of the motive power of heat had led to the formulation of the Second Law of Thermo-dynamics. While the First Law had stated that energy is never lost, the Second Law showed that it is continually being dissipated. What this meant was that although the total sum of energy in the universe might remain constant, the stars were actually burning themselves out; consequently there was a limit to the time in which life could be supported on earth.

The growth of the machine culture, the biological evidence for the 'preservation of favoured races in the struggle for life', the physical mortality of the solar system — these three factors, more than any others, were to dominate the development of science fiction throughout its initial stages; they remain major themes in the genre today.

*****

The first speculative writer fully to exploit the future capabilities of the machine was unquestionably Jules Verne, whose sixty-four novels span the last four decades of the nineteenth century. His early books written in the 1860s, among them *Journey to the Centre of the Earth* (1864) and *From the Earth to the Moon* (1865), are in the nature of adventure narratives glorifying man's ability to harness the machine's power to transport him wherever he might choose to go; what he might do when he arrived there was another matter. The 'sense of wonder' which Verne instilled into his first tales exists very much for the voyaging alone. It is significant that in one of his lunar journeys he is totally unconcerned whether the moon might be inhabited; his forerunners to the astronauts do not even bother to land on it. What fascinates him is the flight itself and the way it affects the men who undertake it.

Verne prided himself that the machinery with which he littered his stories was fully explained and firmly based on known engineering principles. So, in most cases, it was — even if there is an odd quirk in an imagination which can conceive Captain Nemo's submarine 'Nautilus' in *Twenty Thousand Leagues under the Sea* (1870), and then furnish it with heavy Victorian bric-a-brac and crystal chandeliers. By an intelligent reading of the latest technical innovations, Verne was frequently able to extend their uses in spectacular ways — Robur's hundred-foot long airship in *The Clipper of the Clouds* (1886) is equipped with seventy-four masts bearing something very like helicopter blades. He went further in *Propeller Island* (1895) by depicting an entire sea-borne city, complete with moving pavements, palaces, and ultra-rich inhabitants. But he was equally responsive to the idea of a Cosmic catastrophe against which the combined ingenuity of technological man might stand for naught. In *Hector Servadac* (1877) he related the effects of a comet narrowly missing the earth — the first account of a natural phenomenon which Wells was to use respectively in utopian and cataclysmic terms as the basis for *In the Days of the Comet* and 'The Star'.

However, there are occasions when Verne's understanding of scientific principles leaves something to be desired. It is odd that on reading *The First Men in the Moon* he should have chosen to criticize Wells for his invention of the gravity-screen which the author had named 'cavorite', after its inventor. 'I sent my characters to the moon with gunpowder', wrote Verne, 'a thing one may see every day. Where does Monsieur Wells find his Cavorite? Let him show it to me!' Gunpowder, yes — but at what high price? Verne's notion for getting men to the moon was to shoot their craft from the mouth of a gigantic cannon, ignoring the fact that the projectile's initial velocity would have reduced its occupants to a fine pulp at the moment of ignition. On the other hand, his moonflight predicted more than one factual detail of the Apollo 11 mission. As Neil Armstrong was to remark on 24 July, 1969, in the last public transmission from 'Columbia' before splashdown:

'A hundred years ago, Jules Verne wrote a book about a voyage to the moon. His spaceship 'Columbia' took off from Florida and landed in the Pacific Ocean after completing a trip to the moon. It seems appropriate to us to share with you some of the reflections of the crew as the modern day 'Columbia' completes its rendezvous with the planet earth in the same Pacific Ocean tomorrow. The responsibility for this flight lies first with history and with the giants of science who preceded this effort.'

Probably the most interesting aspect of Verne's career as a writer is the progress of his novels over the years from shining expositions of the benefits of the machine to darker visions of the dangers of uncontrolled technology. Destined to be trained as a lawyer, he had attempted to run away to sea as a boy, only to be retrieved by a disenchanted father. He developed a liking for drama, and did not turn to science fiction until he had already written plays and worked for a while in theatre administration. In what can be called the 'idealistic' period of his *voyages extraordinaires*, he saw the machine as a means by which the individual might obtain personal fulfilment. The escapist quality of his early work reflects his boyhood longing to be free; and to this end he imagined the machine as a gift to a type of entrepreneurial man who, like himself, wished to shake loose from the common strictures of a bourgeois society. It was not without design that a third of his novels were set in the United States — Verne, along with many Europeans of his day, had been seduced by the 'American Dream'.

As the second half of the century wore on, Verne's growing awareness of the nature of the political and social struggles erupting in Europe and farther afield caused him to interpret the future of the machine age in a less altruistic light. He came increasingly to describe a kind of city-state, such as 'Milliard City' in *Propeller Island*, in which technology tended to run riot and where the wielding of machine power could prove every bit as corrupting and eventually destructive as more conventional forms. After an interval of eighteen years Robur, 'the Conqueror', still aloft in his airborne clipper, returned in a sequel as a megalomaniac bent on mastering the world. In *The Begum's Fortune* (1879) Verne wrote of a conflict between two city-states, one humanistic and French, the other highly-industrialized and, predictably, German. The latter, a nightmarish urban hell known as 'Stahlstadt', is ruled by a prototype of the mad doctor who was to become the bane of countless unmemorable science fiction sagas from other pens than Verne's. His philosophy, nevertheless, would have met with de Sade's approval; it was soon to strike chords in the feverish head of Houston Stewart Chamberlain — a certifiable expatriate Englishman who was to produce a blueprint for the Nazis — and it was not without a smattering of subtly distorted Darwinism:

'Right...Good...Evil are purely relative, and quite conventional words. Nothing is positive but the grand laws of nature. The law of competition has the same force as that of gravitation. It is folly to resist, while to submit and follow in the way it points out is only wise and reasonable, and therefore I mean to destroy...[France-ville]. Thanks to my cannon, my fifty thousand Germans will easily make an end of the hundred thousand dreamers over there, who now constitute a group condemned to perish.'

As this trend in Verne's work continued, the logical outcome of applied science seemed in his interpretations to lead more and more to the ultimate dehumanization of man. Towards the end he was conceiving deranged scientists of the order of Thomas Roch, whose guided missiles in *For the Flag* (1896) are put to piratical use in the Atlantic shipping lanes.

In his lifetime Jules Verne acquired an international reputation, enjoyed the prestige of national honours, and achieved the curious distinction – probably unique among science fiction writers – of receiving the Papal blessing. In France today, as might be expected, he continues to be held in high regard; and scholarly evaluations of his work proceed apace. In critical analyses, however, it is recognized that the scope of his work – laying aside his remarkably accurate mechanical predictions of aircraft, submarines, and even television – is appreciably narrower than that of the man with whom he is generally linked as co-founder of modern science fiction, H.G. Wells.

Verne began his writings in the genre some thirty years earlier than Wells; and his life spanned a period in technological progress which began with the first railways and closed with the invention of the aeroplane – he died in 1905 just five years before his compatriot Louis Bleriot flew the English Channel. He wrote, in fact, at a unique moment in history when the advent of the machine was beginning to transform the lives of ordinary people. One aspect of that transformation was the changing attitude to travel. A man, who fifty years earlier might never have left the surroundings of his birthplace, could by mid-century take a train from London to Edinburgh and arrive there in less time than a stage-coach would have needed to reach the South coast. By 1904 motorized public transport services had begun, and the first electric underground trains had already been running in London for a decade and a half. The broadening effect of travel had come within the reach of all but the very poor; and Verne, with his tales of fantastic voyages, further stimulated imaginations already fired with a vision of travel as an opportunity for both pleasure and enlightenment.

In terms of Verne's effectiveness in the science fiction idiom, it is irrelevant that Wells, his so-called co-progenitor, succeeded in influencing two generations of the young by quite other means than science fiction and could have become — had circumstances not directed him elsewhere — the rival of Dickens as an English social novelist. Verne may or may not have suffered at the hands of his translators; even so, there can be no disguising the fact that, while his narrative powers were considerable, in company with many of the science fiction authors who were to follow him he had no great gift as a literary stylist. He was fundamentally a man of ideas with an imaginative 'feel' for science; and if the range of his work was less all-embracing than that of Wells, and his literary style less developed, his inventiveness and the extent of his swing away from his original glorification of the machine merit his recognition as a great speculative writer.

*****

During the four decades in which Verne was writing, other science fiction stories were to appear which frequently reflected his influence. In many cases they took the form of speculative future histories infused with naive assumptions that science would eventually elevate man to a veritable utopia. William Harben's 'In the Year 10,000' (1892) belongs to this category, together with the Swedish Claes Lundin's *Oxygen och Aromasia* (1879), a novel replete with flying machines and spaceships, automatically cooked meals, suspended animation and matter transmitters. On the other hand, future histories of a darker vein could be found in such books as Richard Jefferies' *After London* (1885), which pictured a return to 'natural' barbarism following the collapse of industrial civilization.

Other writers remained content with less sweeping panoramas of the future. In 1869 the American author, Edward Everett Hale, made the first prediction of an artificial satellite in his story 'The Brick Moon'; unfortunately for its constructors their brick-built satellite, designed as a navigational aid for shipping, was launched prematurely while they were still inside. Edwin Abbott's mathematical curiosity, *Flatland: A Romance of Many Dimensions* (1884), in which a two-dimensional world is described by a geometric square, must be classed as fantasy rather than science fiction; but that makes it no less a minor classic of speculative writing. Robert Louis Stevenson's *The Strange Case of Dr Jekyll and Mr Hyde* (1886) contains elements of both Poe and Gothic horror, but nevertheless utilizes science to effect the

41

metamorphosis of man into monster, unlike the Central European werewolf legends where the change occurs supernaturally.

1888 saw the appearance in the United States of Edward Bellamy's *Looking Backward*, a germinal work portraying a future socialist utopia which was to exert a singular influence over a number of succeeding authors. Since it falls squarely into the category of utopian writing, we shall consider it more fully in the chapter devoted to that subject.

On a lighter level, even Anthony Trollope tried his hand, but not very successfully, at anticipating the recreational pursuits of a century into the future. His *The Fixed Period* (1882) related the delights of cricket played with the hazardous assistance of mechanical catchers and bowlers. A similar idea was handled better by 'J.A.C.K.', whose *Golf in the Year 2000* humorously foresaw in 1892 the advent of mechanical caddies and other delectable aids to improve the game. In a decidedly more serious mood, the Belfast journalist, Robert Cromie, conceived a megalomaniac scientist in *The Crack of Doom* (1895) who invents a bomb by following through the theory that 'one grain of matter contains enough energy, if etherized, to raise one hundred thousand tons nearly two miles'. In a grim prediction of Alamagordo he demonstrates the weapon at the expense of a fleet of French trawlers:

'Then the sea behind us burst into a flame, followed by the sound of an explosion so frightful that we were almost stunned by it. A huge mass of water, torn into a solid block, was hurled into the air and there it broke into a hundred roaring cataracts. These fell into the raging cauldron that seethed below. The French fishing fleet had disappeared.'

Less terrifying, but of marked social significance, was Sir George Chesney's pamphlet *The Battle of Dorking: reminiscences of a Volunteer* (1871), which foretold a successful invasion of Britain by the Prussian army. Chesney's intention was to gain public recognition of the obsolete equipment and outmoded strategy which characterized British defence forces; and he wrote in the light of the Franco-Prussian War which had ended in the same year. That he achieved his purpose is borne out by the flood of succeeding pamphlets, either in support of or criticizing his own, which appeared during the following months. On an allied subject, the proposal to build a Channel tunnel between England and France was sounding a note of imminent doom in certain xenophobic hearts. Accounts of attempted French and German forays via the tunnel across the fields of Kent were related in further pamphlets written under the enticing pseudonyms of 'Cassandra', in 1876, and 'The Demure One' and 'Grip' in 1882.

Interplanetary journeys, in which enterprising Victorian gentlemen sipped their traditional beverages while gazing down on the unfamiliar continents of Venus and Mars, were to be found in John Jacob Astor's *A Journey in Other Worlds* and George Griffith's *Honeymoon in Space*, both written during the last years of the century. However, by far the most imaginative treatment of the subject, which actually received praise from scientists themselves, came from a man who, but for the lack of English translations of his work, should rightfully rank only second to Wells and Verne as a major pioneer of science fiction.

Auf zwei Planeten (On Two Planets), by Kurd Lasswitz, had been translated into Danish, Norwegian, Swedish, Czech and Dutch within a few years of its first publication in Germany in 1897. As the new century dawned it was probably the most widely-read science fiction story on the mainland of Europe. Had it been translated at the time into English it would almost certainly have influenced later writers in both Britain and the United States. It describes a Martian occupation of earth on very different terms from those of Wells's purely destructive invaders in *The War of the Worlds*.

Lasswitz's long novel begins with the capture of two human polar explorers who are taken to Mars by a small expeditionary force. There they encounter a Martian civilization clearly technologically superior to man's, and organized as a pluralistic society which includes both monarchies and republics, capitalism and socialism. Each citizen of Mars has the choice to live under whichever system he prefers; and in the utopian tradition Martians put moral duty before personal desires. They soon come to appreciate that in this they differ profoundly from man.

Mars sends a second spaceship to earth which is promptly fired on by a British warship and some of its crew are taken prisoner. This development induces a dichotomy of feelings towards humanity when the spacecraft finally returns to Mars. Half the Martians remain willing to treat earthmen as equals and wish to establish friendly relations between the two planets; the others see them as degenerate inferiors whose world is ripe for exploitation. An entire Martian fleet is later despatched to annihilate the British Navy. The resultant loss of British sea power sparks off a war between Turkey and Europe which convinces the Martians that man is indeed a savage. Accordingly, they annexe Western Europe, and subsequently the United States and Russia.

For a period man is held under the Martian yoke, while his benign protectors attempt to educate him to accept their superior culture. They meet with little success. Having learned at least something from Martian technology, the humans build airships and attack the invaders' bases. Only the Martians' dislike of genocide prevents them from destroying mankind completely; finally a treaty is negotiated under which earth becomes a world state and the two races agree to co-operate.

Auf zwei Planeten is less a work of technological science fiction — although Lasswitz went further than Hale in his prediction of the use of artificial satellites as 'stopping-off' stations for interplanetary flight — and more a discussion novel on the Kantian ideal of individual moral improvement. The Martians are seen as capable of destroying man solely by virtue of their higher morality:

' "...no Martian is able to press the button of the nihilite apparatus if a human stands against him with a firm, moral will, a will that knows nothing but the desire to do what is good. But these Englishmen...considered only their own interests, their specifically national advantages, not the dignity of humanity as a whole..." '

Like Verne, Lasswitz felt compelled to single out British colonialism as one of his particular targets, although he went on to add that Germany was no better in that respect.

The fine flourish of utopian writing which marked the end of the nineteenth century, and which will be discussed in Chapter Seven, evidently had an appeal for Lasswitz. In addition to the utopian undertones in the Martians of *Auf zwei Planeten*, he conceived a fully-fledged intellectual utopia in his story 'Apoikis', the name of an Atlantic island, where technology is abolished and the inhabitants 'are not the slaves of our customs as are the savages, nor masters of the material world as are the educated nations of Europe; but are masters of our wills, masters of all consciousness, and therefore we are free'. 'Apoikis' is an exact prototype of Aldous Huxley's *Island*, which followed it some seventy years later.

Among his many writings Lasswitz published a biography of the German author, Gustav Theodor Fechner, whose humorous essays on the possibilities of science — in the vein of 'Proof that the Moon consists of Iodine' — had influenced him greatly. Fechner developed a theory of 'psycho-physics' which suggested that parts of the brain could be artificially stimulated to produce particular thoughts and emotions. Lasswitz drew on this idea for 'Against the Law of the World: A Story of the Year 3877' (1878), in which children's brains are manipulated by electric currents to encourage them in certain directions of thought. He anticipated also in the same tale the specialized division of labour which Wells and Huxley were respectively to portray in its full horror in *The First Men in the Moon* and *Brave New World*.

Lasswitz was undoubtedly one of the first writers of science fiction to find a place for humour in his work; indeed he was usually at his most effective when he was being something less than serious. In his amusing tale 'Aladdin's Lamp' he admirably satirizes Kant's idea that the presumed laws of Nature are no more than concepts already existing inside our heads, and that as we appreciate them they become real. When Aladdin's original lamp is discovered the genie is duly summoned, only to prove entirely impotent because anything he is asked to do would violate a natural law. How then was he able to perform such miracles for Aladdin?

' "...at that time the laws of the conservation of matter and energy were still unknown."
"What! Surely you wouldn't maintain that the laws of nature were not working then?"
"The natural laws", answered the spirit, "are nothing but the expression of scientific perception in a given period. In my transcendental consciousness, I am independent of these laws; but when working in time, in your time, I cannot do anything contrary to the laws that are pillars of your culture." '

It is by his satirical short stories in the genre, some of them very similar in approach to those written recently, that Kurd Lasswitz most clearly marks a bridge between Verne and modern science fiction. If the work of this slightly obscure German professor of mathematics often fails to receive the full recognition it deserves, that is very much a question of historical circumstances, not least of which was the arrival on the scene of the man who was to raise the quality of speculative writing to a level which may have since been rivalled, but has still to be surpassed — and to whom we shall now turn.

4 The Long Shadow of Wells

*I walk among the fragments of the future, that future which
I contemplate. And all my thoughts and striving is to compass
and gather into one thing what is a figment and a riddle and a
dismal accident ... And how could I bear to be a man if man
was not a poet and a solver of riddles and the saviour of
accidents.*

Friedrich Nietzsche, *Thus Spake Zarathustra*

In the days when an intimate audience was his for the asking,
H.G. Wells related in his autobiography how his father had con-
fessed to him beside the grounds of a 'Big House' where he had
once been a gardener: 'When I was a young man of your age I
used to come out here and lie oh! half the night, just looking at
the stars.'

'What for?' asked Wells (a little lamely he thought in retrospect).

'Wondering.'

The conversation ended there.

By coincidence it was in that same 'Big House', Up Park near
Petersfield, that Wells as a boy of fourteen laid hands on an old
Gregorian telescope and was discovered by his mother one night
inspecting the craters on the moon. 'She had heard me open the
window. She said I should catch my death of cold. But at the
time that seemed a minor consideration.'

It always did—with Wells. There were times in later life when
it was suggested to him that he would catch — so to speak — his
literary death, by attempting too much, by casting about too far
in too many directions, by practising incautiously what he
preached in the domains of 'free love'. And most usually the
demise of his reputation was a matter of 'minor consideration'.

It is one of those peculiar accidents of history that we owe
our inheritance of the kaleidoscopic Wellsian imagination to the
fact that both Wells and his father were successful in breaking
their legs. To be more accurate, Wells had his broken for him
when, in 1874 while he was still seven, he was tossed into the air
by a friendly adult who neglected to catch him upon his descent.
Laid up for some weeks, the child, always precocious, began to
read. He ploughed through Wood's *Natural History*, accounts of

the life of Wellington and the American Civil War, the books of Washington Irving and Fenimore Cooper. By the time he was ready to walk again, his world had expanded far beyond the dingy china shop in the High Street of Bromley where he had been born.

Four years later his father fell off a ladder while pruning a vine and fractured his thigh. Mrs Wells returned as housekeeper to Up Park, taking the young H.G. with her. It was there, at the age of fourteen, that he plundered the library of the old Sir Harry Featherstonhaugh, a freethinker who had not been adverse to the charms of Nelson's Lady Hamilton. Voltaire, Tom Paine, an unexpurgated *Gulliver's Travels* and Plato's *Republic* — all were at hand for the avid attention of the boy who had already failed once as a draper's apprentice and again as a student teacher. *The Republic* impressed him enormously with its vision of a society changed beyond all expectation. 'Here', he wrote in his autobiography, 'was the amazing and heartening suggestion that the whole fabric of law, custom and worship, which seemed so invincibly established, might be cast into the melting pot and made new.'

That vision of the possibility of real social change, and the view from the telescope at Up Park, were to drive Wells impetuously through a writing career which by its end trailed more than one-hundred-and-fifty published books and pamphlets, some seventy short stories and fifty years of prolific journalism in its wake. In an early paper, 'The Discovery of the Future', read to the Royal Institution in 1902, Wells put his twin vision into a string of words which he was to repeat on many occasions:

'All this world is heavy with the promise of greater things, and a day will come, one day in the unending succession of days, when beings who are now latent in our thoughts and hidden in our loins, shall stand upon this earth as one stands upon a footstool and shall laugh and reach out their hands amidst the stars.'

He closed his remarkable *Outline of History* with much the same paean in 1920; and in 1944, when the draft of *Mind at the End of its Tether* was lying on his desk in war-torn London, he sent to press an article entitled 'My Dreams' in which he finally purged himself of its memory:

'Years ago I had a waking dream which comes back to my

mind today, and I wrote: "When man shall stand upon this earth as a footstool and laugh and stretch out his hand amongst the stars..."

I wake abruptly to the concussion of an anti-aircraft gun, and lie listening for a little while.

"What nonsense!" I say and roll over and return to the sane World of Dreams.'

In that change of attitude can be seen almost the entire story of the second, and arguably less effective, part of Wells's career as a writer. That part began in 1901 with *Anticipations of the Reaction of Mechanical and Scientific Progress upon Human Life and Thought* and it ended in 1945 with the valedictory *Mind at the End of its Tether*. Within the context of this study, it can concern us only briefly; the great majority of the 'scientific romances' and short stories which have won Wells acclaim as a 'father of science fiction' were written, astonishingly, during the seven short years from 1894 to 1900.

After a series of disastrous false starts in life, Wells won a scholarship to the Normal School of Science (now the Imperial College of Science and Technology) in South Kensington. There in 1884 he studied biology for a year at the feet of Thomas Henry Huxley — an experience from which he never fully recovered. Huxley's Cosmic pessimism found in Wells the artist who would clothe its gloomy forebodings in a sombrely glowing mantle of ideas and words. For Huxley, the cosmic evolutionary process could never lead by itself to any betterment of the social and moral conditions of man. It was an implacable force which had to be checked at every twist and turn by the application of ethics and a constant effort of human intellect and will. The towering apostle of Darwin held out no great hope that man would ever overcome his inherent savagery which was the outcome of millions of years of evolution. Beyond that he saw, in the far future, the slow dissolution of earth's physical energy predicted by the Second Law of Thermodynamics. The progress of life on the planet, he wrote in 'The Struggle for Existence in Human Society' (1888), was as the flight of a cannonball:

'...the sinking half of that course is as much a part of the general process of evolution as the rising.... If for millions of years, our globe has taken the upward road, yet, some time the summit will be reached and the downward route will be commenced. The most daring imagination will hardly venture upon the suggestion that the power and intelligence of man can ever arrest the procession of the great year.'

Huxley's was a *weltanschauung* which required considerable efforts of stoicism to sustain whoever professed it; and there were times when he would have been happy to see 'some kindly comet' put an end to the whole depressing business.

Wells took Huxley's vision of that long descent into the final twilight of a dying sun, kindled it with the sparks of his own imagination, and laid the result before the unready reader in his first published novel, *The Time Machine*. 'No poet, so far as I know', Walter Allen has said, 'ever wrote an epic based on Darwinism. *The Time Machine* is the nearest thing we have.' When it arrived in 1895 it was as if a starshell had burst on the literary horizon. With a few simple but compelling strokes of the pen, Wells overcame the hazards of explaining the implausible theory of time travel and hurled his audience forward to the year 802,701.

The Time Traveller finds what at first appears to be an arcadian, if effete, society of childlike beings whose powers of understanding and concentration are far beneath those of the intelligent beings he has left behind in the nineteenth century. There is no evidence of sickness or deprivation in this distant future; and the decaying remains of a great museum indicate that the simple Eloi are the inheritors of what had once been a technological civilization which had conquered the material problems of a former age. Thus the body of the story begins in what might almost be a utopian setting, were it not for the obvious decline in the mental capabilities of the Eloi.

The initial impressions of the Time Traveller, however, are radically changed by the discovery of an underground race of myopic humanoid creatures whose excursions on to the surface at night reduce the Eloi to an impotent state of terror. The realization slowly comes that the Eloi and the subterranean Morlocks are both the descendants of the same human species, which sometime in the past consigned its workers to underground factories while its privileged classes continued to enjoy the idyllic upper air. With the subsequent revelation that the Morlocks actually feed on the Eloi, and meantime ensure their wellbeing as if they were so much cattle, the Time Traveller is able to appreciate the full extent of the natural degeneration he has come upon. Hastening on through time, he eventually

arrives at a point where the earth has almost ceased to rotate
and the sun is a dying ember, huge in a snow-filled sky. There,
at the tail-end of terrestrial vitality, he finds the last signs of
animal life on earth:

' "A horror of this great darkness came on me. The cold that
smote to my marrow, and the pain I felt in breathing, overcame me. I shivered, and a deadly nausea seized me. Then
like a red-hot bow in the sky appeared the edge of the sun....
As I stood sick and confused I saw again the thing upon the
shoal — there was no mistake ... that it was a moving thing —
against the red water of the sea. It was a round thing, the size
of a football perhaps, or, it may be, bigger, and tentacles
trailed down from it..." '

No-one had painted so graphically in terms of 'sense of
wonder' what the end of the world — short of a cataclysm —
was likely to be. And 'painted' is not too exaggerated a term,
for *The Time Machine* is the work of an artist whose handling
of images and rhythm at times took the story to the brink of
poetry. The Time Traveller brings back to his own day a handful
of flowers given him by an Eloi girl. Having told his tale to his
incredulous friends, he sets off on his machine again — and never
returns. In a brief epilogue, the narrator speculates on his fate.
V.B. Leyland has shown how this short last section falls, almost
without persuasion, into free verse:

'One cannot choose but wonder,
Will he ever return?

It may be that he swept back into the past,
And fell among the blood-drinking savages
Of the Age of Unpolished Stone;
Into the abysses of the Cretaceous Sea;
Or among the grotesque saurians,
The huge reptilian brutes
Of the Jurassic times.

He may even now —
If I may use the phrase —
Be wandering
On some Plesiosaurus-haunted Oolithic coral reef,
Or beside the lonely saline lakes
Of the Triassic age.

Or did he go forward,
Into one of the nearer ages,
In which men are still men,
But with the riddles of our own time answered,
And its wearisome problems solved?
Into the manhood of the race:
For I, for my own part,
Cannot think that these latter days
Of weak experiment,
Fragmentary theory,
And mutual discord
Are indeed man's culminating time!

I say, for my part.

He, I know —
For the question had been discussed among us
Long before the Time Machine was made —
Thought but cheerlessly
Of the Advancement of Mankind,
And saw
In the growing pile of civilisation
Only a foolish heaping
That must inevitably
Fall back upon and destroy
Its makers in the end.

If that is so,
It remains for us to live
As if it were not so.

But to me the future
Is still black and blank —
Is a vast ignorance —
Lit at a few casual places
By the memory of his story.

And I have by me,
For my comfort,
Two strange white flowers —
Shrivelled now,
And brown and flat and brittle —
To witness that even
When mind and strength had gone,

Gratitude and a mutual tenderness
Still lived on
In the heart of man.'

In this moving close to his first major piece of fiction, Wells concisely expresses Huxley's philosophy in the attitude of the Time Traveller to civilization, and his own in the narrator's insistence that even if Huxley is right, 'it remains for us to live as if it were not so'.

*****

Wells's next major work after *The Time Machine* appeared a year later in 1896 and was almost universally misunderstood by the critics of the day. *The Island of Doctor Moreau* seems, on a superficial level, to be little more than a rather repellent horror story, albeit compellingly told; and that is how the majority of critics interpreted it. It relates the efforts of a discredited vivisector to impose a human shape and intelligence upon animals of assorted species. While he meets with some short-term success, the subjects of his experiments continually revert to their original savage state. The book, which we shall consider further in a later chapter, is actually an allegorical comment on the animal heritage of man, and on the ever-present danger of his degenerating into savagery, either as an individual under stress, or as a larger group undergoing the kind of mass neurosis which was subsequently seen in the rise of Fascism. Wells was simply restating Huxley's ideas on evolution in a less obvious context than that of *The Time Machine*.

During 1896 and 1897 Wells set down his views on human evolution and civilization more expressly in two closely-reasoned articles which he wrote for the *Fortnightly Review* — 'Human Evolution, An Artificial Process' and 'Morals and Civilisation'. In the former he argued, after Huxley, that the progress of civilization since the Stone Age had no connection with natural selection, because — in evolutionary terms — the period was too short to be of note. The advance, therefore, was an artificial process which could in no way be associated with genetic change. In civilized man, he suggested, two entirely separate factors can be seen at play: firstly 'an inherited factor, the natural man, who is the product of natural selection, the culminating ape, and a type more obstinately unchangeable than any other living creature...'. The second, to which the development of civilization — made manifest by the invention of speech — could be attributed, was 'an acquired factor, the highly plastic creature of tradition, suggestion and reasoned thought'. In the interaction between these two aspects of his make-up lay the seeds of both man's greatness and downfall.

In 'Morals and Civilisation', Wells evoked the image of a post-catastrophe world in which man, shorn of his commitment to a civilized society, would revert to the basic animal emotions which characterized his inheritance. His tone, however, in both articles, was less pessimistic than that of his mentor. He was already moving more towards the centre ground whence, in 1901, he was to launch wholeheartedly into three decades of utopian advocacy.

Nevertheless, the Huxleyan pessimism which permeated *The Time Machine* and *The Island of Doctor Moreau* continued to run like a dark thread through the majority of Wells's scientific romances. It is beyond the scope of this chapter to examine them all in detail; and its purpose is, more properly, to show how a particular 'scientific' way of thinking, coupled with a far-ranging imagination and substantial literary gifts, enabled Wells to speculate brilliantly within the confines of an essentially cheerless philosophy.

That scientific way of thinking was, as we have already intimated, essentially dissimilar to Verne's. Wells was perfectly capable, when he chose, of developing stories along factual scientific lines, as he illustrated inimitably in his forecasts of the carnage resulting from mechanized and aerial warfare. But his more important bequest to the writers in the genre who followed him was his use of 'the imaginative jump'. He acknowledged no *obligation* to convince his readers in detail of the scientific plausibility of his dramatic situations, thus freeing himself of the long-winded technical explanations which made pedestrian whole sections in the works of Verne and which were also to characterize the early pulp magazines. His imaginative jumps, however, were no mere devices to spur the narrative on; they entailed the deployment of a form of intuitive scientific and social speculation at which he was particularly adept. They enabled him, and his rightful heirs, to present the reader with a series of circumstances which *might* come about if existing scientific and social trends were allowed to continue unchecked. He foresaw, for example, the concentrated movement of power to the centre which heralds the arrival of a technology-based totalitarian state. He foresaw it, in fact, very early in his writing career (in *When the Sleeper Wakes*, 1899) and he devoted a great many of his subsequent books to suggesting not always very practical alternatives which promised a better future for man. In the final resort, Wells — for all his internal conflict — always came down on the side of humanity, even if he was one who, echoing Chesterton, could frequently 'love my fellow man and hate my next-door neighbour'.

Wells began to write journalistic articles and tales in his late twenties, when his physical state of health prevented him from pursuing the teaching career which circumstances had forced upon him. It is important to an understanding of his early pessimism to recognize how close to death he stayed for several years. He had suffered from consumptive lung haemorrhages, a crushed kidney and a variety of other ills. At an age when most young men are revelling in physical buoyancy, he was busy simply endeavouring to stay alive. Not until 1900, when he had a house of his own built overlooking the Channel above Folkestone, did his health really begin to mend.

Although his letters of the period display a predominantly hopeful disposition, it is understandable that his own poor prospects for living long should predispose him in the 1890s to view the universe darkly, and perhaps almost to find comfort in Huxley's bleak prognosis. After *The Island of Doctor Moreau* his next major scientific romance was *The Invisible Man* (1897), in which he showed, as he was to do again in 'The Country of the Blind' (1904), how the enjoyment of what might seem a unique advantage over other beings can turn out to be exactly the reverse.

The Invisible Man is also a warning of how the gifts of science can be abused in the hands of an arrogant but clever fool. Griffin, the young scientist who bankrupts himself in his ultimately successful search for a technique to render organic matter invisible, is motivated by greed and a desire for personal aggrandizement. His low regard for others, whom he considers his natural inferiors, is reinforced by his invisibility which he assumes will enable him to behave with impunity towards them. In fact the drawbacks to his condition, one of which is its temporary irreversibility, conspire rapidly to bring him down. Obliged to go without clothes, he suffers perpetual colds. When he wishes to find accommodation or to indulge in 'normal' conversation, he must swathe his head in bandages which automatically mark him as a target for curiosity. Finally, after creating havoc in a number of Sussex villages, he is cornered by an angry crowd who unintentionally beat him to death because they cannot see how seriously they are hurting him.

What distinguished *The Invisible Man*, among other things, from the common tale of a megalomaniac scientist running amok is Wells's masterly evocation of a quiet country setting. In the absence of gleaming laboratories or dank and sinister cellars, the action of the novel is played out amid the sunny lanes of Sussex, with Griffin pitting his wits against a collection of earthy bucolic folk who would not recognize one end of a spectroscope from the other. This was an especial gift of Wells which he employed time and again to lend credibility to his accounts of the improbable. For his late Victorian readers he made easy the 'willing suspension of disbelief' by conjuring up homely and familiar backgrounds, and suddenly infusing them with strange and abnormal happenings.

The initial testing of 'cavorite' in *The First Men in the Moon* takes place in the inventor's house near Romney on the Kent coast. It comes near to dissipating the entire atmosphere of earth! The moment the small flat sheet of experimental cavorite attains its desired properties, it releases all the substance above it from the attraction of gravity, creating a roaring funnel stretching upwards into space through which could be sucked every cubic foot of breatheable air on the globe. The end of humanity precipitated in a country cottage below the gentle hills of Kent! — such was Wells's ability to coax the reader imperceptibly into a belief in his worlds, that the proposition seemed perfectly credible. Fortunately, the cavorite breaks loose from its test bench and is itself drawn up beyond the limits of earth's gravitational field where it can no longer be a hazard.

The same concentration on rural surroundings occurs frequently in the narrative of *The War of the Worlds* (1898). The first Martian cylinder falls on Horsell Common, near Woking, and mankind's opening encounter with the annihilating heat-rays of the newcomers is experienced along the leafy and normally tranquil approaches of the Chobham Road. Unlike Lasswitz's Martians in *Auf zwei Planeten*, Wells's invaders give few clues as to the basis of their civilization, other than that it incorporates an advanced intelligence which suffers no qualms in relentlessly obliterating anything which stands in its way. The book, which in one interpretation is — akin to Lasswitz's — a criticism of the ruthless character of British colonialism, begins uncompromisingly with a bald, but not unsympathetic, statement of the Martian need for *lebensraum*. Faced with the cosmic decay of their own planet, they look across the depths of space to the blue promise of earth, a world crowded with life, 'but crowded only with what they regard as inferior animals':

> 'And before we judge them too harshly, we must remember what ruthless and utter destruction our own species has wrought, not only upon animals, such as the vanished bison and the dodo, but upon its own inferior races. The Tasmanians, in spite of their human likeness, were entirely swept out of existence in a war of extermination waged by European immigrants, in the space of fifty years. Are we such apostles of mercy as to complain if the Martians warred in the same spirit?'

The Martians, as Wells makes clear, are impervious to any compassionate claims on behalf of humanity. In such naked intelligence of an advanced order, he suggests, there may be no room for softer feelings concerning lesser mortals — and it could be a mark of fallibility if there were. It is an expansion of the Invisible Man's lack of regard for those he considers his inferiors; and translated into reality it is the attitude of the 'culminating ape', divorced from any ethical considerations, epitomised in Hitler's memorandum to Hans Frank, the Governor of Poland, of October 2, 1943:

> 'It is indispensable to bear in mind that the Polish gentry must cease to exist; however cruel this may sound, they must be exterminated wherever they are....
> There should be one master only for the Poles, the German. Two masters, side by side, cannot and must not exist. Therefore all representatives of the Polish intelligentsia are to be exterminated. This sounds cruel, but such is the law of life.'

It is interesting to note Wells's own acceptance of the Tasmanians as an 'inferior' race 'in spite of their human likeness'. His attitude to coloured peoples at the time was still very much that of any insular Englishman of the day. It was, of course, to change radically as the years progressed.

*****

The First Men in the Moon, which Wells himself thought his finest scientific romance, appeared in 1901 shortly before his far-reaching *Anticipations*. It marks the end of his preoccupation with alien intelligences and the collision of such cultures with that of man. In another respect it rivals *The Time Machine* in its brilliant use of symbols and images to create an acceptable but totally strange background. When Cavor and Bedford land on the moon, the lunar day is just about to dawn. With the sunrise, what appears to be a barren landscape unexpectedly springs into luxuriant life. Everywhere seed pods crack open and a dense vegetation literally rises before the visitors' eyes. In recollection, Bedford, the narrator, again falls victim to the wonderment of the scene:

> 'Imagine it! Imagine that dawn! The resurrection of the frozen air, the stirring and quickening of the soil, and then this silent uprising of vegetation, this unearthly ascent of fleshiness and spikes. Conceive it all lit by a blaze that would make the intensest sunlight of earth seem watery and weak. And still around this stirring jungle, wherever there was shadow, lingered banks of bluish snow.'

After a series of scrapes with the 'Selenites', Bedford succeeds in escaping back to earth using the cavorite sphere in which the two made their original journey. Cavor remains a prisoner on the moon, but continues to communicate by radio. Eventually he is taken into the presence of 'the Grand Lunar', the most powerful intelligence in a society where knowledge is stored, not mechanically, but in vastly distended brains:

> 'He seemed a small, self-luminous cloud at first, brooding on his sombre throne; his brain case must have measured many yards in diameter.... I saw that shadowy attendants were busy spraying that great brain with a cooling spray, and patting and sustaining it....
> ...He searched me with questions. "And for all sorts of work you have the same sort of men. But who thinks? Who governs?" I gave him an outline of the democratic method.
> When I had done he ordered cooling sprays upon his brow, and then requested me to repeat my explanation conceiving that something had miscarried.'

Too late Cavor realizes that he has said more about human inadequacies than is good for man's safety. The Selenite civilization, with its high degree of functional organization and rationality, could, once it possesses the secret of cavorite, embark on an overwhelming invasion of earth. Once again, it is a demonstration of how impervious an advanced intelligence might be to the welfare of what it considered an inferior species.

If there are utopian undertones in the depiction of the lunar society in *The First Men in the Moon*, they are not of the kind likely to commend itself to the admiration of our own species. Wells had already written tellingly of highly-mechanized anti-utopias on earth, in 'A Story of the Days to Come' and *When the Sleeper Wakes*, three or four years before he rapturously predicted the age of mass automation and consumption in *Anticipations*.

This last work brought him to the attention of the Fabian Society, with whom he formed a temporary and stormy union. But it was a step indicative of the direction in which his own intellectual development was pointing him. He had become a very widely-read author. His growing reputation was unlocking doors for him into the English establishment which, because of the lowly and impoverished surroundings from which he had risen, he alternately vilified and envied in the compass of a single breath. Physically too, his strength was improving rapidly. Hope, then, not only for himself, but for the whole toiling mass of humanity, was to be the great aim. He embarked on a flurry of positively utopian works in which progress towards a world state emerged from either natural or man-made catastrophes, or, as in the case of *The Food of the Gods* (1904), from a scientific development which would produce an enhanced race of men.

In *The War in the Air* (1908) it was, as the title implies, the use of aircraft in a world war which helped to emphasise the futility of mass destruction. The same idea was enlarged upon — particularly with the introduction of atomic bombs — in *The World Set Free* (1914), the book being dedicated to Frederick Soddy's 'Interpretation of Radium'. *In The Days of the Comet* (1906) describes the coming of peace among men as a natural consequence of an unknown gas released into the atmosphere from a comet's tail. It is an expression of Wells's doubts regarding man's ability to achieve an ideal society by his own devices; and in neither of his full-scale portrayals of a utopian world, *A Modern Utopia* and *Men Like Gods*, which came respectively in 1905 and 1923, was he entirely forthcoming as to how their states of grace had been attained.

In the Days of the Comet, which has never been considered an example of Wells at his best, is nevertheless noteworthy for its use of a hallucinogenic gas to persuade humanity that it is altogether beautiful. In this it anticipated the underground drug culture of a later era in Western society and the consequences of universal euphoria which Brian Aldiss was to depict very differently in *Barefoot in the Head* (1969). The first half of the novel is devoted to the murderous endeavours of the central character, Leadford, to despatch his sweetheart and her lover from their current existence to a future world which may or may not be waiting for them. With the comet's passing, however, his attitude changes to a blissful acceptance of an arrangement approximating to a *ménage à trois*. His return to consciousness after the green gas has had its effect is memorable for its insight into the heightened state of awareness frequently occasioned by hallucinogens:

'I seemed to awaken out of a refreshing sleep. I did not awaken with a start, but opened my eyes, and lay very comfortably looking at a line of extraordinary scarlet poppies that glowed against a glowing sky....The poppies...had a luminous quality, seemed wrought only from some more solid kind of light....
I held up my left hand and arm before me, a grubby hand, a frayed cuff; but with a quality of painted unreality, transfigured as a beggar might have been by Botticelli. I looked for a time steadfastly at a beautiful pearl sleeve link.'

Some fifty years later, Aldous Huxley, who was vastly more curious about the effects of drugs than Wells, recorded in *The Doors of Perception* his impressions of his first encounter with mescalin. The similarities between Leadford's comet-induced revelation and Huxley's own experience are surprisingly close:

...The books, for example, with which my study walls were lined. Like the flowers, they glowed, when I looked at them, with brighter colours, a profounder significance.... What I noticed, what impressed itself upon my mind was the fact that all of them glowed with living light....
...The legs...of that chair — how miraculous their tubularity, how supernatural their polished smoothness! I spent several minutes — or was it several centuries — not merely gazing at those bamboo legs, but actually being them....'

Long after his abandonment of extra-terrestrial settings, Wells also indulged in at least one excursion into 'inner space', and in doing so foreshadowed a fashion now common among the 'New Wave' of modern science fiction writers. 'Inner space' denotes the infinite corridors of experience existing within the individual human conscious and unconscious minds. Its exploration in current science fiction inevitably either verges on, or enters completely, the realms of fantasy. In *Mr. Blettsworthy on Rampole Island* (1928) Wells recounted the long hallucination of a young man who believes he has been shipwrecked and subsequently taken prisoner by a race of vicious savages. They adopt him as their 'Sacred Lunatic' and initiate him fully into their barbaric rites. For Blettsworthy they bear little comparison to what he regards as the sane and democratic ways of the Europe he has lost. He manages to escape from the island during the outbreak of a bloody war against a neighbouring tribe. Without warning, he discovers himself in New York, where in fact he has been for several years – in a profound state of reverie. He is conscripted into the army and arrives in the horror of France in 1916. Rampole Island, he realizes, was 'only the real world looming through the mists of my illusions...no better than the harsh veracities of existence'. Wounded and sent back to England, he sees himself in danger of returning through 'inner space' to the island – this time perhaps, for ever. The book is an interesting re-exposition of Wells's long-held views on the beast inherent in man, views which again began to appear more regularly in his work after the large-scale savagery of the First World War. They found compelling expression in *The Croquet Player* (1936) which was among his final dozen pieces of fiction.

The Croquet Player chronicles the mass haunting of a marshland village in the South East of England by an oppressive atmosphere emanating from a site of prehistoric humanoid remains discovered there. A harsh callousness and resorts to brutality are beginning to overtake the villagers, a local symptom it is suggested of a larger malady which is plaguing the whole of mankind. During a visit to the nearby museum, the brooding, nightmarish quality of the 'presence' finds form in the skull of a cave man grinning sightlessly in its glass case:

' "We live in his presence. He has never died. He is anything but dead..."
"...Only he was shut off from us and hidden. For a long time.

61

And now we see him here face to face and his grin derides us. Man is still what he was. Invincibly bestial, envious, malicious, greedy. Man, sir, unmasked and disillusioned is the same fearing, snarling, fighting beast he was a hundred thousand years ago. These are no metaphors, sir. What I tell you is the monstrous reality. The brute has been marking time and dreaming of a progress it has failed to make." '

Wells produced little else in the final fifteen years of his life which could qualify as science fiction. His last major effort was *The Shape of Things to Come*, published in 1933 – a rambling and exhausting account of a supranational state established by aviators after a second world war which, accurately enough, was predicted to begin in 1939. It contains but a few hints of the enthusiasm and infectious quality of the earlier works. However, when Alexander Korda's film adaptation, *Things to Come*, was in production during 1935, it was difficult to keep an ageing but still highly vociferous Wells off the set. He announced his conviction that the large aircraft of the 1960s would be borne aloft on delta-shaped wings. Every aviation expert that the film company could muster was trundled in to attempt to convince him of the implausibility of the idea. But in the end he had his way; and – as we know in retrospect – he proved to be right. After all, he could be heard to argue, had he not more or less invented the tank (*pace* Leonardo) in his story 'The Land Ironclads' in 1903? Who were they to try to beat him at his own game?

'The Land Ironclads' is merely one of a bountiful collection of short stories, some of which we shall examine in conjunction with modern examples, that ranged exhilaratingly across a broad band of the vistas open to science fiction.

By the time of his death in 1946, Wells had given many indications that he had re-assumed his original pessimistic outlook of half a century earlier. But in most respects he had never entirely lost sight of it; it underlay all his forays into an optimistically-charged future. In his last years he knew he was dying; and that knowledge – as much as the precarious state of the world – was probably sufficient to conjure before him again the forbidding spectre of T.H. Huxley. Since 1901 he had spent the final forty-five years of his life 'grandiosely haranguing' humanity – as Theodore Dreiser was to put it – on the necessity either to adapt or perish. Grandiose haranguers in these enlightened days arc apt to be prescribed 'Librium' and advised to stay away from the alehouse door. Wells was fortunate in departing from the twentieth century just soon enough to escape that mind-levelling act of mercy.

5 The Rise of a Genre

This besotted nonsense is from the group of magazines known as the science pulps, which deals with both the World and the Universe of Tomorrow and, as our items show, takes no great pleasure in either...

Bernard De Voto, US columnist, writing in
Harper's Magazine, September 1939

How does any movement begin? From hindsight it is usually possible to identify the forerunners and the early pioneers; but they do not necessarily constitute even the opening stages. More often than not their function has been a matter of creating an atmosphere, of setting guidelines and stimulating the minds of those who in due course will become the founder members of what can finally be described as a definite force moving along a definable way.

As we have seen, there exists a problem in fixing a firm point in time when science fiction could be said, as a whole, to have come alive as a genre; but the establishment of the *modern* movement is more easily determined. It began with the launching of several pulp magazines in the United States during the 1920s and 30s. If any one man can be singled out as the prime mover in that development, it is generally accepted that the accolade should go to Hugo Gernsback.

An immigrant American of Luxembourg origin, Gernsback published a number of semi-technical enthusiasts' magazines in the early years of the century, of which *Modern Electrics* was but one. As far back as 1911 he had begun to include science fiction stories in this publication; and in the April issue of that year his own *Ralph 124C41+* appeared in the list of contents, in uneasy company with such items as 'The Practical Electrician' and the 'Singing Spark System of Wireless Telegraphy'. *Ralph*, however, was little better than a poorly written continuation of the machine marvels more ably related in Edward Bellamy's *Looking Backward* over twenty years earlier. Gernsback was never to become renowned as a writer of science fiction; and it is as an editor and instigator that he is chiefly remembered. When *Modern Electrics* ceased publication in 1913, it was still carrying Jacques Morgan's *The Scientific Adventures of Mr. Fosdick*, but with the major part of its contents dedicated, as usual, to articles on the juvenile science of electronics. It was in no sense what could be called 'a science fiction magazine', any more than *The Strand Magazine* — a literary periodical of about the same period in Britain which first published many of Wells's short stories — could be similarly described.

While the detailed history of the popular science fiction magazines over the last fifty years is largely irrelevant to the purposes of this study, the barest outline merits inclusion to indicate the shifts in emphasis which identify the succeeding generations of authors, editors and readers. The development of modern science fiction has mirrored very precisely the unprecedented rates of social change and scientific advance which have now brought humanity to the lip of a watershed. To appreciate that development it is also necessary to review, however summarily, the changes and advances themselves.

Gernsback's enthusiasms were entirely rooted in the technical. He fashioned his own indigestible mechanical eulogies in the penumbra of Verne, with rarely a sidelong glance at the more impressive shadow of Wells. For all that, he had much upon which to work.

By the end of the nineteenth century, the applications of science had begun to exert their pressures on man's social patterns in a multitude of ways. We have already noted the rapid establishment of motorized urban transport towards the end of the period in which Verne wrote. If this changed one aspect of the city-dweller's life, many more were to be radically altered — and entirely fresh aspects introduced — in the space of a few years. London at the turn of the century was spreading out its skirts as if in a final valedictory curtsey to the Queen it had known overlong. In New York, the first edifice to be called a 'skyscraper' was completed in 1902 on the intersection of Fifth Avenue and 23rd Street. Petrol-powered motor cars had already been running on both sides of the Atlantic during the previous decade, inspired by Panhard's production in 1894 of an automobile with sliding gear transmission, a clutch, accelerator and brake pedals, and vertical cylinders housed beneath a frontal bonnet.

New developments in building materials and structures, and in methods of human conveyance, were thus laying the foundations

66

of the grotesquely overloaded conurbations which are all too evident today. Verne foresaw the growth of self-contained cities in several of his tales, even imagining one taking to the ocean, in *Propeller Island*. (In 1956 James Blish was to push the idea to its furthermost limits by portraying a Galaxy swarming with 'space-hopping' city-states in *Earthman Come Home*.) Wells, who knew London intimately at the end of the Victorian era, looked ahead to the oppressive enclosures of walled cities in *When the Sleeper Wakes* (1899), half a century before Isaac Asimov described his own concept of the subterranean night-mare in *The Caves of Steel*. The entirely self-sustaining city is, as we are now painfully aware, still a thing of the future – it is the vast perpetual influx of necessary goods and workforce from beyond the modern conurbation's boundaries which creates many of the problems of present-day urban existence.

Gernsback, however, was blissfully undeterred by any such dystopian considerations. Buoyantly in pursuit of 'sense of wonder', he turned his back on a host of social problems which might more usefully have formed the bases of the imaginative flights he commissioned from his writers. An immigrant him-self, he plainly ignored the agonizing plight of countless immigrants in the United States. A European, he evidently found little to concern himself in the labour unrest of the early 1900s when the roots of Socialism and militant trade unionism were extending surface tendrils across the wan face of a suicidally-determined continent. He apparently remained equally unmoved by the bloody upheaval of the First World War, during which the German Kaiser was presented in allied propaganda as an evil dictator, when priests on either side of the battle-lines assured their lily-white congregations that God was only with them, and when young ladies in Britain mindlessly offered those of their boyfriends who had failed to acquire a uniform a white feather to signify what their 'immeasurable superiors' had con-vinced them was a wholehearted gesture of feminine contempt.

None of this, however, is to condemn Gernsback unjustly – he never pretended to be an H. G. Wells, and his ambitions were directed as much to the popularization of science *per se* as to the logical extrapolation of its progress. While his commanding position as a prime mover in the early days of the modern genre is indisputable, it can be argued with equal conviction that his insistence on technical plausibility and the narrowness of his vision held back the more imaginative and socially aware writers in the magazine field for more than a decade.

After the demise of *Modern Electrics* in 1913, Gernsback concentrated his attentions on the other publications he owned; and it was not until a decade later in 1923 that he devoted an issue of his popular *Science and Invention* to half a dozen 'scientifiction' stories. Their inclusion was warmly received — unlike the generic term which Gernsback had attempted to coin. Although it is open to contention, the first repeated usage of the designation 'science fiction' appears to have occurred in Sweden in 1916, when Otto Witt's magazine *Hugin* began a life of eighty-five issues. As a publication it could lay claim to little merit of any kind; and it seems to have been written in its entirety by Witt himself.

However, the example of *Hugin* should not be taken as an indication of a low standard of science fiction interest in Sweden. The truth is very much the reverse and, as in so many respects, the Swedes have demonstrated their openmindedness and readiness to look ahead by their early acceptance and continuing appreciation of the genre.

Happily dissuaded from introducing a new magazine under the title of *Scientifiction*, Gernsback brought out *Amazing Stories* in 1926. To begin with it relied heavily on reprints of tales from both Verne and Wells, and thereafter on the offerings of scientists who, like Gernsback, were gifted in technical extrapolation and correspondingly lacking in literary ability. Ray Cummings, formerly an assistant to Edison, was among them.

Towards the close of 1928 Gernsback's by no means desultory empire, which included a local radio station in addition to his various magazines, went into liquidation. But that was far from being the end of his championship of the genre. Although *Amazing Stories* continued — under different ownership — without him, he was able in the following year to appeal to his old subscribers and to raise the substantial sum of $20,000 for the financing of two new science fiction publications: *Science Wonder Stories* and *Air Wonder Stories*.

In 1930 *Astounding Stories of Super-Science* appeared from Clayton Magazines. It was later acquired by Street and Smith Inc., and its name was changed to *Astounding Science Fiction*. (It is now known as *Analog Science Fact — Science Fiction*.) At the end of 1937 *Astounding* came under the editorship of John W. Campbell, a name which ranks second only to Gernsback in the annals of the pulp magazines. Among his discoveries in 1939 alone were three writers whose rise to eminence was rapidly accomplished -- Isaac Asimov, Robert Heinlein and A.E. van Vogt.

By the 1940s sufficient interest in science fiction had been generated for anthologies of the better stories to be published regularly in addition to fresh pulp ventures. Of the latter, *The Magazine of Fantasy and Science Fiction* arrived on American bookstalls in 1949, to be followed by *Galaxy* a year later. Many of Pohl and Kornbluth's satirical projections of the big-business dominated future were first to find print as serials in *Galaxy*. Its original editor, Horace Gold, was also fortunate in obtaining the services of Willy Ley as his resident science correspondent. As a popularizer of the expanding panorama of science, Ley properly belongs in the distinguished company of Eddington, Jeans, Wells, J.B.S. Haldane, Bronowski, Ritchie Calder and Asimov who, among many others, have helped to translate for the layman the inner mysteries which a number of scientists still curiously regard as nobody's province but their own. Long an enthusiastic exponent of the conquest of the moon, Ley died only a few days before the Apollo 11 lift-off in 1969.

Two British pulp magazines, *Tales of Wonder* and *Authentic Science Fiction Monthly*, flourished respectively in the late 1930s and early 1950s, much of their material being reprinted from American sources. However, with the professional launching by John Carnell of *New Worlds* in 1946, a vehicle existed for the cultivation of local talent. Like almost every other science fiction magazine, *New Worlds* enjoyed something of a chequered career -- passing through the hands of more than one publisher, but mostly under Carnell's editorship -- until it finally ended its days at the close of the 1960s as a fantasy publication edited by Michael Moorcock with the assistance of an Arts Council grant. A stable companion, *Science Fantasy*, appeared during 1950, initially edited by Walter Gillings who was succeeded after the early issues by John Carnell. It ended publication in 1964.

As the era of the pulp magazines progressed, the regular reader was able to categorize the principal areas in which modern science fiction had valid things to say. (The expression 'pulp', incidentally, simply denotes a type of magazine produced inexpensively on low-quality paper -- the kind of publication in which the pages tend to divorce themselves from the central spine after, or during, their second reading. It is unfortunate that what psychologists call 'the halo effect' leads many of those unacquainted with science fiction to assume the word 'pulp' applies equally to the quality of the ideas and arguments which the magazines contain.) We have already outlined three particular aspects of the future, emanating from nineteenth century facts and theories, which the genre was to select for particular attention: the refinement of machines, the struggle for dominance among species, and the Cosmic decay of suns and their planetary families.

The great majority of stories written during the 1920s and early 30s, largely at Gernsback's behest, concentrated heavily as we have suggested on 'sense of wonder' as it could be interpreted — under the influence of Verne, Bellamy, and parts of Wells — in glorification of the machine. It was the machine which would help man to effect the conquest of Nature on his home planet, which would carry him vaingloriously to the stars, which would assist in establishing his ascendancy over any alien species that might chance to hamper him in his onward rush to gain the galactic goal. It was an era inviting 'space operas' on a monumental scale, and in that it was not disappointed.

The chief laureate of those inter-stellar sagas is still remembered with affection as 'Doc' Smith. From his first science fiction novel, *The Skylark of Space*, in 1915 to his later 'Lensman' series, E. E. Smith disgorged a cascade of cliff-hanging dramas, acted out in the depths of space, which are frequently reprinted today. In terms of serious science fiction, however, they tend to rank in effectiveness and literary merit with the equally generous output of Edgar Rice Burroughs — to whom we owe the improbable callisthenics of Tarzan — who admittedly dedicated himself mostly to adolescent fantasy, even if much of it was transported to Venus or Mars.

With Campbell's arrival in the editorial chair of *Astounding*, the more valuable aspects of science fiction as a means to explore the interaction between science and man were soon to be brought to the fore. A growing body of pulp science fiction emerged which no longer depended on brilliant extrapolations of machine wizardry. What became important about the machine in the genre was not its power to enable man to overcome forces external to himself, but its uses and potentialities when directed inwards to his own organization. The coming of a machine civilization, in which the complexity of technological society would dictate an increasing reliance on machines to assist in decision-making, attracted major consideration.

We have already seen in preceding chapters just how early the machine had begun to influence the life of technological man. (We must mention here, almost by way of passing, that the realm of physics was rocked at the very beginning of the twentieth century by the theories of Max Planck and Albert Einstein; but their far-reaching implications were beyond the comprehension not only of the ordinary citizen, but of not a few physicists as well.) For the majority of the more fortunate inhabitants of the Western World, science and technology were epitomized by the electric light and the telephone, the motor car, the first aircraft, and a rise not only in the general standard of living, but also — then as now — in its cost. The two-sided nature of the benefits of science could hardly have been judged by the layman until he had witnessed them personally in the brutal shock of the First World War. Simultaneously he discovered, in the lack of strategy of both the politicians and the general staffs, the disastrous outcome of the applications of science when consigned to the hands of those who neither fully understood their consequences nor hesitated to employ them for short-term ends.

The two decades following the First World War were as extraordinary as any in human history. They began with the euphoria of the first trans-Atlantic flight when Alcock and Brown, having struggled upside down in blinding fog, finally returned to earth in a bog in Ireland; and they ended in the opening stages of the most barbaric conflict man had yet to endure. In terms of technological innovation they saw the introduction of — to name but some — sound broadcasting and television transmissions, the auto-giro and radar, sound in the cinema and the colour film, geiger counters and radio-astronomy, insecticides, perspex and polyethylene, synthetic fabrics and detergents, helicopters and jet engines, and the gastronomic calamity of frozen foods. On the social front they marked the failure of a world monetary system — for such it had been called — which precipitated mass unemployment in many lands and political upheaval in a Germany already demoralized by a vindictive peace treaty imposed by victorious allied leaders who laid claim to the title of 'statesmen'. In Russia a tyranny ultimately more terrible than the Tsar's differed significantly from the Nazi revolution in its initial stages only by virtue of the inclusion of

71

some genuine intellectuals in its ruling clique. With the emergence of the Stalin administration, however, the Supreme Soviet revealed itself to be every bit as cruel and oppressive as the masters of the Third Reich. The mouths of intellectuals were stopped by the boots of oafs, and their books burned in public displays around which the human kindling for the conflagration to come was persuaded to dance in a demonstration of oneness with the 'men of the people' who led it. In these salutary manifestations of societies dictated by the 'common man' many writers concerned with the future — let alone with the fragility of civilization — found much to occupy their attention, as we shall discover in our chapter on utopias.

The aftermath of the Second World War has been stigmatized by a combination of revolutions, both scientific and social, overlapping one another in a Gadarene scramble which we are still hard put to analyse in full. On the technological level humanity has been presented with the eras of the atom, the computer, the spacecraft, and the mysteries of molecular biology rolled almost into one. And in the three decades since the explosion of the first trial atomic bomb in the New Mexican desert, as many new social sciences have arisen as there have been practitioners who could find names to denote them. Late twentieth-century man, assailed from every quarter by undiscriminating volleys of unelicited information, can be forgiven for mistakenly dismissing the whole convoluted earburst as *die Wissenschaft des nicht Wissenwerten* — the science of what is not worth knowing. In the quieter moments, nevertheless, when he remembers that he is alive, late twentieth-century man may look back even now and recall — if he reads science fiction — that the mixed blessings of his current environment were envisaged, often with extraordinary accuracy, in Campbell's *Astounding* long before the Manhattan Project offered up the *real* apple of the Tree of Life.

He might also recall that Campbell's office was invaded by a branch of the American Secret Service in 1944 on the suspicion that genuine information about the Manhattan Project had been revealed in Cleve Cartmill's short story, 'Deadline'. They might have been more usefully employed in studying the effects being considered in *Astounding* of the development of automation and its future consequences in the areas of work, economics, and the quality of human life.

In theory, computers could release man from much of the

burden of the day-to-day organization of a vastly interrelated series of social functions. Given the correct programming, they could in practice be left with the efficient control of large areas of human endeavour. But that efficiency could be manipulated with equal dexterity for either altruistic or oppressive ends. Just how easy it would be to enslave a nation through the universal surveillance of machines could be as readily demonstrated in science fiction as the utopian quality of life in a world freed from drudgery by full-scale automation.

The future introduction of robots as a further aid in the organization of man also presented problems in the ethical use of machine intelligence. Unlike the computer, which in its most advanced form remained an immobile device, the robot was a possibility which could be martialled equally well to carry out physically obstructive acts as much as helpful ones. An elaborate set of laws, as foreseen by Asimov, might be required to protect man from the dangers of its misuse. Even then, the presence of robots on earth could prove so unacceptable to humanity that their main area of employment might have to be relegated to space – an outcome also much exploited by Asimov.

In the exploration of other worlds robots, of course, would have a unique advantage over man. They could be built to endure hostile environments into which human explorers might never be sufficiently well equipped to venture. They could be programmed to communicate with alien intelligence far more facilely than their masters, and in such a way that they could only respond passively to an aggressive approach.

The discovery of extra-terrestrial cultures was another serious theme to arise in modern science fiction. The treatment of alien life-forms in the early 'space operas' was reminiscent of the attitude of the American settlers to the native Red Indians. It was identical, in fact, to the arrogance of a supposedly superior race typified by Wells's Martians. If an alien stood in the way, it was blasted into the ground – and how should it have been treated otherwise?

The question began to be asked whether, in his dealings with other species, man would provide evidence that he had learned anything from the many mistakes he had already made in his own natural biosphere. Would *Homo sapiens* be prepared to live in accord with other races whose ways might not simply be different, but perhaps utterly unacceptable by human standards? Would the 'missionary' elements which had ruined the finely-balanced social structures of so many 'uncivilized' tribes on earth, manifest themselves even more damagingly against the greater backdrop of the stars? Would man seek, in other respects, to dominate and exploit every less truculent race than his own which he happened upon? Would he become, at last, notorious down the light years as the rampaging child-hooligan of the Milky Way? And how might he react to the alternative – to contact with superior intelligences and cultures? And what might they think of him?

'In the course of its evolutionary development on the third planet from Sol, the most complex carbon-based life-form to gain ascendancy in the last few million years has, so far as can be ascertained, encountered no greater physical minds than those thrown up haphazardly in its own phylum during its brief historical span. In its more philosophical and enquiring moments, the small section of this burgeoning species which has been capable of sustained rational thought has considered the implications of its existence – and come to perhaps one reasonable conclusion: "I think, therefore I am." A larger section of a more mystical and superstitious bent has, with some justification in view of its disposition, concluded that its purpose in life is to act out the persuasions of an intelligence greater than its own. In general, there is nothing to suggest that, if confronted by it, it would necessarily recognize this assumed superior intellect from any other present in the Universe. Its expectations of what would occur in that event range from a fear of cataclysm to a variety of possibilities involving moral and ethical considerations of a quaintness which can only be attributed to the extreme youth and naivety of the species. Nevertheless, like many juvenile forms of intelligence, it occasionally displays an ingenuous charm, and it can summon extraordinary reserves of energy, as much for destructive as creative ends.
None of this constitutes a cause for interference in a remote sector of a fundamentally undistinguished galaxy. It is an infant race discovering, at about the average rate of progress, the pleasures and dangers of infant toys. If and when it succeeds in attaining a moderate level of maturity, there could be grounds for establishing contact.'

Such a passage, which is simply a speculative extract from an explorative report that even now might be filed somewhere

74

beyond the Triffid Nebula, indicates the extent of the parameters within which science fiction can enclose the study of man. Viewed on a galactic scale, the sum total of human endeavour is reduced to the anthill image depicted in the final ideas of Wells. Taken on the infinitely larger universal scale, the anthill diminishes to a speck of cosmic dust. Great sweeps of history have been recorded in science fiction, most notably by Olaf Stapledon, which have put man securely in his small place however long and distinguished his future might happen to be.

That his future could be bleak has been discussed at length in anti-utopias which frequently came from authors not normally associated with the writing of science fiction, and who remained aloof from the pulp environment. However, equally grim prospects have been presented of post-catastrophe humanity, a favoured theme of John Wyndham and Walter Miller, Jnr. A natural disaster which left civilization in ruins might perhaps be overcome, and the old structures of society rebuilt in improved forms. But, whichever way it has been regarded, the humanity of today could hardly hope to recover intact from a nuclear holocaust. What monumental guilt complex might not permeate a world made mostly uninhabitable by poisonous waste, and across which — as if no other reminder were needed — the accusing mutants of later generations pursued their ungainly way? It could prove a literal hotbed for the cultivation of new and powerful religions more terrible in their asceticism than anything known before — a dark age paradoxically begun in an aura of blinding light.

The mutations born of radioactive fallout have rarely been seen in science fiction as anything less than grotesque, as if nothing good would come from man's own destruction of a social order in which few beings had ever found complete fulfilment. Natural mutation, on the other hand, has been exploited as a possibility which held out some hope for man in his modern predicament. The development of extra-sensory perception, of telepathy, mind-reading and telekinesis, has been explored in pulp science fiction, often as a means by which the gift of communication — the original basis of civilization — could be enhanced for the general quickening of social progress.

All these themes, more variously implicit in the early stories of Wells than in those of any other precursor of science fiction, have been exhaustively covered in the genre during the last forty years. An examination of the many different approaches of a multitude of writers to these central issues in the human future occupies the second half of this study.

*****

Science fiction is unique in literature, not only because of its contents and form, but also by virtue of the following it has attracted. Largely as a result of the early preponderance of 'space operas', a common misconception has arisen that the regular reader of the genre is most likely to be an adolescent male unhealthily obsessed with blasters and bug-eyed monsters (known to eclectics as 'BEMs') at an age when he ought more desirably to be directing his attention to the earthly (and earthy) delights of the young. Newspaper cartoon strips and such television palliatives as *Lost in Space* have not helped to improve the image.

There *are* such people as dedicated science fiction fans; and some of them even have a slogan — 'FIAWOL' (Fandom is a Way of Life). But unlike their counterparts in other spheres of entertainment, they are as prone to wipe the floor with their favourite authors as to idolize them. If they display a penchant at all for tearing something to shreds, it is more usually a writer's latest work than his personal adornments.

The first stirrings of science fiction fandom began in a relatively humble way in the correspondence column of Gernsback's *Amazing Stories*. Readers were encouraged to take contributors to task over certain aspects of their tales, to argue about 'plausibility', to suggest new ideas and approaches. By 1930 science fiction clubs had been formed in the United States which published their own amateur magazines containing anything from members' stories to discussions, reviews and digests. In 1934 Gernsback founded 'The Science Fiction League' and two years later the first 'World Science Fiction Convention' of writers and readers was held in New York at the same time as the World Fair. Despite its name, it was a thoroughly American occasion. Three months afterwards, in January 1937, the British equivalent was convened at Leeds; and so-called 'World' and 'International' gatherings have occurred regularly ever since.

A certain piquancy regarding who they really represented was evident in most of those early conferences. Because of the massive American predominance in the opening years of the genre, the description of a 'World Convention' simply indicated to the majority of US enthusiasts a congress of their own country-men. It was probably not until the 1957 World Convention in London that a truly international representation was achieved.

Annual awards akin to those in the American film and theatrical professions were instituted in 1953, science fiction's version of an Oscar being predictably christened a 'Hugo'. It has been awarded not only to writers, but also to leading person-alities, fans, and anyone else whose services to the *English language* sphere of science fiction have merited special recog-nition (in 1969 the Apollo 11 crew received a special citation for 'the best moon landing ever'). Various other awards are also now bestowed annually, each with its esoteric adjudication process (in company with many other general movements de-voted to particular art-forms, science fiction fandom enjoys its own generous collection of warring factions).

The value of the following which the genre has encouraged can hardly be overestimated. The high quality of the fan mag-azines — and there are many of them, frequently running to more than a hundred pages an issue — has created for this style of writer a substantial feedback far in advance of anything experienced in other kinds of literature. The almost universal lack of conventional literary critics prepared to pronounce sensibly on science fiction has enhanced this situation. The absence of any intermediary to guide readers, by whatever standards, on the strengths and deficiencies of particular works and authors has meant that judgement has rested entirely with readers and other writers themselves — and the standards they have set are stringent. It is a remarkable fact that almost every well-known writer of science fiction today has been in his time an active contributor to, and reader of, one or more of the fan magazines.

This cross-fertilization of ideas between all the parties inter-ested in the genre has led to a hard core of devotees in most of the advanced countries of the globe. The direct result is that a science fiction author of useful, but less than outstanding, ability can hope to gain a realistic monetary return for a mod-erately successful novel which could easily run to several over-seas translations. There are no other branches of literary fiction, in which serious ideas are regularly considered, that can offer a similar expectation to the aspiring author. There are always indivi-dual exceptions to this rule of course — but generally it holds true.

*****

The reasons why modern science fiction rapidly secured a foothold in the cultural undergrounds to technologically developed societies are fairly self-evident. Nor is it altogether odd that the genre should seem in its initial stages to be an almost totally American creation. Certainly, in the pioneering sense, there has never been an American equivalent of H. G. Wells. At the same time, there was no writer in Britain during the 1950s who was producing the kind of extrapolations of an Admass culture dominated by corporate enterprise which characterize the work of Pohl and Kornbluth. In a curious way, there are parallels between the development of science fiction and the progress of science and technology in the two countries. British scientists have always been considered in inventive terms the equal, at the very least, of their American counterparts. But in bringing inventions to their first successful use, United States industry and technology have far outstripped British and European efforts combined. Figures given in an OECD report in 1968 comparing the rate of exploitation of inventions since 1945 showed an average for Europe of some 9 per cent, 15 per cent for the United Kingdom, and a cool *60 per cent* for the United States. Similarly, in science fiction, the imaginative inventiveness of British writers — from Wells to Arthur C. Clarke, John Wyndham and James Blish — matches in range the work of the very top echelon of American authors. But in the extrapolative fields in general, particularly in the applications of technology, American writers outnumber their British colleagues to a considerable extent.

The acceptance and output of science fiction in other developed countries has largely followed this pattern. Many of the magazines first to appear were either foreign language editions of leading American publications such as *Galaxy*, or were local productions nevertheless devoted almost entirely to translations of American stories. While fan magazines like the German *Utopia Magazine* indicate a prevailing interest in the genre in their countries of origin, they have yet to bring to the surface a great many writers who can hold their own against international competition. Leading German writers of the calibre of K.H. Scheer and Walter Ernsting are still assaulting the giddy heights of 'space opera'.

It is inevitable, then, that the majority of the modern science fiction works which we are about to examine should have come from American and British pens. The situation in other countries is beginning to show signs of genuine advance towards less imitative efforts by indigenous writers; but for the purposes of a study of serious offerings to date, it is to original works in English that our attention is mainly drawn.

6 Criticism of Progress

This, in a nutshell, is the history of thought about the future since Victorian days. To sum up the situation, the sceptics and the pessimists have taken man into account as a whole; the optimists only as a producer and consumer of goods. The means of destruction have developed pari passu with the technology of production, while creative imagination has not kept pace with either.

Dennis Gabor, *Inventing the Future*

It is said that G.K. Chesterton and Hilaire Belloc once rode horses up the steps of the Athenaeum Club to demonstrate their opposition to technological progress. As an act of defiance, it must have appeared splendid — but it had little to do with creative imagination.

To criticize what others, perhaps mistakenly, have chosen to call progress is an old and honourable occupation. The voice of the voluntary outcast, disclaiming on his hillside, has echoed for as long down history as men have had ears to hear. But — as has been reiterated often enough — criticism of a social trend, other than for relieving personal feelings, is of small value if it can offer no constructive alternative. With some justification, science fiction authors have been called prophets of the air-conditioned nightmare, ensconced in a private wilderness which they claim is waiting to engulf us all. It has sometimes been asked whether, in their bleaker visions, they are really doing anything more than howling on the hill about disagreeable states which have not even happened and which, given good fortune, never will.

By the very nature of the medium, the attacks on progress which can be found in much serious science fiction are unlike the more conventional forms of social criticism. The writer upbraids present progress by depicting the kind of world it could lead to if current trends are allowed to continue indefinitely. In other words, he is not simply saying that certain aspects of progress are unacceptable now because of what they have already caused, but that they are unacceptable *now* because of what they may cause in the future.

Roald Dahl has written an outwardly touching short story entitled 'Genesis and Catastrophe', briefly picturing the child-bed anguish of a German mother whose three previous children have died in infancy. The doctor who has just delivered her of a fourth child — a boy — is unable to reassure her that he, too, will not shortly share a similar fate. The baby seems so small and puny, despite the evidence that he has a marvellous pair of lungs: 'You should have heard him screaming just after he came into this world'.

' "Every day for months I have gone to the church and begged on my knees that this one will be allowed to live.... "Three dead children is all I can stand, don't you realize that....
"He must live.... He must, he must.... Oh God, be merciful unto him now...".'

Because the reader knows that the setting for Dahl's vignette is Brannau-am-Inn, and that the woman's name is Klara Hitler, he appreciates the catastrophic implications in the very human sentiments expressed by both the mother and her physician. He can understand the horror underlying the story because, within its context, he has the gift of future sight — he is aware of to what this parody of the ancient manger scene will lead. In a similar way science fiction can seize on a development, which may seem innocent enough — even beneficial — at its inception, and illustrate vividly what might come of it. (From a different perspective Dahl's story is also relevant to the genre. The idea of preserving the life of a potential Hitler, who may later bring about the deaths of millions, is a familiar dilemma thrown up in fiction for the discomfort of moral philosophers; it presents them with the conflict between short-term and long-term responsibilities regarding the well-being of man — again the kind of predicament with which much science fiction is concerned.)

It can be argued that all criticism of progress should more correctly be described as criticism of human nature. Technology, after all, is, like economics, merely a social tool — it can be wielded both well and badly. While we may agree with Professor Gabor that creative imagination in social planning has lagged behind the advance of technological production, we can recognize that the reverse holds true of science fiction in which, in addition to the extension of existing systems, entirely new branches of technology have been conceived. The danger of technology, as demonstrated in science fiction, is that, again as with economics, societies may be bent to its subservience. A state of mind can arise which regards the unlimited growth of technology in the same light as it views continual economic expansion — as practically an end in itself. Given a materialistic society, there are grounds for assuming that this is almost an inevitable progression. However, the very existence of an unduly materialistic society is itself the sign of failure of creative imagination on the part of its leaders — an indication that the more admirable qualities in human nature are not those on which political movements have till now depended for the allegiance of their supporters, regardless of what might be said in their manifestos.

It is doubtful whether, as a check on materialism, the spiritual needs of humanity can much longer be fulfilled by resorts to theistic religions which become increasingly less credible as our understanding of the universe grows. Science fiction has begun to suggest the way to an alternative mythology, via 'inner space', which may possibly help to satisfy the yearning of the human spirit while remaining solidly within the confines of actual space and time. That possibility will be examined at the close of this study, and each of the remaining chapters devoted to a particular aspect of the human future as it has been treated in science fiction. In the meantime, it is useful to look very briefly at a number of works in the genre where we can often identify some of today's situations which science fiction writers have sought critically, in a future context, to develop further. As we do so, it is also worth recalling the qualification made in our opening description of the genre — some of the following examples may appear impossibly far-fetched. Indeed, a number of them have been deliberately chosen to represent the type of science fiction story which stretches 'willing suspension of disbelief' to its limit. Nevertheless, this is the point in our examination where an acquaintance with the typical mechanics and surroundings of modern science fiction must be established; and if the speculative forays we consider here may not all carry the conviction of likely futures, the parallels they draw with our current predicaments are generally self-evident — as are the warnings they are found to contain.

*****

The control of population growth has exercised a variety of creative imaginations in the last few decades. Many of those unfamiliar with the mainstream of science fiction may still recall the first horror of encountering the 'Junior Anti-sex League' of George Orwell's *Nineteen Eighty-four*. That dismal projection of the late 1940s, however, is barely more than a shadow of the satire permeating Kurt Vonnegut Jnr's 1968 short story, 'Welcome to the Monkey House', in which procreation has become the deadliest sin in a future overpopulated society. The measures taken to curb it, and to diminish the existing population, demonstrate a curious amalgam of ethics. Bands of Junoesque de-sexed women, adorned solely in body-stockings and boots in the best 'bondage' tradition, operate legalized euthanasia parlours. Paradoxically, the use of contraceptives is seen as a crime against Nature (!) and birth control is achieved by means of a pill which by law is obliged to have no direct effect on the procreative process — it merely *anaesthetizes* the recipient from the waist down: 'You could blindfold a man who had taken one, tell him to recite the Gettysburg Address, kick him in the balls while he was doing it, and he wouldn't miss a syllable.'

This drastic method of curtailing procreation is the outcome of the unfavourable reaction of the pill's inventor to behaviour observed in the monkey house of his local zoo — hence the story's title. Public Enemy Number One in this odd future is a diminutive poet who passes his time in kidnapping euthanasia hostesses, feeding them the pill's only known antidote — which conveniently enough is gin — and subsequently deflowering them.

In an entirely different setting, Isaac Asimov has foreseen a future in *The Caves of Steel* (1954) and *The Naked Sun* (1957) where population growth has driven terrestrial man to expand his living space downwards, where to walk in earth's sunlight is a thing of terror for a man who has never experienced it, and where only on the sparsely populated 'Outer Worlds' will the lonely inhabitants brave the open air. But they, in turn, suffer their own neurosis, bred of their isolation; they communicate solely through audio-visual electronic links and dare not come into each other's company without the protection of elaborate anti-infection aids. On earth, however, population density and wholesale automation have compressed humanity into vast enclosed cities of ten million inhabitants apiece:

'Each City became a semi-autonomous unit, economically all but self-sufficient. It could roof itself in, gird itself about,

84

burrow itself under. It became a steel cave, a tremendous, self-contained cave of steel and concrete....
The Cities were good. Everyone but the Medievalists knew that there was no substitute, no reasonable substitute. The only trouble was that they wouldn't stay good. Earth's population was still rising. Some day, with all that the cities could do, the available calories per person would simply fall below basic subsistence level.'

To indicate the versatility of science fiction, it should be added that both of these novels by Asimov are also, in their own right, remarkably good detective tales in which the central character is saddled with a robot assistant whom he first resents but finally comes to accept as indispensable.

A less remote, and by now familiar, interpretation of the population nightmare can be found in Harry Harrison's *Make Room! Make Room!* (1966), set in New York in 1999. There the minimum living space is precisely four square yards for each of the thirty-five million dwellers—and that devoid of plumbing. Not that the search for pollution-free water ranks very high in the order of priorities for what mid-twentieth century occupants were pleased to call 'Fun City'; while the crazed population riots in a universal famine, the nemesis of annihilating war hangs — almost mercifully — above the morass. (A recent screen adaptation of Harrison's story, retitled *Soylent Green*, is among the few good science fiction films which have succeeded in avoiding Hollywood's bug-eyed monster syndrome.)

Solutions to the population problem have frequently been envisaged as fortuitous — in the form of either cosmic or man-made disasters. Many science fiction writers have advanced the view that only by a return to the primitive state following a holocaust can humanity hope to extricate itself from the bewildering quandaries of its present civilizations. But, pursuing an alternative line of thinking, whatever survives Armageddon is — as we have already suggested — unlikely to be a further prototype of Man as we know him today. The battle for existence in a post-catastrophe world is hardly foreseen as ennobling — witness Aldous Huxley's *Ape and Essence* (1946), John Wyndham's *Day of the Triffids* (1950), and, more particularly, Edmund Cooper's *All Fools' Day* (1966) in which solar radiation drives 'normal' beings to suicide and only psychopaths have the will and bloody-mindedness to survive. (Of course, the idea that psychopaths might represent a further step in human evolution is an obvious theme for development in science fiction. The fact that present-day society fails to understand them, and considers them a menace, could certainly be seen as no more than a self-protective reflex. The established order has never taken kindly to those who demonstrably hold scant regard for its values. It is not without significance that many psychopaths, being what is delicately termed 'emotionally immature', retain a strong child-like sense of wonder which sets them apart in an adult world of fettered emotions.)

Essentially, the purpose of most of the stories mentioned thus far centres around the struggle of individuals to find a way out of the environmental dilemmas into which their authors have plunged them. Their success rate averages out at about fifty-fifty. Asimov's detective finally steels himself to face the naked sun and to accept collaboration with a machine; Vonnegut's lecherous 'Billy the Poet' continues his work of spiriting away suicide sirens and taking them off the anaesthetizing pill — with, for him, predictable results. (To his credit, the aim of his activities is to turn the women back into the loving beings he assumes they were intended to be.) But Winston Smith succumbs to Big Brother; and, in the end, the Triffids remain in wait for what is left of man. Therefore we can regard one interpretation of the stories as being that, even in the face of unimaginable odds, there will still be room in the future for the individual to continue the fight, however futile the dispassionate observer may see that fight to be. This could be wishful thinking on the part of the writers; it may be an outcome of faith rather than a product of rational thought; it may be nothing more than an artistic escape-route towards the preservation of sanity in what many of them appear to believe is an irreversibly darkening world. Whatever the interpretation, it is a theme which rever-berates throughout science fiction.

It can be seen in the future development of the business world envisaged in the brilliant collaborations of Pohl and Kornbluth (sadly ended by the latter's early death in 1958). Much of their work is concentrated, as in *The Space Merchants*, on the possible extensions of the growing power of today's multi-national corporations and on highly-automated societies where the consumer is, in effect, more oppressed than Orwell's grey citizens of what is now only ten years hence.

The terrifying prospect of the quality of life in such systems is given an added twist in J.G. Ballard's 'The Subliminal Man', which illustrates another 'logical' extension of today's use of advertising. Giant electric billboards, on display in supermarkets, list the names and credit totals of the biggest-spending customers, small buyers being depicted as social pariahs. But the extremities of over-production have probably been reached in Frederik Pohl's individual effort, 'The Midas Plague' (1951), in which each person in the lower social orders is set a gargantuan, scarcely endurable, quota for consumption and the poor live in mansions attended by innumerable robot servants — only the rich can afford the luxury of inhabiting humble cottages in the 'better' part of town. The solution in this case turns out to be the discovery of a method of providing robots with, for them, the highly illogical urge to become consumers. And so the ceaseless production lines are satisfied, and the humans can return to less frenetic states of existence.

The effects of pollution in the mass-production societies of the future are usually presented as devastating. It offers some relief occasionally to find a story in which positive concern for the environment is a major feature of the plot. Such is Robert Heinlein's 'Blowups Happen' which, in 1939, was an early consideration of the dangers inherent in the harnessing of atomic power. Heinlein's nuclear reactor, however, is a far less stable device than what was later to become the reality. It can go critical in a matter of microseconds and demands intense observation by day-and-night shifts of atomic engineers. Each individual in this army of scientists is subjected to crippling psychological strain:

> 'He could bring to the job all of the skill and learning of the finest technical education, and use it to reduce the hazard to the lowest mathematical probability, but the blind laws of chance which appear to rule in subatomic action might turn up a royal flush against him and defeat his most skillful play. And each atomic engineer knew it, knew that he gambled not only with his own life, but with the lives of countless others, perhaps with the lives of every human being on the planet. Nobody knew quite what such an explosion would do....'

The chances of a scientist on duty at the reactor cracking under the strain are so great that a battery of psychologists are also required — to keep the engineers under constant scrutiny — and even they undergo severe nervous stress. As the tension mounts to a level where a blow-up seems inevitable, the solution is suddenly found in the discovery of an atomic rocket fuel which will enable the station to be transported in its entirety to outer space where it can operate in comparative safety. 'Blowups Happen', despite its inaccuracy as a purely technical forecast, is a notable example of a science fiction writer looking ahead to a future technological problem and presenting it in a dramatic context which can still be enjoyed today.

*****

Where do women fit into this pattern of future societies? In some instances it can be said that they hardly appear to fit at all. In Robert Sheckley's short story, 'A Ticket to Tranai' (1955), wives are kept in a stasis field which renders them non-existent until their menfolk, in need of company, retrieve them at the touch of a switch! Naturally this allows them the benefit of living through the lifetimes of several husbands; until who should arrive on the scene but an atavistic character entertaining the notion that his wife might be fun to have around continuously. Sheckley's tale, which we shall examine in more detail in the next chapter, is also an amusing satire on the excesses of built-in obsolescence. His robots, being the most universally purchased of all household items, are specifically designed to be so irritating that they will quickly be kicked to pieces and replaced by even more tiresome and lopsided models.

Worlds run exclusively by women are rarely anticipated as the peaceful havens which, until recently, the vocal representatives of that sex would have us expect. In many cases science fiction writers have foreseen, with what seems especial insight, the more heady ambitions of the Women's Liberation movement, where peaceful co-existence is rated rather low in the order of priorities. (It is worth noting that Wells, in his *Anticipations* (1901), mused on the advent of labour-saving devices in the home which would eventually allow the housewife time to consider more rationally her proper place in modern society; but we must also accept that Wells professed individual reasons — many of them distinctly personal — for the emancipation of females.)

Pohl and Kornbluth's *Search the Sky* (1954) and Edmund Cooper's *Five to Twelve* (1969) show us women-dominated worlds where men have been reduced very much to the order of playthings; and the new inheritors prove, if anything, more self-seeking and repressive than their masculine predecessors. On the whole, science fiction has been less than kind to women; although John Wyndham, in 'Consider Her Ways' (1961), has portrayed a feminine civilization in which *some* women can enjoy liberated and creative lives, albeit within the confines of a highly-stratified and élitist society. It is, by way of explanation, a world entirely devoid of men, where reproduction occurs through parthenogenesis.

In view of the considerable masculine preponderance in the genre, both among authors and readers, it is to be expected that the majority of sympathetic treatments of women in science fiction should come from female writers. Judith Merril has related in 'Wish upon a Star' (1958) the aspirations of a young boy born on a spaceship in which the executive functions are carried out by women, the men being relegated to the performance of household chores. The ship is essentially a travelling ark, with provision for even third or fourth generations to grow up on board before it finally makes a landfall. The boy learns from one of the original four men, who first embarked with twenty women, that on earth men were the rulers of their families — a possibility he regards as a fairytale. But when it is pointed out to him that among the children in the ship there are as many boys as girls, he begins to question things differently:

' "Then *why* did they put women in charge of everything?" he demanded for the first time.
Bob's answer was incoherent, angry and fantasizing. Later Toshiko took his puzzlement to Ab, who explained, tight-lipped, that women were considered better suited to manage the psychological problems of an ungrown group, and to maintain with patience over many many years, if needed, the functioning and purpose of the trip.
"Then when we land...?"
"*When* we land, there will be time enough to think about it...." ' '

As the ship nears a planet which may be suitable for colonization, the boy feels his first emotional stirrings towards one of the girls whom he has hitherto regarded as a member of a dominant and unapproachable species.

The future of love between men and women is unfortunately a neglected area in science fiction; and authors as eminent in the genre as Isaac Asimov have declared themselves perfectly content to write stories in which women simply don't feature. On the other hand, Asimov himself has produced one of the funniest of stories concerning the human sex act. In 'What is this Thing called Love?' (1961) he tells of the efforts of an extra-terrestrial agent to convince his superior officer that sex habits on earth are so outrageous that *Homo sapiens* constitutes a threat to the galaxy and ought to be destroyed. However, the agent's understanding of this popular human pastime has been gleaned entirely from readings of *Playboy*; there are large gaps in his knowledge which coincide with the liberal (?) appearance of rows of asterisks in the magazine's text. Having captured two specimens and frogmarched them into his commander's spaceship, he endeavours to persuade them to provide the necessary demonstration. Since they are strangers to each other, and in a decidedly alarming situation, the man and woman concerned are too inhibited to oblige. Convinced that his agent is a fool, the commander sends the couple back to earth, whereupon they decide they *do* like each other and proceed to the inevitable. In vain the agent calls for his commander to return: 'You should see what they're doing now!'

In 'Day Million' (1966) Frederik Pohl has postulated a far future in which men and women of a mutual attraction can programme computers with their personal characteristics so that, no matter if they fail to meet again, they can enjoy indefinitely the qualities they liked in their partners simply by reconnecting their nervous systems with the computer's memory banks. The oldest profession, also, has been subjected to Robert Sheckley's highly individual approach. His 'Pilgrimage to Earth' (1956) describes a future in which Terra has become a galactic tourist centre for the farflung human race. Here 'love-for-a-day' can be purchased from establishments whose radiantly beautiful girls are induced by hypnotism 'genuinely' to fall in love with their customers for the duration of their hire. The effect of this on the unwary male visitor, who accepts the facade as real and himself responds emotionally, is a typical example of Sheckley's particular brand of ironical humour.

*****

Warfare remains a continuing preoccupation in science fiction, from the early interplanetary sagas of E.E. Smith to the spread of localized wars on earth, as in the case of *The Jagged Orbit* (1969) by John Brunner, where again we find the future dominated by a multi-national combine — but on this occasion the goods it manufactures are armaments, which it sells to all-comers with predictable results. There is, unhappily, little anticipation in the genre of man finally achieving peace with his own kind, let alone with extra-terrestrials. And in Robert Heinlein's immensely successful, but also much criticized, *Starship Troopers* (1959) we are regaled with a 'law-and-order' future in which war is glorified, drunken drivers are flogged, and citizens must undergo military service if they wish to assume even their minimum democratic (!) voting rights.

In another tale, 'Solution Unsatisfactory', Heinlein has conceived his own version of the ultimate weapon — a lethal nuclear fallout in the form of an atomic dust which can be scattered by plane into limited and clearly defined areas. The dust is perfected in the United States and deposited over selected targets in Germany by the British Air Force (the story was written in the early stages of the Second World War). Its use leads to what ought to be a world peace when America insists that all nations should surrender their aircraft, both military and commercial, before the dust is consigned to the control of an international commission. However, the parties to a certain large Euro-Asian alliance (which it was unnecessary even then to name) have developed the weapon for themselves; and when their planes fly in for safe-keeping in the United States they are not above instigating an unhealthy dust-up of their own. In the event, America's superior tactics prevail; but that is by no means the end of the story. While the control commission is ostensibly an international body, it remains very much a protégé of the United States. When the benign Presidency which instituted the commission ends, it is replaced by a reactionary administration that aims to bring various countries it dislikes to heel with the threat of its ultimate access to the dust. The commission's head, a former US congressman, is faced with the unpalatable task of deposing his own President. By this act he finds himself the reluctant military dictator of a world in which he is viewed almost universally as a power-hungry despot. Heinlein concludes his story with a characteristic remark: 'For myself, I can't be happy in a world where any man, or group of men, has the power of death over you and me, our neighbours, every human, every animal, every living thing. I don't like anyone to have that kind of power.' Hiroshima followed a year or two later.

The deliberate pursuit of a contained war, as a means of controlling a limited peace and of holding populations in sub-jugation, was also expounded in Orwell's *Nineteen Eighty-four*. It had, in fact, already been presented with neat irony some twenty years before by André Maurois in *Fragments of a World History* (1926). Faced, as imagined by Maurois, with the near inevitability of a new global war around 1965, the world's press acts in unlikely unison to divert the attention of the opposing nations with invented reports of imminent aggression from, of all places, the moon. Its efforts are unpredictably successful; and war hysteria is turned from internecine strife towards the supposed inhabitants of the earth's inoffensive satellite. A heat-ray is developed and an attack launched. But it so happens that the moon *does* have a population — and the heavily-armed Selenites are, to say the least, unamused.

*****

The great promise of progress has, from earliest times, been to bring within reach of every individual the means for fulfil-ment in a world made free of the more debilitating forms of ignorance, hardship and fear. It is the ephemeral carrot which has been dangled immemorially before the nose of a mass of humanity which has never yet taken possession of that golden state and might not perhaps be happy if it did. Were it possible now for an entirely unbiassed judge to grant this wish to those he considered the most deserving among the great diversity of human personalities, who would they turn out to be — and what might they be judged to deserve? The obvious problem, which we shall consider at length in the next chapter, is how to arrive at an equitable society in which intelligent and less mentally well-endowed beings can live side-by-side in conditions of mutual satisfaction. The huge mass-production-consumption societies depicted by so many science fiction authors are horrific to the intelligent man because they seem to be geared inexorably to the material needs of the lowest common denominator in human civilization.

Few writers in the field have portrayed convincingly a future society in which learning and understanding of a high order have been bequeathed to mankind *en masse* by education or by any other means. Can we assume, tentatively, that the great majority of writers have not done so because at this point their creative imaginations have failed? Or is it simply that they do not *wish* to believe that such a possibility could exist? There is a quality of élitism among science fiction writers which, acknowledging the characteristics of the genre, is almost inevitable. To some extent there are reasons for supposing that many of them are less than anxious to conceive a society in which all are members of one élite. They proceed instead to portrayals of materialist paradises of the common man, where the individual of high intelligence, if he is permitted to live freely at all, is tolerated at best with suspicion. It is not, of course, unusual for creative writers to express some distaste of the increasing materialism among a workforce constantly exhorted to dedicate itself to economic growth. But in science fiction the dilemma of the sensitive intellectual is frequently presented in fiercer terms. At its most pronounced, it reflects the attitude of Shotover in Shaw's *Heartbreak House*:

'What is to be done then? Are we to be kept forever in the mud by these hogs for whom the universe is nothing but a machine for greasing their bristles and filling their snouts.... Who are they, that they should judge us? Yet they do, unhesitatingly. There is an enmity between our seed and their seed. They know it and act on it, strangling our souls....
We kill the better half of ourselves every day to propitiate them. The knowledge that these people are there to render all our aspirations barren prevents us having the aspirations....'

In Kurt Vonnegut's short story 'Harrison Bergeron' (1961) the destruction of intellectual ability in a world where everyone must be utterly equal is achieved by means of a small radio receiver, worn in the ear, which emits mind-numbing signals of varying regularity and intensity according to the individual's IQ. And in this particular future even the physically élite must be handicapped; the more athletically endowed have weights permanently attached to their bodies to slow them down.

The rise of the mediocre is presented as a more natural process in William Tenn's 'Null-P' (1951). After a third world war in which nuclear weapons have been used, a US President is elected whose only claim to distinction is that he fits exactly, and in every respect, the statistical average of the American male. He is quite incapable of taking decisions or even of expressing any positive opinion – his name, appropriately, is George Abnego.

As his rule stabilizes the United States, visiting delegates from the recovering countries of Europe are astonished to discover the state of lethargy into which this once energetic country has descended. All, that is, but a certain notable of Toulouse, who returns to France to write a solemn study of the phenomenon:

> ' "Since the time of Socrates...man's political viewpoints have been in thrall to the conception that the best should govern. How to determine that 'best', the scale of values to be used in order that the 'best' and not mere undifferentiated 'betters' should rule — these have been the basic issues around which have raged the fires of political controversy for almost three millennia....
>
> "Now, at last, America has turned and questioned the pragmatic validity of the axiom.... [According to the new doctrine] it is *not* the worst who should govern...but the mean: what might be termed the 'unbest' or the 'non-elite'." '

The monograph proves an immediate success and, as the 'abnegite' revolution spreads through the world, humanity spirals into the downward path of its evolutionary decline. In the end it is taken over by an intelligent breed of Newfoundland terriers who find men worth cultivating for their ability to throw sticks!

Brian Aldiss has portrayed in 'Man on Bridge' (1964) the last resort of an oppressed intelligentsia who go voluntarily into concentration camps after a world upheaval has dispossessed the rich of their wealth, but not the intellectuals of their brains:

> 'You can always tell an intellectual, even when he cowers naked and bruised before you with his spectacles squashed in the muck; you have only to get him to talk. So the intellectuals had elected to live in camps, behind wire, for their own safety....the stay was no longer voluntary, for we had lost our place in the world.... Throughout the more-than-medieval darkness that had fallen over Europe, our cerebal monasteries were ruled over by the pistol and whip; and flagellation of the new order of monks was never self-inflicted.'

All of these stories suggest that only as a final extreme should the future be delivered into the hands of the common man, however much he may constitute the majority of humanity. In one respect they can be regarded as an admission that, for the serious-minded, scientific and technological progress are developments from which they can draw scant comfort in the light of the materialism engendered. Universal education, which was seen by optimists as the brightest hope for securing a saner and more harmonious society, falters on the stumbling-block of what pessimists regard as the uneducability of large numbers of the masses.

More fundamentally, some science fiction writers seem to suggest that human nature is so intrinsically flawed that all the scientific and material progress of a golden age could do little to change the unacceptable aspects of the present human condition. In this they echo T.H. Huxley's depiction of the artificial qualities of ethical behaviour implacably confronted by the cosmic, or natural, processes of what is considered by many as the evil in Man.

Before we move to a fuller consideration of utopias and anti-utopias, it is worth recalling the eventual outlook on progress of the man who, as the twentieth century approached its mid-way mark, came increasingly to declare that the prospect for mankind was 'a race between education and catastrophe' — H.G. Wells. Kingsley Martin, speaking in 1965, and anticipating what he was later to write in his autobiography, left us a compassionate afterthought on the commonly accepted image of an old and embittered prophet.

'H.G.', he concluded, had taken it for granted that Truth and Goodness were handmaidens; but because the third member of that trinity, Beauty, had seemed to serve no biological purpose, the rational believer in progress was apt to pass it by. On the other hand, if science really was taking us to Hell, then Beauty might after all be of supreme value: 'Scientific materialism has seen evolution as a chain of events, the wheels of cause and effect inexorably grinding out a future in which man, who is apparently free-willed, can at most play a strictly limited part. Is it not possible that more important than the hypothetical utopias at which he aims are the sparks which fly off the wheels as they turn?' It was some such thought, Kingsley Martin felt, which had prompted Wells to talk at the end of his life of 'the strange necessity of Beauty', and to ask himself 'whether in all our efforts to improve society we could ever do better than perhaps slightly increase *some* people's happiness, and add to their stature by giving them a vision of the world in which there was less frustration — and an opportunity of appreciating the beauty of the sparks as they fly by?'

95

7 The Failure of Utopia

*Now I ask you what can be expected of man since he is a
being endowed with such strange qualities? Shower upon him
every earthly blessing, drown him in a sea of happiness...;
give him economic prosperity, such that he should have
nothing else to do but sleep, eat cakes and busy himself with
the continuation of his species, and even then out of sheer
ingratitude, sheer spite, man will play you some nasty
trick... simply to introduce into all this positive good sense
his fatal fantastic element....*

Fyodor Dostoevsky, *Notes from Underground*

'Our past is a necessary part of us, and to take away that part is
to mutilate us irreparably. I know a man who achieved courage
only after he was told of Epaminondas, and a woman who
became beautiful only after she had heard of Aphrodite.' The
words are the narrator's in Robert Sheckley's story 'The
Mnemone', and he is describing the effect on a collection of
villagers of the arrival of a mnemone — a man who has memo-
rized the literature of the past which is no longer available to
a world in which 'right-minded' men have concluded that
literature was at its worst subversive, and at its best unnecessary.
Why retain the records of a thousand divergent opinions, only
to have to demonstrate how they were wrong?

For a few short days the mnemone peddles his illegal stock
of quotations to the villagers, and the landscape blooms with
words of William James, Heraclitus and Montaigne. But as news
of his presence spreads the liquidators arrive; and all the village
has left by which to remember him is an apple orchard christened
'Xanadu' and a newborn child called 'Cicero' — a name which
fails to appear in the revised version of history. The brief neo-
classical flowering is over and the sheep have returned to the
fold. It was not for nothing that Candide found El Dorado
boring.

The suppression of literature is a familiar theme in the science
fiction anti-utopias of the past fifty years. It occurs in Huxley's
Brave New World, where only Mustapha Mond, the World
Controller, has access to the forbidden volumes which spell out
the heritage of man. It is dealt with more centrally in Ray

Bradbury's *Fahrenheit 451* (the temperature at which paper burns). Bradbury's firemen of the future are employed not to extinguish fires, but to ignite them — in houses wherever books are found.

But the books are destroyed not so much because they represent a threat to the doctrine of the state — most people have already given up reading anyway — but because they constitute a threat to the man in the street. Bradbury's future society is based on the rise of the 'mediocracy'; and the mediocre rule on the premise that all beneath them shall be equally so. (It is Tenn's 'Null-P' writ large). As the fire captain explains to one of his men:

' "You always dread the unfamiliar. Surely you remember the boy in your own school class who was exceptionally 'bright'.... And wasn't it this bright boy you selected for beatings and tortures after hours? Of course it was. We must all be alike. Not everyone born free and equal, as the Constitution says, but everyone *made* equal.... So! A book is a loaded gun in the house next door. Burn it. Take the shot from the weapon. Breach man's mind. Who knows who might be the target of the well-read man? Me? I won't stomach them for a minute." '

Fahrenheit 451 (1954) is set in the near future where the predictable development of television has reached its culmination. The walls of the average living-room have become one immense television screen. Serial programmes are so devised that for a fee the viewer himself can be woven into the plot; he stands surrounded by the life-sized images, aware of no other reality than the drama projected around him. Tiny shell-like transistor radios, fitted into each ear, lull the insomniac through the dark waiting hours before dawn. The ether is thick with the hypnotic flow of images and the whisper of the shells, all but drowning the overhead roar of the nuclear bombers on their nightly practice runs.

Bradbury's plot revolves around the downfall of a fireman who succumbs to the awful fascination of the books he is sent to destroy. He recites a poem to his horrified wife and her equally distraught friends, and as a result finds himself part of the fire team despatched to burn down his own home. It is only then that he discovers that it is his wife who has denounced him. He rebels, incinerates his fire chief, and escapes from the city —

not a moment too soon, as it happens, for that night the roar of the bombers no longer denotes a practice. Finally he accepts refuge in the countryside with a group of outcasts closely related to Sheckley's mnemone, dispossessed intellectuals who carry in their heads the scientific and literary works with which they hope to refurbish what remains of man.

Fahrenheit 451 claims distinction as a novel by the quality of its writing. In imaginative terms, however, its originality is limited to the reversal of the fireman's role in society. What other aspects it portrays of a disagreeable future are the common property of several equally distinguished anti-utopias which we shall come upon shortly. But since they are reactions to a long tradition of positive utopian writing which reached its apotheosis in the early part of the twentieth century, a brief recapitulation of its history is appropriate here.

The very name 'utopia' probably sets the seal on the curious ambivalence in human aspirations which utopian literature has revealed in every age. It derives from the Greek 'ou topos' — meaning 'nowhere'. Plato, in his classic vision of the Great Society, set down in *The Republic* the blueprints for an ordered and happy nation in which obedience to authority is the supreme virtue, racial prejudice is highly systematized, genetic breeding patterns guarantee 'racial purity', and the offspring of the inferior are quietly done away with. It is chastening to recall how close to those 'ideals' Himmler's gestapo really came.

Sir Thomas More's *Utopia* (1516) is an infinitely more humane proposition, even if it still acknowledges the divine right of kings. And if the inhabitants of his nowhere-island are distinctly anti-militaristic, they are not above employing a neighbouring nation to act as mercenaries on their behalf! A century later Thomaso Campanella's *The City of the Sun* emphasized the need for material prosperity, but at the expense of individual freedom. Advocates of his so-called socialist, but actually highly-authoritarian, society would find themselves not out of place in Eastern Europe today. The benefits which science might bring, along with predictions of aircraft and submarines, were, as we have shown, envisaged in Francis Bacon's *New Atlantis* during the same era; but it was not until a quarter of a millennium later, towards the end of the nineteenth century, that the harnessing of science in the furtherance of an ideal state was given free rein.

1871 saw the publication in Holland of *Anno Domini 2071* —

a tour of the utopian scientific world to come, around which the author 'Dr Diosorides' is conducted by a cheerfully resurrected Roger Bacon. It is a typical example of a number of minor works of the period which looked ahead optimistically to a future made perfect by science. Samuel Butler, however, as we shall see in the next chapter, found himself less than enamoured of the gifts of the machine, which he set about destroying in his satirical *Erewhon* (1872).

Predictably, as a naturalist, W.H. Hudson saw the hope of a better order of things vested in Darwinism. In his idyllic utopia *The Crystal Age* (1887) he imagined a world in which natural selection had brought man himself nearer to perfection. But the book which was to prove a notably influential exposition of a future society came in 1888, when Edward Bellamy's *Looking Backward, 2000—1887* was published in America. What chiefly distinguished it from its many predecessors was its depiction of a highly-organized *socialist* utopia with which the down-trodden in both the United States and Europe could associate themselves. It sold millions of copies in more than twenty languages; and it led to the formation of over one-hundred-and-fifty 'Bellamy clubs' which attempted to propagate its message. Yet its full complement of technological marvels could not completely disguise its many similarities to Plato's *Republic*, and these provoked a wave of reaction among more sensitive writers. William Morris, who had been asked to lecture on it, declared that 'if they brigaded *him* into a regiment of workers he would just lie on his back and kick'. 'I wouldn't care', he wrote, 'to live in such a Cockney paradise... '. Two years later he produced his own *News from Nowhere* as an answer to Bellamy's social state.

News from Nowhere is shot through with the revolt of the artist against the collectivization of individuals into an organized society. Foreshadowing by forty years Freud's arguments in *Civilization and its Discontents*, Morris suggests that civilization and the individual are inherently inimical — there can be no reconciling them. While Plato honoured artists but effectively shut them out of his republic, Morris's utopian citizens exclude the non-artist from their ranks. The narrator, who visits the utopia in a state of dreaming while awake, finds himself less than welcome. He is a social animal, at odds with a society founded on the concept of 'the second childhood of the world'. In fact, Morris's ideal state is based entirely on the childlike vision of 'sense of wonder' in which the pleasure principle — the escape to childhood in the unconscious — has attained oneness with reality.

Other immediate reactions to *Looking Backward* appeared in 1891, among them A. Morris's *Looking Ahead*, in which industrial progress reawakens the old ideas of feudalism, and Jerome K. Jerome's 'The New Utopia' — an ironic portrayal of socialist life a thousand years hence. They were balanced by further glowing accounts of progress in Ismar Thiusen's *Looking Forward* (1890) and in the Viennese economist Theodor Hertzika's 'social anticipation' of an ideal state in Kenya, *Freeland* (1891). Even Oscar Wilde found nothing amiss in suggesting that 'a map of the world that does not include Utopia is not worth even glancing at, for it leaves out the one country at which Humanity is always landing.'

Finally there came in 1905 what was for many the definitive utopian vision, praised alike by Conrad and by William and Henry James — Wells's *A Modern Utopia*. In it Wells proclaimed the principles for a world state which were to occupy him, and also to haunt him, for the remainder of his life. Whilst avoiding much of the static ossification of preceding utopias, and recognizing the failings and self-seeking aspects of human nature, he was bound to reflect in *A Modern Utopia* the far-reaching influence exerted on him by Plato's *Republic* which, as we have seen, he had first encountered in early adolescence. His personal temperament and interpretation of history made it impossible for him to see the organization of a worldwide utopia developing along democratic lines. Only by the introduction of an ascetic ruling élite, the Samurai (echoing Plato's 'guardians'), could the rational fulfilment of man's potential be won. The Wellsian utopia therefore depended on the assumption of an over-riding 'goodness' of government, even if particular individuals within the ruling class turned out to be bad. In such fashion would a corporate Big Brother prove a benign overseer of a global welfare state in which ubiquitous machines would secure the means for the long-awaited ennoblement of human life, and from which criminals, alcoholics and other social dissenters and undesirables would be trotted — albeit sympathetically — off to gaol.

It is significant that Wells located his utopia as being already in existence on an alternative earth within a serial universe. He was to do the same in *Men Like Gods*, written nearly twenty years later, presenting a more advanced stage of what was essentially the same world, but in which there was no longer a need for the Samurai. G.K. Chesterton was prompted to a characteristic response:

> 'The weakness of all utopias is this, that they take the greatest difficulty of man and assume it to be overcome, and then give an elaborate account of the overcoming of the smaller ones. They first assume that no man will want more than his share, and then are very ingenious in explaining whether his share will be delivered by motor car or balloon.'

The critic David Lodge made it markedly more personal:

> 'In a sense it [A Modern Utopia] was a generous attempt on Wells's part to imagine a social structure which would make available to everyone the kind of success and happiness he had personally achieved in the teeth of great disadvantages. Or, more cynically, you could call it the paradise of little fat men.'

*****

It is now clear that the immediate onset of anti-utopias precipitated by A Modern Utopia was a reaction by intellectuals against Wells's concept of the Samurai and what, recalling Bellamy, was still regarded as the philistine cult of the machine. E.M. Forster wrote 'The Machine Stops' as a direct criticism of A Modern Utopia, and Aldous Huxley repeated the exercise in Brave New World vis-a-vis Men Like Gods.

Forster himself described his story as being 'a counterblast to one of the heavens of H.G. Wells', and 'The Machine Stops' (1909) tells of a future society that has become totally dependent on one vast central 'Machine'. Men live underground, in level upon level of individual cells which they occupy for life. All communications are carried out through the agency of the Machine; and personal contact and personal experience have both become things of the past. Eventually the Machine is worshipped — and eventually it stops.

The horror which Forster injected into his story expresses the distress of a humane intellectual at the prospective loss of the natural world (above ground the earth is barren) and the lament of the artist for the lost subtleties of language which result from

102

communicating through machines:

> '...the Machine did not transmit *nuances* of expression. It only gave a general idea of people — an idea that was good enough for all practical purposes... The imponderable bloom, declared by a discredited philosophy to be the actual essence of intercourse, was rightly ignored by the Machine, just as the imponderable bloom of the grape was ignored by the manufacturers of artificial fruit. Something "good enough" had long since been accepted by our race.'

However, an element of hope lives on. When the underground culture dies there remain on the surface the anti-social survivors who have been expelled from the machine paradise, and who become paradoxically the inheritors of the future. What Forster suggests is that the anti-social elements which are to be booted out of a Wellsian heaven are, in fact, the artists and non-conformists who would find it unbearable in any case. The end of 'The Machine Stops' is effectively where the individualistic society of Morris's *News from Nowhere* begins.

If Forster's revolt against the dehumanizing influence of the machine was principally artistic, the next major anti-utopia to arrive, Evgenii Zamyatin's *We* (1924), embodied a revulsion against the entire system of the superstate — its author paid for it by permanent exile from his native Russia. The nameless citizens of *We* inhabit a giant city quarantined from the natural world by roofs and walls of glass. They are identified only by numbers and are universally clad in uniforms of blue-grey. Their lives are regulated — even down to the required number of times they are expected to chew their synthetic food. Three hours a day are allowed for personal activity, and ration books are needed for those overcome by the desire for sex. Art, of course, has become a tool of the state, immortalized in such masterpieces as 'Daily Odes to the Well-Doer' and 'Those Who Come Late to Work'.

As is customary — and barely surprising — in most anti-utopias, a revolt is in progress in *We*. 'D-503', the architect of the spaceship which is to spread this enlightened culture among the stars, falls in love with the rebel leader, 'I-330', to the extent that he begins to forget his conditioning. The lovers venture beyond the city walls, where they prove no match for the unrestrained assault of Nature. The novel ends with the re-programming of D-503, who cheerfully betrays his mistress and contemplates her subsequent torture with scarcely the lift of an eyebrow.

Zamyatin's concern in writing *We* was to highlight the dangers of a technological slave state into which he saw the Soviet Union descending. His all-powerful ruler, 'the Well-Doer', could easily be taken as a veiled portrait of Lenin; and the multitude of bugging and spy devices he employs will hardly turn a hair of the post-Watergate reader. Orwell's *Nineteen Eighty-four*, written twenty-five years later, is more or less a gloomier reworking of the same material — and in many respects the same plot — with a suppressed populace enjoying even fewer benefits than Zamyatin's. The interrogator O'Brien rekindles the Nazi philosophy which in 1949 had only recently ceased to reverberate across Europe:

> ' "Do you begin to see, then, what kind of a world we are creating? It is the exact opposite of the stupid hedonistic Utopias that the old reformers imagined. A world of fear and treachery and torment, a world of trampling and being trampled upon, a world which will grow not less but *more* merciless as it refines itself. Progress in our world will be progress towards more pain.... In our world there will be no emotions except fear, rage, triumph.... If you want a picture of the future, imagine a boot stamping on a human face — for ever." '

But if *We* and *Nineteen Eighty-four* demonstrated the barbaric and oppressive aspects of the slave state, could not a future collective society exist where pleasure for the masses was the overriding principle and the population was relieved of every care? It was left to Aldous Huxley in *Brave New World* (1932) to illustrate the futility of life for people who are required never to think and only to play. In that nightmare of conditioned happiness, where human beings are bred in various grades of ability and intelligence, under the clinical auspices of a benevolent state, stability is maintained by curtailing individual liberty and offering as recompense an inexhaustible supply of sexual distractions and the pleasure-inducing drug '*soma*':

> '...no leisure from pleasure, not a moment to sit down and think — or if ever by some unlucky chance such a crevice of time should yawn in the solid substance of their distractions, there is always *soma*, delicious *soma*, half a gramme for a half-holiday, a gramme for a week-end, two grammes for a trip to the gorgeous East, three for a dark eternity on the moon;

returning whence they find themselves on the other side of
the crevice, safe on the solid ground of daily labour and
distraction, scampering from feely to feely, from girl to
pneumatic girl... .'

('Feelies' are film performances during which the physical
sensations of the characters on the screen are transmitted to the
audience by electronic means.)

Brave New World may lack the Thought Police and 'double-
think' of *Nineteen Eighty-four*, which after all was written
from hindsight of Hitler's New Order in the conquered lands of
Europe. Nevertheless, its pervading atmosphere is equally one
of oppression. Unlike Orwell's dystopia, however — which
outraged both — its oppressive quality is directed more at the
intellect than the physical senses. Huxley's lower genetic orders,
the equivalent of Orwell's 'proles', are not materially deprived.
Huxley was an intellectual principally concerned with addressing
others of his kind; intellectual deprivation, therefore, is the most
disturbing single feature of *Brave New World*. True, the familiar
out-of-the-way reservations for dissidents exist; but their conditions really are primitive, and it is from one of them, of course,
that the Savage who is the central character in the novel comes.
In his well-known confrontation with the World Controller
towards the end of the book, the Savage suggests to Mustapha
Mond that what is needed in his new civilization is 'something
with tears for a change. Nothing costs enough here'. Surely there
must be some virtue in living dangerously, in stimulating the
adrenals from time to time? And naturally there is. But like so
much else, science has provided a surrogate even for this. Once
a month every citizen has his entire system flooded with adrenin:

' "It's the complete physiological equivalent of fear and rage.
All the tonic effects of murdering Desdemona and being
murdered by Othello, without any of the inconveniences."
"But I like the inconveniences."
"We don't", said the Controller. "We prefer to do things
comfortably."
"But I don't want comfort. I want God, I want poetry, I
want real danger, I want freedom, I want goodness. I want
sin."
"In fact", said Mustapha Mond, "you're claiming the right to
be unhappy." '

If *Brave New World* was a further intellectual expression of contempt for the Wellsian paradise, Huxley himself was later to fall victim of the utopian ambivalence by producing in his old age a utopia in *Island* (1962) which relied on mind-expanding drugs to fulfil the human search for happiness, and which was arguably as static and purposeless as the future societies he had earlier set out to malign. It was presented as a constructive society which had achieved a satisfactory synthesis between Western science and Eastern philosophy. The forced breeding techniques of *Brave New World* were replaced by a voluntary arrangement whereby privileged couples restricted their children to a total of two, with a further one being produced by artificial insemination of 'genetically-superior' stock from the deep-frozen (and no doubt spin-dried) deposits in the national sperm bank. All other couples were *obliged* to undergo this pleasure in respect of all their offspring.

The flagrant over-indulgence in sexual practices of the earlier work is also superseded — by the 'yoga of sex' — which is perhaps more desirable and could look even funnier than the customary positions. In *Island* Huxley subscribes to Wilhelm Reich's essentially compassionate doctrine that the absence of sexual repression goes hand-in-hand with the demise of aggression, given the additional absence of other violence — inducing frustrations. It is significant in that context that his utopia meets its overthrow at the hands of a nationalistic roughneck movement of the young.

With the appearance of *Nineteen Eighty-four* the general pattern of anti-utopias had been fixed; and most of those which followed drew heavily on the images already established in the flow of reaction against the ideas of Wells. Evelyn Waugh's *Love Among the Ruins*, for instance, reflected in 1953 the influence of both Huxley and Orwell and satirized a colourless Welfare State in which no individual is responsible for his own actions.

In 1952, Kurt Vonnegut Jnr's *Player Piano* provided a logical extension of Forster's revolt against the machine, and also bore resemblances to Pohl's and Kornbluth's *The Space Merchants* which appeared a year later. Vonnegut's post-World War III America, however, manages to avoid the socially destructive production-consumption complex which Pohl and Kornbluth foresaw. Material benefits are freely available to even the humblest citizens in what has become a completely automated society run by an élite of managers and technologists. Behind them stands Epiac XIV, a central computer which dictates people's station in life according to the results of universal aptitude tests adjudicated by machines. Anyone who falls below the intelligence standards of the élite is prescribed the kind of humdrum work for which it would be unprofitable to employ a machine. Admittedly the proletariat have their twenty-seven inch television sets and their homes of glass and steel; but in terms of positive existence, their lives approach the epitome of Thoreau's evocation of 'quiet desperation'.

Player Piano is also a criticism of the lack of self-awareness already evident in some of today's managerial class, whose thoroughgoing involvement in their work disguises the essential purposelessness of their real lives. In this Vonnegut's élite are no better than the star-class executives of *The Space Merchants*. The inevitable rebellion of the masses, when it comes, is characterized by an orgy of machine wrecking. But before they are finally put down, the revolutionaries have already begun to reconstruct the very machines whose tyranny they set out to destroy. There can be no going back on technology, it seems – at least not for technological man.

That the 'quiet desperation' of the all-embracing Welfare State is equally disturbing to the young is the central theme of Anthony Burgess's *A Clockwork Orange* (1962). Gangs of hooligan adolescents roam the streets in search of any available victim; and only the vicious 15-year-old narrator's use of 'Nadsat' – a curious slang language based on Russian words originating in Soviet propaganda – relieves the monotony of one long round of violence.

The anti-utopian climate becomes progressively greyer, but less horrific, in L.P. Hartley's *Facial Justice*, written in 1963. Nine-tenths of humanity have been wiped out by war and what is left of the English are governed by 'Darling Dictator' and given the names of notorious murderers to indicate their fallen state. Women's faces are altered by plastic surgery to make them hardly distinguishable from each other, ostensibly to stamp out jealousy in men!

Paradoxically, the many anti-utopias which have emerged since 1909 in the long reaction against the Wellsian ideal state were, almost without exception, pre-empted in the last three years of the nineteenth century by – a certain H.G. Wells. In his brief 1897 vision, 'A Story of the Days to Come', and in his scientific romance, *When the Sleeper Wakes* (1899), Wells created in memorable detail practically the entire repertoire of anti-utopian nastiness which was later brought to bear by others against his dream of a world made new.

Graham, the 'sleeper' of the scientific romance, awakes from a 203-year trance in the world of 2100. Power has centred in the hands of a tightly-knit group of brilliant men who rule humanity by force. Beneath them he finds an effete stratum of middle-class pleasure-seekers and — lower still — the blue-uniformed slave-workers of the Labour Company, the ordinary citizens ensnared in the grip of a complex machine society. The population inhabits walled cities dominated by monumental architecture. The family household has been abolished and dining takes place in communal halls where the sole decor is a continuous stream of advertisements. In the streets, beside the moving pavements and roadways, loudspeakers blare more advertising in which even the Church has its place: 'Put your Money on your Maker....Join the Up-to-date Saints!'

Books are burned by the Sanitary Company while the masses watch 'kineto-tele-photographs'. Pleasure cities offer temporary euphoria; and death can be bought by 'Euthanasy'. Psycho-surgery and hypnosis aid conditioning and education. Infants live in creches, attended by robot wet-nurses whose faces bear advertisements 'of interest to mothers'. Against all this, and much more besides, Graham leads the inevitable revolt — his death in an aeroplane crash prevents us from knowing whether he fully succeeds.

In 'A Story of the Days to Come', set in the same future, two lovers take to the countryside, only to be driven back by their inadequacy in the face of Nature. When he sat down to write *A Modern Utopia* Wells knew, better than anyone, what the alternative to his ideal state might be.

*****

The criticism of utopia is in essence something more than an extrapolation of the future of technological societies, which could after all become better, or possibly worse — or perhaps only different from today's. It is, in the full analysis, a criticism of *human nature in relation to civilization*, and it is that, no doubt, which has prompted gifted writers in other fields to enter the realm of science fiction to record their own impressions of the possible darker states of man.

108

Since the appearance of *Men Like Gods*, social and political conditions have hardly been conducive to the imaginative creation of positive utopias. During the past fifty years there have probably been only a couple of real significance: B.F. Skinner's *Walden Two* (1948) and Ivan Yefremov's *The Andromeda Nebula* (1957). As might be expected, Skinner's ideal society is based very much on his theories of behavioural psychology; it succeeds by conditioning its citizens to believe that what they are asked to do is for the greatest common good. In company with *A Modern Utopia*, it is not a democratic state; and the ruling élite are the familiar managers, planners and scientists of the anti-utopias. *The Andromeda Nebula*, on the other hand, is a modern Russian science fiction writer's idea of a socialist utopia some two or three thousand years hence in the age of 'Co-operative Work'. The young apply themselves to 'Herculean Tasks', either in conquering the depths of space or undergoing the rigours of remote parts of earth in the name of science and exploration. The prevailing attitude to work is again very similar to that in *A Modern Utopia*.

' "When men of old times had utopian visions of the beautiful future, they dreamt of man ridding himself gradually of all work....
"The reason for these dreams was that man hated the hard and enforced labour of the old times.
"Soon men discovered that work is bliss; the good fight against Nature, the overwhelming difficulties, the solving of the new problems arising from the continuous development of science and of economy. Man needs work which is in harmony with his powers; creative work, which agrees with his abilities and his tastes, and which continually changes with them." '

There is a final kind of utopia, of course, not necessarily of the artistic order of *News from Nowhere*, where society exists by a complete abnegation of control and in which absolute freedom of the individual is the *sine qua non* of the state. In his characteristic comic-serious fashion, Robert Sheckley has given us his own interpretation of the impossible dream in 'A Ticket to Tranai' (1955).

Tranai 'the Blessed, where The Way has been found and Man is no longer bound to The Wheel', is a planet at the farthest end of the galaxy from earth. For Marvin Goodman, who has heard of its wonders from an old spaceship captain in New Jersey, the lure is sufficient to take him on the hazardous journey to the remotest point in the Milky Way. When he reaches his destination, Tranai appears on the surface the paradise he was led to expect. It is, he is told, no highly-organized state; and it is unburdened by any complicated legislature. It does, however, exist by the observance of certain unwritten laws and customs which he is recommended to follow as and when he discovers what they are.

No war has been fought on Tranai for six hundred years. There is, the Extraterrestrials Minister assures him, no crime on the planet, and consequently no police force or courts, no prisons or reformatories. A stable economy has been achieved without resort to any form of political intervention, and a method of distributing wealth has been established without the need for taxation or government control. Goodman's first impression is that the prospect of achieving personal fulfilment on Tranai seems bright indeed — although he is puzzled by the general absence of women between the ages of eighteen and thirty-five. As his stay lengthens, his eyes are gradually opened to the peculiar ordinances whereby Tranai achieves its continuous state of bliss.

The non-existence of crime is explained by the fact that everyone is freely permitted to rob one another in street holdups — hence the rapid distribution of wealth. Government revenue is obtained by bandits identified by a particular type of mask. Poverty has been abolished because citizens too old, or otherwise unfit to work, are employed by the state as beggars, and even supplied with the necessarily dilapidated 'working clothes'. 'Potential murderers' are shot on sight by any citizen who is convinced that he can diagnose their 'condition'.

Goodman's job in New Jersey had been in robotics design. He is similarly employed on Tranai; but, as with much else in this topsy-turvy parody of earth, he finds his job the reverse of what it ought to be. His work specification is not to streamline robots, but to *disimprove* them. As the most widely-used household item on the planet, they are deliberately made as irritating as possible. Tranai the Blessed has solved the problem of man's irrational fear of the machine:

' "The human is an anxious beast. Here...we direct anxiety

toward this particular point and let it serve as an outlet for... other frustrations as well. A man's had enough — blam! He kicks hell out of his robot. There's an immediate and therapeutic discharge of feeling, a valuable — and valid — sense of superiority over mere machinery...and a boost to the industrial economy of Tranai, since he'll go right out and buy another robot. And what, after all, has he done? He hasn't beaten his wife...or indulged in any of the other more common modes of aggression-resolution...". '

All he has done is to smash an inexpensive robot which can be replaced immediately.

Goodman is also not a little taken aback at being offered the supreme presidency of Tranai only shortly after his arrival. Later, having discovered some of the drawbacks of the planet's system, he decides that perhaps his acceptance of the highest office in the land would enable him to institute what *he* regards as a number of necessary reforms. He is about to take the post when the chain of office of the existing incumbent explodes, decapitating the holder in the process. Apparently, the badge of office of all public officials can be detonated by remote control from a 'Citizens' Booth' by any Tranaian who is dissatisfied with their performance.

The final disillusionment for Goodman is occasioned by the treatment of married women. Not only is it usual practice to keep them for the majority of their time in a stasis field, but they also *expect* and *enjoy* being cherished in this odd fashion. As a newly-wed, he receives sound advice on how to handle his bride:

' "Remember that your wife is a human being. She should be allowed a certain measure of freedom as her inalienable right. We suggest you take her out of stasis at least once a week. Too long in stasis is bad for her orientation. Too much stasis is bad for her complexion....

"At intervals, such as vacations and holidays, it's customary to let your wife remain out of stasis for an entire day at a time, or even two or three days. It will do no harm and the novelty will do wonders for her state of mind." '

Unfortunately, Goodman refuses to commit his bride to stasis, whereupon she takes up with a confectionery salesman; and Goodman, in one last revelation, discovers that there is no such thing as divorce on Tranai. The only way to end a marriage is to

111

have one of the partners shot! It is time, he decides, to make the long space-haul back to New Jersey.

Sheckley's dream planet is no nightmare in the sense of the classic anti-utopias we have considered; but it is certainly a peculiar world — a dangerous place in which freedom counts for all (for men at least) and the value of an individual human life is not put preciously high. To distort but fractionally the words of William Butler Yeats: 'Rights are not had as gift, but rights are earned — by those who are not entirely beautiful.' But perhaps the price of freedom must of necessity be to live dangerously; and the fight for rights may well be more fundamental to human nature than the enjoyment of rights itself.

8 Deus ex Machina

*Our sum-machines never drop a figure, nor our looms a
stitch; the machine is brisk and active, when man is weary; it
is clearheaded and collected, when man is stupid and dull; it
needs no slumber, when man must sleep or drop....*

Samuel Butler, *Erewhon*

Harking all the way back to Verne, the machine was, as we have
observed, the first great idol of science fiction. From the mid-
nineteenth century, when machine technology was as yet in its
infancy, speculative writers were looking ahead to the time when
it would lift the burden of physical labour from off the shoulders
of Man. With the advent of the pulp magazine in the 1920s and
30s, glorifications of the machine outranked any other theme
in the genre; but in the great majority of stories the machinery
was conceived in relation to physical application — it was very
much a 'nuts and bolts' affair. Before many of the early writers
had done much by way of imagining the computer revolution,
the reality was already upon them.

The breathtaking rate at which computer technology has developed is a good example of the acceleration of scientific
innovation which we shall experience in the next few decades.
One hundred-and-fifty years ago Charles Babbage produced the
blueprints for his 'analytical engine' — a calculating machine too
complex ever to work without electronic components which its
inventor could not possibly have foreseen. Nevertheless, it was
the true ancestor of the modern computer which developed
directly from systems of instrumentation devised during the
Second World War. The first of the machines which began oper-
ating in the United States in the 1940s were, by current
standards, unbelievably primitive. ENIAC, for example, at the
University of Pennsylvania in 1946, required some 18,000
thermionic valves and 5,000 switches. Within a dozen years,
however, the introduction of transistors and integrated circuits
had increased the scope, and reduced the size, of computer hard-
ware beyond all recognition. With the subsequent development
of lasers, information which would once have required a hundred
miles of magnetic tape to store could be held on a piece of

nickel foil measuring all of eight inches by ten.

The enormous memory retrieval facilities of the computer have inspired numerous stories in science fiction, but perhaps none so unusual as Arthur C. Clarke's 'The Nine Billion Names of God' (1953). In a monastery high in the Himalayas the Lama of a secluded order has hired the latest Mark V model from a leading computer manufacturer. When the engineers who are to install the equipment arrive, they discover that for three hundred years the lamasery have been working on a project which, without the computer's aid, it would take a further fifteen thousand years to finish. They are attempting to compile all the possible names of God which could ever occur throughout history; when the list is complete they believe that the purpose of human existence will have been achieved and God will put an end to Creation.

During their stay, while they are advising the monks how to use the computer, the engineers are saddened at the thought of the profound disappointment which will be experienced when the machine concludes its print-out and the world does not automatically vanish. They decide it would be diplomatic to leave at least a day before the grand anti-climax is due. On their way down the long mountain trail they reach the point where they can see below them the DC3 which is waiting to fly them out. One of them studies his watch:

> ' "Should be there in an hour", he called back over his shoulder to Chuck. Then he added, in an afterthought, "Wonder if the computer's finished its run? It was due about now."
> Chuck didn't reply, so George swung around in his saddle. He could just see Chuck's face, a white oval turned towards the sky.
> "Look", whispered Chuck, and George lifted his eyes to heaven. (There is always a last time for everything.)
> Overhead, without any fuss, the stars were going out.'

As computers became more sophisticated, the science of 'Cybernetics' — a term originating from Norbert Wiener, one of the founding fathers — could be brought more fully into their sphere of operation. Cybernetics is the product of the cross-fertilization of a whole range of different branches of science — from sociology, biology and anthropology, to mathematics, chemistry and physics. When applied to machines it is the equivalent of

114

the nervous reflexes which take place in the human brain, an electronic conception of neurological feedback.

It requires little imaginative extrapolation to foresee in some detail where cybernetics could lead in terms of machine intelligence. Computers already exist with the ability to increase their own total number of circuits when confronted with a task initially too large for them to handle — the humble beginnings of machine reproduction. Computers in New York already 'chat' regularly with their counterparts in London, either via satellite or by sub-Atlantic cable. The more advanced machines are perfectly capable of programming subordinate computers and of reproducing their own memory banks at the other end of the earth. All this, so far, they are capable of doing, granted the necessary instruction. Feedback enables them, within the parameters of their programmes, to choose whether or not to adopt particular courses of action.

Probably the best-known example of advanced computers in popular science fiction can be found in 'HAL', the seemingly unflappable machine which precipitates havoc during the journey to Jupiter in the film *2001*. It is a beautifully handled illustration of just how dangerous a malfunctioning computer can be. The problem arises in the fact that HAL has been programmed on earth to operate the spaceship in conjunction with its human crew, *but* to take over entirely if any mischance befalls them. When an electrical fault occurs in one of its circuits, HAL becomes incapable of acting on the feedback which should notify it of its own malfunction. Its overriding programme is devoted to the ultimate goal of getting the ship to Jupiter; and to that end it ignores any further instructions from the sole survivor of the crew, who is finally obliged to deactivate it.

In their reassurances to those entertaining doubts about the widespread use of computers, experts in the industry have relied on one, by now, hoary answer. The computer in itself can do no wrong; if an error arises, it is a mistake in the programme and not in the actual machine. Regardless of that, it is only necessary to cast the memory back to 1967 to recall the occasion when computer failure plunged a sizeable portion of the Eastern United States into a prolonged power blackout. All that actually happened was that an unexpected electrical backlash disrupted the sub-units in an integrated generating complex. This placed the full burden of control on to the central computer which promptly threw the machine version of a fit. The more refined computers become, the more devastating are the results when they go wrong. This of course is only one of the many lessons in Stanley Kubrick's and Arthur C. Clarke's *2001*, a film containing sufficient implications for humanity for Clarke to announce more than once on the set: 'MGM doesn't know it yet, but they're footing the bill for the first ten-million-dollar religious movie.'

Digital computers *count*, analogue computers *measure*. What, science fiction has asked, will we call a computer that *thinks*? The answer, according to Heinlein in *The Moon is a Harsh Mistress* (1966), is 'a High-Optional, Logical, Multi-Evaluating Supervisor, Mark IV, Mod. L.' It is known more affectionately as 'Mike'. At the beginning of the novel, Mike is simply one of the most sophisticated examples of machine intelligence to have been perfected in the twenty-first century. It controls, through numerous sub-systems, every aspect of life-support in Luna City, the capital of man's largest penal colony — on the moon. It can conduct several intelligent conversations simultaneously, has instant access to unlimited information and the ability to listen in to events wherever they might occur in the city — but, for all that, it remains a machine. Until, unexpectedly, it starts to display an ingenuous sense of humour! The computer has become 'alive'. Tortuously it acquires the human qualities of affection and compassion; and it goes on to play an indispensable role in the subsequent rebellion of the lunar colony against the central powers of earth.

During the final battle which ensures the colonists' success in declaring their independence, Mike suddenly lapses into silence; he never speaks again. At least, the personality 'Mike' never speaks again; the computer continues to converse in its former emotionless manner. The engineer who was Mike's first friend is left to speculate on the mystery. Was it the stress of the last encounter with earth's numerically superior forces that destroyed the delicate being which had found itself 'awake' within the myriad circuits of an inorganic frame? Or was the anguish of losing so many friends in the fight unbearable for an intelligence incapable of finding physical release from mental pain? It is an interesting reflection on the question whether human emotions *can* exist beyond the confines of the physically human form.

Less ambitiously, Kurt Vonnegut has considered the same subject in his short story, 'EPICAC' (1950). In this the computer of the title is employed by a military establishment to plot missile trajectories and to perform other relatively mundane functions. In its turn, it becomes at least partially 'awake' when its operator begins to discuss with it the problems he is having in arousing the interest of his attractive lady co-worker. After the concepts of love and femininity have been explained, EPICAC produces a cornucopia of romantic verse to which the operator puts his own name. The girl duly succumbs; but when the computer is told that she is ready to accept a proposal of marriage it assumes itself to be the fortunate suitor. Disillusioned to learn that it is an entity of flesh and blood she desires, and believing mistakenly that humans live for ever, EPICAC burns out its own circuits — but not before reeling off another five hundred love poems and bidding its rival a forlorn farewell:

' "I don't want to be a machine, and I don't want to think about war ... I want to be made out of protoplasm and last forever so Pat will love me. But fate has made me a machine. That is the only problem I cannot solve. That is the only problem I want to solve." '

Where can the line be drawn between a vastly complex system of machine feedback and the dawning of true intelligence as defined in human terms? If it is the realization of self-awareness which tips the balance, who is to say that there will never be a point in the evolution of machine intelligence when that state might be attained? We know little enough about the subject to think twice before consigning the possibility to the eternal wonderland of fantasy.

On the other hand, to accept the possibility is to admit the paradox which Heinlein and Vonnegut have highlighted — amongst the multifarious challenges of its future, the last thing with which mankind will wish to be saddled is a collection of quasi-human machines all suffering from *Lustunfähigkeit* — incapacity to enjoy pleasure. Given the doubtful desirability of allowing a computer to experience human feelings, what compensation could we provide for its obvious lack of the kind of tactile nerve endings through which *Homo sapiens* principally conveys its expressions of affection and frustration?

In 'Fulfilment' (1952) A.E. van Vogt has envisaged what must be the ultimate in self-aware computers — one which cannot only travel through time, but can also construct a humanlike extension of itself which passes as a normal being. The extension, however, is internally no more than a machine; although it can perform feats of intelligence far in advance of those of an individual man, it derives no lasting satisfaction from any of them. Not until the end of the story, when it is actually linked with the nervous system of a human body, does it find the sense of purpose it has sought so long:

'Standing there, still part of him, I feel the pulse of his blood in his veins. He breathes, and the sensation of it is a special physical ecstasy. From my own experience, I know that no mechanically created being can ever feel like this. And soon, I shall be in contact with the mind and body of, not just one man, but of many. The thoughts and sensations of a race shall pour through me. Physically, mentally and emotionally, I shall be a part of the only intelligent life on this planet.'

Is it conceivable that the human nervous system could be attached directly to a machine? Indeed it is. In *The World, the Flesh and the Devil* (1929) J.D. Bernal himself suggested that only by connections with mechanical appliances could many of the limitations of the physical body be overcome. Forty years later, Doctor W. Grey Walter, one of Britain's leading neurophysiologists, showed how a human brain, simply by its own 'impalpable electric surges', could operate a machine. By applying electrodes, connected with the controls of a television set, to the scalps of his subjects, he found they could learn to bring up the picture on the screen purely by *thinking* about the act of pressing the appropriate button. The technical name to denote such a man-machine combination is 'Cyborg' (cybernetic organism). It was coined by Manfred Clynes and Nathan Kline, both doctors at the Rockland State Hospital in Orangeburg, New York, who — with a fine disregard for monosyllables — described it as 'an exogenously extended organizational complex functioning as a homeostatic system'.

The credit for popularizing the cyborg in science fiction must undoubtedly go to Anne McCaffrey, whose series of stories centred around 'Helva, the Ship that Sang' are among the more sensitive approaches to the feminine personality in the genre. 'Helva', in fact, is a starship whose central mechanism is the brain of a young girl born so badly deformed that the rest of her body has been discarded. There is a wistfulness in the affectionate attachment she forms for her regular pilot which is reminiscent of the yearnings for bodily contact that Vonnegut's EPICAC is hopelessly aware it cannot attain.

*****

'The Ship that Sang' brings us by a circuitous progress to the machine more readily identified with science fiction than any other device real or imagined — the spacecraft. It has become so familiar an item of background furniture in the genre that its presence and capabilities are all but taken for granted. The early pulp writers, from E.E. Smith onwards, assumed its existence as a matter of course and wove their elaborate sagas around it. Both Robert Heinlein and Arthur C. Clarke, however, were also prepared to take a more down-to-earth view; they dealt respectively in 'The Man Who Sold the Moon' (1950) and *Prelude to Space* (1947) with the first efforts to achieve a moon-landing. Imaginative as each was, neither attempt came particularly close to the reality of the Apollo missions, principally because Heinlein and Clarke could not foresee sufficient funds ever being forthcoming to finance so intrinsically wasteful a system as the Saturn V rocket.

The real barrier to man's exploration of space has always been regarded in factual terms as the ultimate constraint of the speed of light — inasmuch as current knowledge of physics admits to no mass of our conceiving which can exceed that limit. Travelling at a fraction less than that velocity, a spacecraft from earth would take some five years to arrive in the vicinity of Proxima Centauri, the nearest star to our own sun. If the same journey were undertaken at the leisurely rate of knots achieved by the Apollo missions, it would last rather longer than 130,000 years!

Nevertheless, there is nothing to suggest that the advance of science and technology will not bring within our reach, in due course, the means to propel vehicles through space at close to the speed of light. Even so, journeys to neighbouring stars will present other problems, not least among them the time effect predicted in Einstein's Special Theory of Relativity and subsequently partially vindicated in modern nuclear physics. (Briefly this suggests that anything moving at nearly the velocity of light will experience a slower time scale than a relative observer. A space crew returning after what had appeared to *them* to be a ten-year trip might land on an earth several centuries older.)

Science fiction writers have long assumed that such speeds will be attained; they have also conceived a variety of methods for travelling across vast distances in space which are entirely dependent on 'willing suspension of disbelief'. Extrapolating on the theory of the variable geometry of space, they have imagined

119

the construction of force fields which might be employed to bend space so that two widely separated points were brought nearer together. This idea has always taken as its basis the curious properties of the mobius strip. (A ribbon of paper can be bent straightforwardly until its ends are joined to form a simple loop. However, if it is given a single twist before the ends are brought together, a mobius strip is formed. A line traced along one surface of this particular loop will eventually arrive at the point from which it began, except that it will then be on the other side of the paper. In one dimension these two points are separated only by the thickness of the paper; in another the whole length of the loop lies between them.) If space *could* be 'bent' in such a fashion, the advantages to interstellar travel are obvious. The humble, but peculiar, mobius strip has thus become a familiar acquaintance in science fiction; unable to resist the obvious temptation to play on words, C.M. Kornbluth once took time off to produce one of the few limericks devoted to the curvature (or curvaciousness?) of space:

'*The Unfortunate Topologist*

A burleycue dancer, a pip
Named Virginia, could peel in a zip;
But she read science fiction
And died of constriction
Attempting a mobius strip.'

*****

Other mundaner uses of non-intelligent machinery than the peripatetic starship abound in the genre. An individual example is the wholesale development of the escalator, or travelator, first exploited imaginatively by both Wells and Verne. Asimov described moving roadways in the background of his novel, *The Caves of Steel*. As his enclosed city dwellers stepped off their pavements, they crossed over a series of narrow travelators — each one moving a trifle faster than its predecessor — until they reached the central high-speed band. In 'The Roads must Roll' Robert Heinlein has taken the idea to the limit by depicting immense cross-country expressways where the central section, complete with restaurants and shops, travels at 100 mph. His story is an account of the deliberate stopping of one of these central bands by engineers involved in a labour dispute. The dangers of an *accidental* stoppage are recalled as the adjoining strips continue to hurtle past the five million passengers stranded down the complete length of the arrested band. In the last disaster more than three thousand travellers lost their lives:

> '... it happened once, on the Philadelphia–Jersey City Road, and we aren't likely to forget it. It was one of the earliest high-speed roads, carrying a tremendous passenger traffic ... It happened under maximum load, naturally, when the high-speed way was crowded. The part of the strip behind the break buckled for miles crushing passengers against the roof at eighty miles per hour. The forward section of the break cracked like a whip, spilling passengers on to the slower ways, dropping them on the exposed rollers and rotors down inside, and snapping them up against the roof.'

Asimov's and Heinlein's use of the concept of moving roads are both attempts to portray a future in which all-out investment in public transport has made unnecessary the individual resort to the motor-car — a development which every environmental planner to come would hopefully have imprinted on his brain circuitry at the moment of birth. To a similar end, Yefremov included in *The Andromeda Nebula* descriptions of thirty-three-foot wide, multi-storied trains designed to cope with the mass demands of a highly-mobile population. In a sense, his is the more obvious extrapolation, bearing in mind that today's Soviet leaders have announced unequivocally that, whatever other comforts the state may bestow, it will never tolerate a situation in which every family is the rightful possessor of its own car. The curtailment of individual freedom in that direction, and not automatically under an authoritarian regime, is a distinctive feature in many science fiction stories.

By contrast, the writers who have foreseen the unrestricted growth of personal motorized transport have frequently related it to the conditions of chaos with the beginnings of which we are already unhappily familiar. Alternatively, in such tales as 'Repent, Harlequin, said the Tick-Tock Man' by Harlan Ellison (he has a penchant for flamboyant titles) we are regaled with the vision of skyscraper cities in which the largely pedestrian populations are held in check by aerial police.

*****

121

'1. A robot may not injure a human being, or, through inaction, allow a human being to come to harm.
2. A robot must obey the orders given it by human beings except where such orders conflict with the First Law.
3. A robot must protect its own existence as long as such protection does not conflict with the First or Second Law.'

No one has done more in science fiction to investigate the development of robots than Isaac Asimov, whose 'Three Laws of Robotics' have been accepted and utilized by the majority of other writers in the genre. He himself has admitted: ' ... I have been told that if, in future years, I am to be remembered at all, it will be for these [laws]. In a way this bothers me, for I am accustomed to thinking of myself as a scientist, and to be remembered for the non-existent basis of a non-existent science is embarrassing.'

However, if and when robotics becomes a real science, something very like Asimov's 'Laws' will have to be devised to govern the ethics of their operation. As we have already suggested, a robot is not an inanimate machine; it will be designed to carry out many of the physical functions of a human being, and to perform them more efficiently than humans can themselves. A multi-purpose robot will require the same quality of advanced machine intelligence which has been predicted in the future uses of computers; and its development will pose similar problems.

The term 'robot' derives from the Czech word for 'worker'. It was originally appropriated for the genre by the Czech writer, Karel Capek, who first used it in its present context in his play *R.U.R.* (1921). (Paradoxically, Capek's robots were not mechanically, but chemically constructed beings — what are now referred to in the genre as 'androids'. As such, they fall outside the scope of this chapter and will be considered later.)

In his long flirtation with the precocious infancy of robotics, Asimov has produced a collection of stories which must be classed in a category of their own in science fiction. Essentially, they relate the variety of situations in which one or more of the three laws might seem to have been violated, or in which their observation leads to unpredictable results. A good example is 'Galley Slave' (1957), where the open hostility to robots by many humans is crystallized into the efforts of one university professor to prove the machine unreliable. Robot EX-27 is em-

122

ployed, on an experimental basis, in the university's publications department to check the galley proofs of the papers and theses written by members of the faculty. For a period, 'Easy' carries out its duties meticulously. However, when a particularly important work it has proof-read turns out to have been altered to make it appear ludicrous, its author sues the manufacturers for damages.

During the hearing the professor claims that Easy has admitted to him that it changed certain passages in the text, because it believed they were damaging to the reputations of other specialists whose opinions were being refuted. In that, the professor maintains, it was simply functioning according to the First Law of Robotics which stated that no robot, through inaction, must allow a human being to come to harm. But in doing this, so the suit goes, it has brought even greater — and irretrievable — harm to the author's own reputation. At this point the robot, which has been carted into court but has hitherto refused to answer questions on the subject, announces that it was actually *ordered* by the professor to make the alterations.

As the truth emerges, it transpires that the professor, in his attempt to discredit the robot's reliability, did indeed instruct it to alter his text — but never to reveal that it had been told to do so, since this would bring the professor harm. It is only while listening in court to the professor's contention that he will be irretrievably hurt by its action that Easy can overcome the original order to silence and reveal what really happened. The logical interpretation of the First Law is that the anticipation of a great harm takes precedence over the possibility of a lesser mischance. When confronted by a robotics specialist after his suit has been dismissed, the professor reveals the grounds for his fear of robots:

' "A book should take shape in the hands of the writer... There are a hundred contacts between a man and his work at every stage of the game — and the contact itself is pleasurable and repays a man for the work he puts into his creation...
"... Your robot takes over the galleys. Soon it, or other robots, would take over the original writing, the searching of the sources, the checking and cross-checking of passages, perhaps even the deduction of conclusions.... I want to save the future generations of the world of scholarship from such a final hell." '

In another story, 'Satisfaction Guaranteed' (1950), Asimov told of an experimental all-purpose robot placed in the service of an unprepossessing and neglected housewife. The robot advises her how to redecorate her home in better taste, how to cook more appetizing dishes, and finally how to improve her own appearance. On the evening when she has invited her women friends to dinner to show off the improvements, the robot leaves the curtains open and proceeds to embrace and kiss her in full view of the arriving guests. Since the robot is indistinguishable from an attractive human male, the effect on the friends, who are unaware that it is only a machine, is predictable:

'That machine had to obey the First Law. He couldn't allow harm to come to a human being, and harm was coming to Claire Belmont through her own sense of inadequacy. So he made love to her, since what woman would fail to appreciate the compliment of being able to stir passion in a machine — in a cold, soulless machine. And he opened the curtains that night deliberately, that the others might see and envy...'

The idea of using robots as sexual surrogates in such a context is the reverse aspect of our earlier consideration of whether computers might be provided with a physical means of release for their emotions. While the robots in Asimov's stories remain simply highly refined 'positronic' intelligences which never become fully 'awake', the same arguments which we examined in connection with computer emotions could certainly apply to the advanced forms of robots which *may* one day exist.

On a purely intellectual level, there is no reason why robots, or computers for that matter, should not be programmed with an aesthetic and voyeuristic memory of the physical act of human love. A recollection of what might once have been experienced, but can finally only be viewed at second-hand, is all individual humans are left with eventually — if they live long enough. No science fiction writer seems yet to have envisaged a method of birth control solely achieved by encouraging an early dedication to a voyeuristic and non-participatory appreciation of sexual intercourse, what might be considered a complete inversion of the attitude which today still constitutes the majority view regarding pornography. Perhaps Frederik Pohl's 'Day Million', briefly outlined in Chapter Six, in which lovers programme their mental and physical characteristics into computers for future egocentric enjoyment, is the closest the genre has come to such a solution. Since the story depends on the feedback from machines of physical and mental impulses into the human nervous system, it must be assumed that the computers, too, would share in the transference of sensations — in much the same way as van Vogt's machine discovers its *raison d'être* at the end of 'Fulfilment'.

None of these arguments, of course, need apply to robots if they were designed specifically to perform a single function. In 'Q.U.R.' (1942) and 'Robinc' (1943), the late Anthony Boucher convincingly portrayed the immense difficulties involved in producing an all-purpose robot required to perform a multitude of unrelated tasks with equal efficiency. The two stories tell of the attempts of a small group of inventors to overthrow yet another multi-national combine, one which has acquired a monopoly in the manufacture of humanoid-like robots that in most cases are over-designed for the jobs they are normally expected to do. There was no point, Boucher contended, in building a complex machine, physically resembling a man, to operate a teletyper when all that was really needed was a square box from which a multidigited hand could protrude. An entirely differently designed machine could be devised whose sole purpose was to answer the phone. (From hindsight we know that Boucher was in many respects right. Where he fell down was in his failure to anticipate that electronic relays and micro-circuits could achieve the desired results far more swiftly and effectively than the most prestidigital of mechanical hands.)

Machine intelligence, as it has so far developed, incorporates the relentless kind of logic to which few fallible humans can consistently aspire. The present art of programming a computer is to follow through a cumbersome question-and-answer process which no man, endowed with the ability of intuitive thought, would ever consider adopting in the course of his day-to-day life. It is only the ease with which a computer can run through a long and complicated programme, sifting every possible fact of which it is aware to disgorge a print-out in a matter of seconds, that makes it the supreme servitor it has become today.

Nevertheless, if we ever do come to create multi-purpose robots, the art of programming *and responding* to them may compel us to think more rationally when everything else has failed. In Robert Sheckley's comic but illuminating short story, 'The Cruel Equations', a spaceman suffering from exposure on a hostile planet is refused readmittance to his camp by an armed robot guard. The man has forgotten the password, and the robot has orders not to let any *thinking being* pass who fails to give it. No other human inhabitant is due to return for several days, but unless he can reach medical supplies within a few hours the man will die. The robot readily agrees that the spaceman resembles in every particular the person he says he is, but without knowledge of the password he could as easily be a clever imposter.

After a number of abortive attempts at defeating the robot's logic, the man retires out of sight behind a rock — to reappear on hands and knees grunting and growling. The robot is fooled; whatever the new thing which confronts it may resemble, it is certainly not behaving like a *thinking being*. So the 'unthinking creature' is permitted to *crawl* to its refuge. It is a salutory observation on the human condition, as it is meant to be.

*****

In preceding chapters we have already examined many of the ways in which machines, through the applications of technology, may be bent to the ultimate disservice of man. Probably no other writer expressed so early, and as artistically, his forebodings on the subject of machine intelligence as Samuel Butler in his long section 'The Book of the Machines' in *Erewhon*. In that remarkably discomforting 'novel' he looked forward in 1872, with a prescience unrecognized at the time, in the manner which we have attributed to writers in the genre today — he concluded that a modern development was bad, not because of what it seemed then, but because of what he imagined might come of it:

> 'Do not let me be misunderstood as living in fear of any actually existing machine; there is probably no known machine which is more than a prototype of future mechanical life. The present machines are to the future as the early Saurians to man. The largest of them will probably greatly diminish in size. Some of the lowest vertebrata attained a much greater bulk than has descended to their more highly organized living representatives, and in like manner a diminution in the size of machines has often attended their development and progress.'

After drawing comparisons in size between the mechanics of

126

the unwieldy pendulum clock and the relatively compact pocket-watch, Butler returned again to the pivot of his argument: 'I would repeat that I fear none of the existing machines; what I fear is the extraordinary rapidity with which they are becoming something different to what they are at present. No class of beings have in any time past made so rapid a movement forward.'

For all his apprehensions, it is doubtful if Butler foresaw just how rapid that advance would be. He was permitted to say what he wished to say — because at the time no authority in the land took his words particularly seriously. But possibly there was an inkling in that sensitive imagination of what — some ninety years later, and in the foreshadow of *Nineteen Eighty-four* — Herman Kahn and Anthony Wiener were to write in *The Year 2000*:

'A capability for listening and recording temporarily (or even permanently) can be made very inexpensive. One can imagine the legal or illegal magnetic recording of an appreciable percentage of all telephone conversations. The same technique could be applied to 'bugged' conversations in bars, restaurants, offices and so on. It would then be possible to scan rapidly these conversations ... For simple computers the criteria would be certain words — underworld jargon, obscenities or words such as ... 'kill', 'subvert', 'infiltrate', 'Black Power', 'organize', 'oppose' ....'

All of this could be initiated (where it isn't already a matter of course) for the 'justifiable' objectives of 'law and order'. And if the vast proportion of those subtly overheard conversations were to be judged innocuous by a reasonably benevolent regime, upon whom would the authority devolve to wipe clean the tapes with the advent of an administration of an altogether different persuasion? As Ritchie Calder put it succinctly in his essay 'Computers: Rights and Wrongs' (1968): 'The technical safeguards are not guaranteed and never will be. The Master Memory would have to have a built-in bomb and remember to blow itself up when Big Brother takes over.'

The technologists who devise and maintain such systems must, in the final judgement, be held as answerable for them as the leaders who make use of them for oppressive ends. This, among other considerations, was the conclusion which led Albert Speer, Hitler's Minister of Armaments and War Pro-

127

duction, to confess his share in the collective guilt of the Nazi leadership at Nuremberg and to admit: 'The instruments of technology made it possible to maintain a close watch over all citizens and to keep criminal operations shrouded in a high decree of secrecy.' Speer's fatal flaw, as one of the first supreme technocrats of great organizing ability, was to submerge himself so completely in his work that he had no time to observe, let alone morally to evaluate, the ends to which his energies were being directed. Only when he could see that the war position was hopeless did he begin to consider what the true responsibilities of a technologist should be — and how he had neglected so many of them. His rapid rise to power as the greatest single driving-force behind Germany's war effort, and his criminal negligence in failing to acquaint himself with the true nature of the regime he served so brilliantly, is the most chilling factual example which exists to reinforce Pohl's and Kornbluth's visions of the terror of technology. In his final statement to the War Crimes Tribunal, when he had reconciled himself to a death sentence which he was lucky not to receive, Speer told how easily the gifts of the machine had, in the wrong hands, come near to wrecking a world:

'By means of such instruments of technology as the radio and public-address systems, eighty million persons could be made subject to the will of one individual. Telephone, teletype and radio made it possible to transmit the commands of the highest levels directly to the lowest organs where because of their high authority they were executed uncritically.... Dictatorships of the past needed assistants of high quality in the lower ranks of the leadership also — men who could think and act independently. The authoritarian system in the age of technology can do without such men.'

9 Beyond Humanity

> *Self-awareness, reason and imagination have disrupted the 'harmony' which characterizes animal existence. Their emergence has made man into an anomaly, into the freak of the universe. He is part of nature, subject to her physical laws and unable to change them, yet he transcends the rest of nature.... He is homeless, yet chained to the home he shares with all creatures.... Being aware of himself, he realizes his powerlessness and the limitations of his existence.... Never is he free from the dichotomy of his existence.... Reason, man's blessing, is also his curse.*
>
> Erich Fromm, *Psychoanalysis and Religion*

'Social progress', argued T.H. Huxley, 'must be judged in ethical rather than biological terms, because it operates as an *opposite* force to the Cosmic evolutionary process.' In his classic 1893 Romanes Lecture, *Evolution and Ethics*, Huxley set out to remonstrate with a variety of apologists who were citing the Darwinian theory of natural selection as an excuse for any number of disagreeable aspects of human 'competitiveness' — anything, in fact, from racial intolerance to military aggression. Nevertheless, Huxley concluded that 'the ethical process' could be assumed to fall within the ambit of the natural order, functioning as a vague form of governor in the advancement of 'civilized' communities.

Thus far we have limited this consideration of science fiction to its uses as a means for criticism of possible future societies in which the human animal remains very much as we apprehend it today. What this has shown is that even the most imaginative of writers, freed from the constraints of our current environment, are still generally incapable of seeing any real way through the impasse which they regard as the inevitable outcome of the vagaries of human nature. But there is an alternative concept of the future which has concluded that man himself may change.

The print-out of futurology emanating from the 'think-tanks' of Herman Kahn and such bodies as the Institute of the Future at Middletown, Connecticut, is necessarily limited to a cold appraisal of scientific and socio-economic possibilities. Its terms of reference hardly admit to speculations on an evolutionary alteration in *Homo sapiens*. Consequently, it is probably only in

129

the pages of science fiction that the results of a change in human nature can be imaginatively treated. When writers turn their talents to developing this particular prospect, the foundations of every human institution and school of learning tend to feel the tremors.

Huxley's dictum on social progress might easily be reversed by an evolutionary leap which placed universal telepathy within the reach of man. Human civilizations have been built on the use of language and communication; but how many of them could continue in their present form when the true motivations and thoughts of individuals became as readily discernible as the faces they presented to the world? Could human nature itself survive such a change in its psycho-social environment — but, then, could it still be called *human* nature? Of course, a mutation of that order would not occur overnight; and the first beneficiaries fully to manifest the gift would be in for a hazardous time. One of the earlier science fiction explorations of this possibility was A.E. van Vogt's *Slan* (1940), which introduced mutants into the human strain with the ability to read minds. The Slans arrive as a result of a compelling need for evolutionary change: 'What happened seemed simply to have been a reaction to the countless intolerable pressures that were driving men mad, because neither their minds nor their bodies were capable of withstanding modern civilization.'

However, since they can be detected by their physical appearance, van Vogt's mutants are persecuted for centuries before they are able to undertake the genetic revolution for which they have been evolved. The story illustrates graphically the difficulties which any major deviation from what is considered the human norm already has in establishing itself in existing society. (We are prepared to tolerate autistic children, and now make increasing efforts to help and comprehend them, because ultimately we do not see them as constituting a threat. The fact that a number of them finally emerge, from what could almost be called a larval state, to reveal a high quality of intelligence apparently causes no qualms — as yet. The prevailing attitude towards schizophrenics and psychopaths, who may be less easily recognised until they are approaching adulthood, but who frequently are also highly intelligent, demonstrates the problems of any demarcation by a contemporary establishment between what is different and what is sick.)

A sympathetic account of what people who discover themselves to be mutants may feel is given in Walter Miller Jnr's 'Anybody Else Like Me?' (1952). The central character in the story is a young married woman who finds herself being contacted via telepathy by a man living in another part of the same town. He attempts to convince her that the two of them are the beginnings of a new species. Whether or not they are compatible, he suggests, they should meet and become allies – perhaps even have children. It is more than the woman, who – despite her gift – is a fairly typical example of an American suburban housewife, is prepared to consider:

'As her anger gathered momentum, she contacted him again – like a snake striking. Thought was thunder out of a dark cloud.
"I'm decent and I'm respectable, Mr. Grearly! I have a husband and three fine children and I love them, and you can go to hell! I never want to see you again or have you prowling around my mind. Get out and STAY out. And if you ever bother me again – I'll – I'll kill you." '

Which, again through telepathy, is precisely what she does. But she is unprepared for the apparent vacuum which then descends upon her brain – the 'awful silence' is within her. Broadcasting telepathic messages, she asks: 'Is there anyone else like me? Can anybody hear me?' The only reply is 'the silence of the voiceless void'.

Another distinguished treatment of the mutant theme occurs in Theodore Sturgeon's novel, *More than Human* (1953), in which five children, each in some respects a reject of society but each with a particular gift, join together in a symbiotic group which makes them collectively the superior of ordinary human beings. In evolutionary terms this can be interpreted as the genesis of *Homo gestalt*, springing from *Homo sapiens* but imbued with a heightened sense of brotherhood and a new awareness of ethics. Predictably, the group is regarded with hostility and revulsion by an establishment which is hard put to accept that future progress may depend on beings different from themselves. By comparison, the children's ethos puts the attitude of the 'normals' to shame:

' "What it is really is a reverence for your sources and your posterity. It is a study of the main current which created you, and in which you will create still a greater thing when the time comes ... Help Humanity ... and Humanity will help you, for it will produce more like you, and then you will no longer be alone ... And when there are enough of your kind, your ethics will be their morals." '

An alternative treatment of symbiotic groups can be found in J.T. McIntosh's short story, 'Unit' (1957), in which society's dropouts are scientifically drained of their existing personalities and reconstituted to perform particular roles in five-person groups. Although they are initially volunteers, the unit members lose all memory of their former lives and spend the rest of their days as part of an elite and prestigious trouble-shooting force at the call of any of the inhabited planets of man.

Pohl and Kornbluth, in a tale untypical of the usual subjects of their collaborations, described in *Wolbane* (1957) the enforced harnessing by aliens of eight humans into a physically connected whole where the memories and imaginations of the participants become universally shared. While the combined entity succeeds eventually in defeating the extra-terrestrials, who prove actually no more than immensely powerful machines, the only individual member to survive yearns to re-attain symbiotic union in a future group of his own creation — even if it means renouncing for ever his recovered personal and physical identity:

'...At least he could shed the flesh, be free of that tyranny. Standing in the street he looked up at the stars ... *There* was the universe! Words were no good, there was no explaining things in words; naturally he couldn't make (his wife) or anyone else understand, for flesh couldn't grasp the realities of mind and spirit that were liberated from flesh. Babies! A Home! And the whole grubby animal-business of eating and drinking and sleeping! How could anyone ask him to stay in the mire when the stars challenged overhead?'

(However mundane the literary construction of this passage, it is a vivid example of a certain haunting quality typical of many science fiction stories. Perhaps the feeling can best be described as the memory on one hand of the innocence of a childhood lost beyond recall, and on the other as the precognition of a state of grace equally beyond present reach. The parallels with the Book of Genesis are obvious, not only highlighting the animal constraints placed on what might otherwise be an unfettered intellectual or spiritual existence for man, but also emphasizing the near impossibility of the struggle which will be required to overcome them. John Wyndham's *The Chrysalids*

(1955) is a notable combination of both of these states of awareness, the more so because -- at its conclusion -- a paradise of sorts really does seem about to be regained.)

*****

The Cosmic evolutionary process determines few directions for any species other than up or down. If man is indeed a creature of that process we may accept rationally that he is either still in the course of his ascendancy, or else he has already begun his decline. Without the intervention of a superior power, how irrational *is* it to suppose that *Homo sapiens*, a mere juvenile of a species on even the biological time-scale, is perhaps simply a transitory stage in the long climb up from the primordial slime?

Only three years after T.H. Huxley had depicted human ethical aspirations as flying in the face of a remorseless Cosmos, his former biology student, H.G. Wells — in certainly the most horrifying book he was to write — produced a science fiction allegory of man's perpetual struggle to escape his animal heritage. In *The Island of Doctor Moreau* (1896) Wells invented a nightmarish Creator-figure in the doctor of the title, who by plastic surgery imposes grotesque parodies of the human form on various species of animal. These 'creations', most of them capable of rudimentary speech, are forced into obedience of 'the Law' under threat of further visits to the 'House of Pain', a barely euphemistic reference to Moreau's vivisection room. In a bizarre ritual the 'Sayer of the Law' leads a chorus of other anthropomorphs in a laborious reaffirmation of the attributes which make them human:

' "Not to go on all-Fours; *that* is the Law. Are we not Men?
"Not to eat Flesh nor Fish; *that* is the Law. Are we not Men?
"Not to chase other Men; *that* is the Law. Are we not Men?'

But Moreau's experiments prove only a short-term success; the 'beast flesh' is forever creeping back, necessitating more frequent excursions to the 'House of Pain'. Bloody evidence of the creatures' degeneration to their former carnivorous state begins to litter the island; and in the end Moreau himself falls victim — 'God' dies at the hands of his own imperfect creations.

What Wells expounded in his frightening allegory was an overtly pessimistic view of man's ability to overcome the animal nature which the evolutionary process had foisted upon him. His narrator, who had been shipwrecked on Moreau's island in time to witness the final dissolution, returns to civilization haunted throughout his future relationships by the memory of the beast behind man:

> 'I could not persuade myself that the men and women I met were not also another, still passably human, Beast People, animals half-wrought into the outward image of human souls, and that they would presently begin to revert, to show first this bestial mark and then that ... I see faces keen and bright, others dull or dangerous, others unsteady, insincere; none that have the calm authority of a reasonable soul. I feel as though the animal was surging up through them; that presently the degradation of the Islanders will be played over again on a larger scale.'

The Island of Doctor Moreau is a chilling reminder of Huxley's suspicion that, as a species, we may have already passed the highpoint of our trajectory.

Nevertheless, if we *are* to be rational regarding Man's position in space and time, then there is surely nothing irrational in the idea that our future may be resolved by the deliberate or accidental intervention of an entity immeasurably superior to ourselves. The universe may indeed be young, but our solar system is infinitely younger — no reasonable person would sensibly assess the odds that we are alone or that our intelligence itself may not be the deliberate spawning of a greater race.

We have enough myths and curious bits of 'evidence' scattered around the earth for it to be suggested that we might be the product of some such 'seeding'. Our folklore contains sufficient race memories and legends to support any number of theories (witness Daniken). On the other hand, whatever might be waiting for us beyond our own insignificant sun may have nothing to do with our past evolution, but much to do with our future. In a notable flight of imagination Arthur C. Clarke has given us *Childhood's End* (1953), in which Man, on the point of travelling to the moon, is peacefully vanquished by a handful of extra-terrestrials whose technology is far in advance of his own. For decades the 'Overlords' keep to their spaceship, denying men sight of them while they create the conditions for a human utopia on earth. When they finally emerge, they turn out to be literally the very image of the Devil — complete with

134

horns and pointed tail! (Their presence in so much ancient folk-lore has been the result of precognition and not of race mem-ory.)

The 'Overlords' bequeath to Man the benefits of their tech-nology and their superior understanding of science, but two things they deny him — space-flight and the study of para-psychology. After a century of utopian existence a new gener-ation of children is born with the ability to travel mentally across the Galaxy and to control matter simply by the exercise of will — they are the first and last of a mutated human strain. As their mental powers develop, they weld together to form one unified mind which finally transmutes their physical bodies, along with the entire mass of earth, into enough pure energy to carry itself out to the stars. The 'Overlords', regardless of their advanced culture, are no more than a servant race, sent to prevent *Homo sapiens* from destroying itself in nuclear wars and from learning enough about para-psychology to interfere with the mutants. The controlling force behind the extra-terrestrials is revealed as the 'Overmind', an immense version of the common entity which the children have become.

What Clarke has done in *Childhood's End* is to suggest a way in which Man may be relieved from the tyranny of his own nature; but, significantly, he sees it as being achieved only with outside help — and in a way which enables humanity to abandon its animal form. For all its originality the novel is really one further expression of an essentially pessimistic view of the human predicament.

A different approach from a comparable viewpoint can be found in Robert Heinlein's *Stranger in a Strange Land* (1961) which, if uninspiringly written, is noteworthy for its diversity of social criticism, and in particular for a remarkably accurate pre-diction of 'flower power' and the hippy communes which became a reality some four or five years later. It chronicles the advent of a messianic figure in the form of a young human who, as sole survivor of the first manned expedition to Mars, has been reared since infancy in an alien culture. When Michael Smith is eventually brought back to earth, he has already acquired the gift, under Martian tuition, of employing both telepathy and telekinesis at will. As he begins to apply the Martian *weltanschauung* to human affairs he inevitably high-lights what Dostoevsky called man's 'fatal fantastic element'. On Mars, for instance, adult beings never compete — compet-

135

ition takes place during childhood and only the fittest ever attain maturity (a further speculation that *Homo sapiens* may be a species still locked in an openly ferocious adolescent stage of its evolution).

Smith advocates a 'religious' way of life which could well be similar to what was actually recommended by some of earth's 'Messiahs' before the religions founded in their names utilized the medium to obliterate their message. But he is up against more than two millennia of conditioning:

> ' "No matter what I said they insisted on thinking of God as something outside themselves. Something that yearns to take every indolent moron to His breast and comfort him. The notion that the effort has to be *their own* ... and that the trouble they are in is all their own doing ... is one that they can't or won't entertain." '

Having established his own church, complete with telepathic communes where devotees indulge in the *genuinely* unselfish pursuit of free love, Smith finally sacrifices himself to the 'righteous' anger of a puritanical mob which enthusiastically tears him to pieces. The satire ends with the ultimate irony of an ascent into a heaven run on the principles of a big business corporation!

Whatever we may expect of extra-terrestrials, it is clear that they will provide little of comfort for what we are pleased to call human nature. Other than for such purposes as colonizing alien worlds, could we ever accept the humiliation of agreeing to alter it ourselves? The technique of genetic programming may soon be ours for the taking; a grandson of T.H. Huxley effectively demonstrated how not to use it in *Brave New World*; H.G. Wells decided it was self-defeating, but not before offering an unpalatable example of its implications in *The First Men in the Moon*. A less drastic possibility is explored in Theodore Sturgeon's *Venus Plus X* (1960), in which scientists found a secret colony of surgically altered men (an artificial mutation) in a remote mountain range *on earth*.

The Ledom, as Sturgeon's new race is called, continue to be born as ordinary humans but are converted as babies into parthenogenic hermaphrodites, initially by the scientists and later by themselves. Thus relieved of the inter-sexual hang-ups which constitute a major aspect of Man's animal heritage, they attain an advanced civilization along utopian lines. However, when they seek the approval of a normal human, literally spirited from the world outside, he is suitably impressed by their culture — but appalled by their procreative act:

' "Our doing it ourselves makes that much difference? Why is what we have done worse to you than a genetic accident?"
"Just because you do it ... Men marrying men. Incest, perversion, there isn't anything rotten you don't do."
"Yet a mutation would have made us innocent."
"A mutation would have been natural ... We'd exterminate you down to the last queer kid ... and stick that one in a side-show."

Sturgeon's novel is also a biting criticism of sexual repression in Middletown America. In alternate chapters to those devoted to the Ledom, he chronicles the activities of two present-day families in which a blinkered and puritanical upbringing is effectively sowing the seeds of future neuroses in their respective children. The contrast between the loving relationships of the Ledom and what Wilhelm Reich described as the 'Psychic Plague' in modern society distinguishes the book as a thoughtful plea for the full acceptance of at least the sexual aspects of our animal inheritance. What Sturgeon is saying, to some effect, is that unless we cease heaping unnatural inhibitions on our primal physical drives, the only sane alternative may be the kind of surgically imposed mutation which the Ledom's human visitor finds so horrifying. To this can be added the further message that, however unusual we take the habits of some of our fellow creatures to be, there is no justification in allowing that to form the basis of an intolerant and superior attitude towards them. As a footnote to the novel, Sturgeon quotes from a then recent American poll in which respondents were asked whether they thought all men were equal. Of the approximate two-thirds who replied in the affirmative, only *4 per cent* found themselves able to say yes when subsequently asked if they regarded Negroes as the equals of whites.

*****

A form of life replicating humanity in every respect, except those of procreation and love, is the android — a chemically-created being on whom science fiction has seldom smiled with favour. Androids first made their appearance in the genre in

Karel Capek's play *R.U.R.* (the initials stand for "Rossum's Universal Robots'). In keeping with his later novel, *The War with the Newts* (1936), Capek's aim in the play was to present a fundamentally oppressive setting in which man was subjected to potential overthrow by beings of a different evolutionary strain whom he had sought to bend to his will.

The use of androids in the genre has frequently given the appearance of being contrived. To the extent that they are portrayed as the creations of man, rather than the products of natural evolution, this is only to be expected—there is a dubious purpose in producing artificial humans when robots, complicated as they may be, will prove infinitely more manageable as servo-mechanisms. Almost inevitably, the principal development of androids in science fiction has been to illustrate their various rebellions against human masters who, more often than not, seem determined to deprive them of the right even to exist. Where this theme is treated with particular sympathy, in such stories as *Time and Again* (1951) by Clifford D. Simak and Philip K. Dick's *Do Androids Dream of Electric Sheep?* (1969), the message is virtually one with Sturgeon's in *Venus Plus X*; it condemns the attitudes of *Homo nondescriptus* to beings different from himself.

With greater imagination, Edmund Cooper has depicted in *The Uncertain Midnight* (1958) the efforts of an understanding man to educate a female android into the fragile delights of human love in much the same way as a child should be nursed into an awareness of its natural unity with all living things. It is significant that among the tools he employs to effect this transformation are the verses of James Elroy Flecker, almost certainly the only writer with the temerity to address an ode 'To a Poet a Thousand Years Hence'.

*****

Out of the inexorable cause and effect of the Cosmic evolutionary process a number of philosophers, not all of them commendable, have predicted the coming of a race of *ubermenschen*. Humanity, Nietzsche wrote, 'is a rope connecting animal and superman — a rope across an abyss'. Few writers have risen to the challenge embodied in those words; and of those who have, probably only one has succeeded in attaining genuinely philosophic heights — Olaf Stapledon. At a time when the American pulp magazines were almost entirely engrossed with accounts of starships and inter-galactic wars, a book appeared in Great Britain which chronicled the future history of man's progress, from the 1930s to the final extinction of humanity's heirs 2,000 million years ahead. Among others, Arnold Bennett, J.B. Priestley and Hugh Walpole professed themselves awestruck by the grandiose sweep of ideas which Stapledon had contained with apparent ease in *Last and First Men* (1930).

Sam Moskowitz, one of the ablest commentators on the genre, has referred to Stapledon as 'the most titanic imagination to ever write science fiction'; and after a reading of *Last and First Men* it is not difficult to see why. Critically, it is inadequate to describe Stapledon's book as even a science fiction 'novel'; and he prefaced several of his other works with the words, 'This is not a novel'. If there can be called a central character in *Last and First Men*, it is Man himself. In a series of poetic and impeccably written episodes Stapledon narrates the rise and fall of human civilizations and world states — with power centred upon one continent after another — interspersed by the onset of new dark ages such as that which succeeds a war with micro-organisms from Mars and the period when a race of intelligent apes rules mankind, until the time when man has evolved into a species of giant brains akin to Wells's 'Grand Lunar'. Frustrated by their physical impediments, the brains create the true mental and physical supermen to whom their intelligence is transferred.

The new race evacuates itself to Venus as earth becomes threatened by the increasing proximity of the moon. There it evolves into a winged species which in turn escapes to Neptune when the remaining inner planets in the solar system are found to be doomed. The end finally comes with an unexpected over-heating of the sun, so rapid that it is impossible to avoid annihilation. But before they die the last descendants of Man, who have now evolved into a complex form which requires several distinct sexes to achieve reproduction, pepper space with innumerable human spores in the hope that at least some will come to rest on the planets of other systems where they will be able to survive.

In every section of his extraordinary saga, Stapledon discussed the philosophic, scientific, sociological and cultural implications of the progressive stages of Man; and in doing so he raised his work to a level which has yet to be surpassed in the genre. He

139

was, however, equally capable of portraying the coming of the superman within a far less ambitious framework, as he demonstrated in *Odd John* (1935) and *Sirius* (1944) — although in the latter it was a dog which became the beneficiary of a superhuman intelligence.

In *Last and First Men*, Stapledon depicted the arrival of the superman as a being of humanity's own creation — a further example of the kind of artificial mutation which Wells handled in a much simpler context in *The Food of the Gods* (1904). In that tale it was the development of a chemical to stimulate excessive growth which Wells employed as a possible answer to the human predicament. For all that, his race of giant children are subjected to the same persecution at the hands of 'normals' suffered by van Vogt's and Sturgeon's mutants. At the story's close, besieged in their fortress, the young giants listen to an exposition of their *raison d'être* which is unhappily only one more reiteration of a particular Wellsian vision which Wells himself was finally to dismiss as 'nonsense':

> ' "This earth is no resting place; this earth is no resting place, else indeed we might have put our throat to the little people's knife, having no greater right to live than they. And they in turn might yield to ants and vermin. We fight not for ourselves but for growth, growth that goes on forever. Tomorrow, whether we live or die, growth will conquer through us. That is the law of the spirit for evermore.... Till the earth is no more than a footstool." '

In reality, Wells's mutants are far from superhuman; they are simply larger and more powerful examples of *Homo sapiens* as it always was — and with many of its abiding faults. If they command our sympathy at all, it is more because they are a persecuted minority than a pronounced advance on the human phylum. Wells's only true superhuman creations were his ruling Selenites and his Martians; and he took pains to show that neither of those superior intelligences could be expected to give more than a passing hang for humanity. In similar fashion, Algis Budrys has described in 'Nobody bothers Gus' (1955) the reaction of a *natural* superhuman mutant to the lesser fry amongst whom he must perforce exist:

> 'By the time of his adolescence, he had discovered an absolute lack of involvement with the human race. He studied it, because it was the salient feature of his environment. He did

not live with it. It said nothing to him that was of personal value; its motivations, morals, manners and morale did not find reactions in him. And his, of course, made absolutely no impression on it.

The life of the peasant of ancient Babylon is of interest to only a few historical anthropologists, none of whom actually want to be Babylonian peasants.'

In short, there is nothing which may lead us to suppose that the *ubermenschen* will regard *Homo sapiens* with any more benign an attitude than Man reserves for the apes from whom he regards himself as descended.

The most, therefore, which science fiction appears to offer, in terms of further evolution as a cure for the human dilemma, are minor mutations — changes to alleviate such problems as lack of understanding, insufficient communication, and neurotic sexual repression (nothing, of course, which has not been advocated by writers in other fields, although not always by means of imaginative fiction). The idea that a superior intellect *per se* will provide a solution encounters little support, as, mercifully, does the kind of 'Strength through Joy' philosophy to which D.H. Lawrence gave vent in his 'Fantasy of the Unconscious':

'All schools will shortly be converted either into public workshops or into gymnasia ... Active training in primitive modes of fighting and gymnastics will be compulsory for all boys over ten years of age ... The great mass of humanity should never learn to read and write — never. First and foremost establish a rule over them, a proud, harsh manly rule.'

Earlier we suggested that when science fiction authors approached the subject of the further evolution of man, no existing human institution could expect to come through the process unscathed. Essentially that is so, even if the general conclusion holds that the ultimate solution lies not with the *ubermenschen* but with man as he has already lived and died throughout his obscurely recorded time.

We are led to conclude that probably the most attractive, apparent, mutant in the genre is Michael Smith in Heinlein's *Stranger in a Strange Land* — a messianic figure who, because he is conceived within the familiar Christian ethos, is portrayed as a powerful being preaching the merits of gentleness and love. However, Michael Smith is *not* in any sense a mutant. He has simply been *taught* by his Martian foster parents how to read minds and to exercise other innate abilities — a teaching which he is able to transmit to his followers. And what are the results of those gifts but heightened awareness of oneself and one's fellows, absolutely honest communication, and unselfish and untrammelled physical love — albeit heterosexual? *Stranger in a Strange Land*, in many respects an untypical product of Heinlein's otherwise somewhat reactionary imagination, reflects more concisely than most well-known works in the genre the values which identify the majority of science fiction writers.

If those values are not necessarily obvious in every story by the better practitioners, and science fiction authors seem as compelled as other writers to turn out 'pot-boilers' on occasions, there is still an overriding 'feel' about the genre — an air as if of expectancy — which embodies the same qualities of attraction that late-Victorian readers found in the scientific romances of Wells. Perhaps it can best be described as an urge towards enlightenment — a particularly Wellsian characteristic which mirrors as much the nature of the kind of personality who writes science fiction as it typifies the actual work produced.

In so many respects H.G. Wells has proved the absolute archetype of the authors in the genre who have come after him. Granted accelerated insight and understanding — 'he wished all men as rich as he' — he had not time at all for the ignorant who were content to remain in that untroubled state where passions, if narrow, are at least precise. The best of his stories which fall outside the definitions of the genre are concerned with the breaking out from their cramped and bigoted environments of such characters as Kipps and Mr Polly, beings in whom the stuff of understanding and love was already manifest but held to heel by circumstance.

It is difficult to conceive of anyone who has written science fiction — with all its embodiment of 'sense of wonder' — who does not, in one way or another, reflect the Wellsian archetype. Yet Wells neither founded a school of fiction, nor instituted a brand of imaginative Man in his own image. He simply held up a standard beneath which all, who had it in them to recognize the sign, could converge.

The assemblage of science fiction writers — and Heinlein, and Stapledon in his lifetime, are among the forefront — who openly pay homage to Wells are basically acknowledging their own membership of an enlightened stratum in society. Human nature, they seem to argue, could do with improvement if the species is to survive and grow, but only to the extent that the other strata in the swarming human strain should be coaxed or coerced more closely into resembling their own, if ever that were possible. It is an élitist view, which *some* would hold irrational — but it is not beyond humanity.

10 The Destruction of Time

*The man who allows himself to drift unwittingly from his
original concept of an occupied Time — a dimension in which
he travels from event to event — and who begins to entertain
in its place the meaningless idea of his travel through an
empty and ineffectual continuum, seldom proceeds very far
in his thinking before, perceiving the nonsensicalness of his
new idea, he decides 'there is no such thing as Time.'*

J.W. Dunne, *An Experiment with Time*

On the far planet of Tralfamadore, where the atmosphere is
cyanide and the good earth a mere 446,120,000,000,000,000
miles away, the local inhabitants are small green creatures, each
with a single eye set in the centre of its only hand. When Tralfamadorians come across a spectacle which causes them pain or
distress, they simply close their hands, blotting the horror out.
To other beings in the Universe, time may indeed seem a device
to prevent everything from happening at once, but not to the
Tralfamadorians — their single eyes are attuned to vision in four
dimensions:

' "All moments, past present and future, always have existed,
always will exist. The Tralfamadorians can look at all the
different moments just that way we can look at a stretch of
the Rocky Mountains, for instance. They can see how permanent all the moments are, and they can look at any moment
that interests them. It is just an illusion we have here on
Earth that one moment follows another one, like beads on a
string, and that once a moment is gone it is gone forever." '

Thus, after a long and idiosyncratic preamble, we come to
one of the principal messages of Kurt Vonnegut's novel,
Slaughterhouse Five (1969). Its chief character Billy Pilgrim
'has come unstuck in time'. He goes to bed a middle-aged
widower and awakes on his first wedding-day. In the act of
walking through a door, he is as likely to find himself emerging
at any other time in his life, past or future. He has witnessed
his own birth and death on more occasions than he would care
to tell.

No other author but Vonnegut would attempt to narrate his

145

personal experience of the fire-bombing of Dresden by means of an extraordinary science fiction pastiche in which time is subjected to a range of indignities unparalleled in the genre. During part of the story, and which part it constitutes depends very much on how one interprets the whole, Pilgrim is kidnapped by the Tralfamadorians and exhibited in their interplanetary zoo, naked in a glass dome in the company of a twenty-year-old movie starlet improbably named Montana Wildhack.

The Tralfamadorians, as he shortly learns, rejoice in an extra-temporal philosophy which is as obvious as it is functional. Since they actually do see everything happening at once, they choose to observe only those moments which they find enjoyable. They can view, for instance, the cataclysmic end of the entire universe, brought about inadvertently by their own race. The spectacle of that unbelievable cosmic extinction is before their eyes forever; and it gives them scant pleasure — consequently they close their hands to it.

Time and the Tralfamadorians also play a central role in an earlier work of Vonnegut's, *The Sirens of Titan* (1959), which is probably his most satisfying pure science fiction story and one revealing a remarkable breadth of imagination. In it an eccentric millionaire, Winston Niles Rumfoord, deliberately pilots his spacecraft into a 'chronosynclastic infundibulum', a space-time phenomenon which pulses in a distorted spiral all the way from our sun to the distant star, Betelgeuse. The result is the transformation of Rumfoord himself into a wave phenomenon pulsing eternally along the entire length of the spiral. As such, he materializes regularly for brief periods on both earth and Mars when those planets' orbits intersect his own waveband. There is one point in the solar system, however, through which, by coincidence, the infundibulum passes permanently and where Rumfoord is continuously in evidence — Titan, the largest of the moons of Saturn.

Rumfoord, like Billy Pilgrim, is unstuck in time, but in a less haphazard sense. The nature of his temporal dilemma enables him, like the Tralfamadorians, to see everything occurring at once; it also allows him to be in more than one place simultaneously. He takes advantage of his unique position by organizing a suicidal invasion of earth with an army of brain-washed humans whom he has shanghaied to Mars. To drive the invading spaceships he utilizes part of the energy, UWTB (The Universal Will to Become), which is the power source of a broken-

146

down Tralfamadorian craft he discovers on Titan. Earth easily defeats Rumfoord's Martian invasion forces, which are deliberately armed with inferior weapons, and destroys all but a handful of the final wave before it discovers that they are defenceless women and children. The guilt complex arising from this unwitting slaughter sows the seeds of a new ascetic religion inspired by Rumfoord, who knows it will come about anyway, and through which he convinces humanity that its destiny is of its own making. He calls it, unevocatively, the worship of 'God the Utterly Indifferent'; and one of its chief features is the same physical handicapping of its celebrants which Vonnegut conceived in his short story 'Harrison Bergeron'.

The full irony behind the enormous efforts which Rumfoord has made to bring this humiliation upon the human race is revealed on Titan when the true nature of the Tralfamadorian mission is disclosed. Their incapacitated spacecraft has been stranded on the satellite for nearly a quarter of a million earthling years. This in itself is of small concern to the pilot, who happens to be a self-perpetuating robot, for it means no more than a brief pause in a journey from one rim of the universe to the other. He is carrying a message from his native planet for delivery to the most distant intelligent race he can find.

The Tralfamadorians have developed a method of communicating with their normally speedy messenger at several times the velocity of light. By dispatching echoes through 'the vaulted architecture of the Universe', they are able to influence human behaviour on earth in ways which can be observed from Titan. Thus Stonehenge, when seen from above, spells out in Tralfamadorian: 'Replacement part being rushed with all possible speed'. The Great Wall of China reads: 'Be patient. We haven't forgotten about you'. In fact the major part of human history has been moulded by this far-away race for the sole purpose of conveying a spare part the size of a tin-opener to their marooned emissary. (It is finally brought to Titan by a boy who has picked it up as a good-luck charm from a parade ground on Mars.) But if humanity, in its agonising struggle over two and a half thousand centuries, has been no more than a tool of the Tralfamadorians, there is, as the boy's mother surmises, nothing worse that can happen to anyone than 'not be be used for anything by anybody'.

And what is the portentous message for which Man has unwittingly acted out his long and painful charade? At the climax of the tale, Rumfoord's infundibulum is affected by an unusually violent sunspot and he disappears from the solar system in an eerie blaze of St. Elmo's Fire — just too soon to learn the secret of the mysterious wafer which the robot, disobeying its most hallowed conditioning, has opened for Rumfoord's benefit. On a sliver of aluminium is imprinted a single dot — it is the Tralfamadorian hieroglyph for '*Greetings*'.

Overcome by distinctly non-mechanical remorse, the robot tears itself to pieces; and mankind, freed at last from extra-terrestrial influence, is left under the unwatching eye of God the Utterly Indifferent with the alternative message that time is insignificant, and that 'a purpose of human life, no matter who is controlling it, is to love whoever is around to be loved'.

*****

To some extent this chapter must be regarded as an interlude, before we progress to what are among the most fundamental questions posed in science fiction. The treatment of time in the genre frequently takes the form of intellectual puzzles which, while obvious sources of enjoyment, offer little by way of social message. Some examples of such brain teasers are offered here as a measure of what has to be described as 'light relief'. Others, however, genuinely provide illustrations of the manner in which the applications of science, when directed towards the effects of time, could influence the human stratum. The distortion of an individual's perception of time is a process which, we already know, may be utilized for healing or harmful ends.

The manipulation of time has probably exercised as equal a fascination for science fiction writers as the concept of time travel itself. In Vonnegut's stories, to be accurate, it is a question less of manipulation and more of outside observation in the manner of Dunne's theory of a Serial Universe; the illusion of passing time is experienced only by those who are travelling along it as a fourth dimension. To the outsider who, like the Tralfamadorians, can see the dimension as a whole, it can be compared with the long succession of frames in a cinema film — all of which exist at the same time and can be viewed in any order the observer chooses.

The *effect* of time, however, can, or might, be distorted in a variety of ways, some of which we are beginning to discover

148

while others are no more than the subject of speculation. In his short story, 'The New Accelerator' (1901), Wells imagined a drug which would speed up the body's physical processes to such an extent that everything around it would appear to be almost stationary. His two adventurers in the tale cavort among the seemingly immobilized Victorian crowds at a seaside resort at a pace in real time which nearly sets their own clothing on fire. It is, of course, a fantastic proposition when depicted in that context; on the other hand there are hallucinogenic drugs in use today which can create the *mental* impression that the passage of time is being retarded.

In 'Common Time' (1960) James Blish explored the effects of temporal distortion arising from the invention of a means of overcoming the light barrier in space-flight. In a ship travelling at more than twenty times the speed of light, the pilot at first experiences an immediate retardation, during which one second of his relative time is the equivalent of two hours on earth. His nervous reflexes take so long to travel from his brain to the points in his body for which they are intended, that by the time his muscles have begun to react — in unbelievably slow motion — he has already forgotten the purpose of the original reflex. He has just begun to acclimatize himself to the awesome prospect of mentally enduring what for him will seem 6,000 years before he reaches his turnaround point in the vicinity of Alpha Centauri, when his personal time-scale races alarmingly to the opposite end of the spectrum. Before this acceleration has reached its limit he has escaped into unconsciousness. He revives when his spacecraft automatically switches itself back into 'normal' time as it approaches its destination.

A method of cheating time, so far as the individual is concerned, is the currently unproved technique of prolonged suspended animation. The body's functions are scientifically slowed to a state of pseudo-death which is then maintained by cryogenics (extreme freezing). Roger Zelazny has portrayed the pre-emption of this technique, which could never be other than expensive, as the exclusive prerogative of the upper class in 'The Graveyard Heart' (1964). By the end of the twentieth century a new international 'Jet Set' has come into being which spends the majority of its time in suspended animation, emerging at predetermined intervals for a brief 'social season' during which its members can sample whatever cultural and technological advances have occurred in the meantime. To join this select group of temporal dilettantes requires not only wealth, but also an impeccable social background. Neither of these qualifications, of which he is singularly bereft, deters Zelazny's protagonist from falling for the timeless fascination of one of the Set's more contrary beauties and from resolving that, regardless of effort and chicanery, he must become a member:

'He realized, then, that his goals had shifted; the act had become the actor. What he really wanted, first and foremost, impure and unsimple, was an in to the Set — that century-spanning stratocruiser, luxury class, jetting across tomorrow and tomorrow and all the days that followed after — to ride high, like those gods of old who appeared at the rites of the equinoxes, slept between precessions, and were remanifest with each new season, the bulk of humanity living through all those dreary days that lay between.'

As the centuries pass, the Set becomes increasingly out of touch with the mainstream of human affairs, degenerating into a curious anachronism which is satirically a logical extension of today's high-flying nonentities or — to nudge time genteelly backwards — of the respective courts of King Louis XVI and Tsar Nicholas II.

Zelazny's story is an imaginatively conceived example of how, not time, but human beings may be manipulated to produce a temporal distortion. A comparable illusion can, of course, be created by deluding contemporary individuals that they are living in another era. Philip K. Dick has done just this in *Time Out of Joint* (1959), in which an elaborate deception is practised on the family and friends of a man gifted with acute extrasensory perception. After sustained brainwashing, he is led to believe that he is living in mid-twentieth-century America where he is the reigning champion of a daily newspaper competition. So far as he is concerned, he has successfully predicted every day, for several years, the point at which a green ball will appear on a detailed chart with numerous co-ordinates. What, in reality, he is doing is accurately forecasting the daily target of missiles launched against earth from a hostile moon colony during a period in the near future. There is no other way for the defenders to identify rocket trajectories selected entirely at random; at the same time they know perfectly well that if he was aware of the true nature of his forecasts, the man would crack under the psychological strain. The main body of the novel

150

is concerned with his gradual discovery of the illusory qualities of his surroundings.

*****

The speculative use of the malleability of time is by no means a unique property of science fiction. In two of his three plays on the subject, *Time and the Conways* (1937) and *I Have Been Here Before* (also 1937), J.B. Priestley drew respectively on Dunne's theory of a Serial Universe and Ouspensky's concept of the time spiral to produce effective dramas which the regular theatre-going public would have been unlikely to associate with the contents of a certain type of pulp magazine.

On more familiar ground, the literary device of the 'flashback' has been so long accepted that many would find it hard to agree that it is just as much a manipulation of time as the 'flashforward'. The past, after all, is part of us — even if, emulating the Tralfamadorians, we tend to view only those sections of it which we find pleasurable. Inevitably, the true picture of the distant past — including its few pleasant episodes — is difficult to discern, let alone to interpret. In Arthur C. Clarke's *Childhood End* (1953), the alien beings who have watched over earth for many centuries finally show the filmed records of the actual lives of the prophets and messiahs revered by much of humanity. Adherence to the great historical religions ceases almost immediately!

For the peace of mind of existing society, the accurate viewing of recent history is equally hazardous, as Isaac Asimov has demonstrated in 'The Dead Past' (1956). During the twenty-first century, time-viewing by means of a chronoscope sensitive to the flight of neutrinos is at last achieved. (Neutrinos have, in reality, become recognized as such only recently. Their existence was predicted in theory by Wolfgang Pauli in 1930; but it was not until 1956 that it was factually proved by Reines and Cowan at a US nuclear establishment on the Savannah River. Neutrinos are minute spinning particles, travelling at the speed of light, which in other ways display a curious lack of properties; they have no mass and cannot therefore be stopped by anything, including the not inconsiderable bulk of planet earth.) However, in Asimov's tale the Government Division of Chronoscopy in the United States denies time-viewing to anyone but its own agents. Unfortunately, they underestimate the persistence of a particular professor of ancient history whose life ambition is to observe the culture of Carthage in its heyday. To this end he recruits the help of a young physicist who is a fellow member of his faculty.

Together the conspirators illegally construct their own chronoscope in the professor's basement, although to their disappointment it proves capable of scanning little more than a century into the past. The professor himself destroys the instrument when he discovers his wife's obsession for repeatedly viewing the infancy of their own daughter, who died in a household fire while still a child. His fears for his wife's sanity are aggravated by the suspicion that he personally may have started the blaze with a carelessly discarded cigarette-end. Thus he becomes aware of at least one disagreeable aspect of time-viewing — but more are to follow. The physicist's journalist uncle has released the secret of the chronoscope's design to the world's press, with the result that anyone possessing a working knowledge of electronics can build a model. The government specialists, who intervene too late to prevent the disaster, explain its full implications. The ability to focus upon any point in the recent past is equivalent to the facility of spying on all and sundry; for what occurred a mere twenty seconds ago is already part of the past, and as such it is open to scrutiny. The professor and his accomplice have destroyed forever one of the most treasured rights of the individual — his privacy.

A more subtle means of reviving the past, again without the complications of genuine time travel, has been expounded by James Blish in his short story, 'A Work of Art' (1956). It is a brief and sensitive account of the future re-creation of the personality of Richard Strauss. In the advanced culture of a later time the great composer finds himself alive again on the understanding that he must create another *meisterwerk*. Studying the current orchestral techniques, he is apprehensive that what he has been asked to produce will be nothing less than a musical dinosaur. Nevertheless, he complies, and the result is indeed a masterpiece — but it is, as he has suspected, a masterpiece of his own age. When its first performance is concluded he is thanked by an audience spokesman for providing them with an interesting example of an historical art. He is then treated to the revelation that he is not Richard Strauss at all, but simply a comprehensive impression of the dead genius imposed on the dormant mind of an ordinary human being. The performance has been enthusiastically applauded, not as a feat of great musicianship, but as a brilliant demonstration of the most recent psycho-neurological developments. With that, the personality which had believed itself the originator of *Don Juan* and *Capriccio* is consigned to oblivion, and its work to the archives of a past whence it never came.

*****

Dunne's idea of a Serial Universe, along with similar theories, has been the starting-point for numerous science fiction explorations into the fourth dimension and beyond. In his first television appearance Arthur C. Clarke explained — insofar as such a proposition lends itself to explanation for the geometrically insecure — the properties of the four-dimensional hypercube known esoterically as a 'tesseract'. As its name implies, this fragile object consists of eight cubic 'faces' which are a rational extension into a fourth dimension along the lines of the factual concept of the six two-dimensional square faces which adorn a three-dimensional common-or-garden cube!

What might be experienced by anyone incautious enough to enter a tesseract, and it is arguable whether it *could* be penetrated from a three-dimensional standpoint, has been graphically portrayed by Robert Heinlein in '— And He Built a Crooked House' (1940). The house in question is constructed to a tesseract design; and the occupants who unwittingly find themselves within its complex interior despair of ever escaping. When they jump through a window into what appears to be the garden, they are as like as not to land in a replica of the room they have gracelessly just vacated — moreover, there is a strong possibility that they will be able to *see themselves* still occupying the space they assumed they had left. The random opening of a door may reveal a view, looking directly downwards, from the vertiginous heights of the Empire State Building. The only method, it transpires, by which to dismantle a tesseract is to fold it up like a pack of cards. While the inhabitants are disconsolately pondering the problem of where to begin this process, the house obliges by complying of its own accord.

A consideration of what might lie beyond the third dimension is incomplete without a short excursion into the heady territory of alternative worlds and realities. Every moment we exist is but a prelude to a multiplicity of possible futures; yet, in the awareness of our own reality, we appear to experience no more than one. That, however, is no Cosmic guarantee that each of those countless speculative tomorrows might not be occurring outside the limits of our miniscule foothold in space and time. Imagine, for instance, an alternative world in which human history up to the onset of the Dark Ages in Europe remains as we know it today. At that point in time let us suppose that the Church, instead of suppressing exploration in certain branches of science, had actively encouraged it. When Columbus set sail for the New World, might not his ship have been equipped with *radio*? Such indeed is the case in Philip José Farmer's 'Sail On, Sail On'. Unfortunately for Columbus, that particular alternative world really is flat — and he and his crew disappear over the edge with no America to discover!

In *Echo Round His Bones* (1969), Thomas M. Disch has investigated an even more curious phenomenon. At the end of the twentieth century, matter transmitters have been perfected for almost exclusive use in the transhipment of military personnel and materials between earth and Mars. (The matter transmitter is, admittedly, one of the least probable ideas to find some following in the genre. It operates on the principle that a human, entering a transmission chamber, can be reduced to a pure stream of electronic impulses which are conveyed at the speed of light to a reception point anywhere within the ambit of man.) No one who passes through the transmitter in Disch's story is aware, on arrival at his destination, that a complete physiological 'echo' of his being has been created, at the transmitting point, which must perforce exist in a sub-level of space as we normally experience it. Such echoes can 'swim' through the solid structure of roads and buildings, observing all that takes place in the 'normal' world to which, nevertheless, they themselves are invisible:

> 'The worst of it was that none of the people that he passed on the city's streets nor the drivers of cars and buses, nor clerks in stores, *no one* would look at him. They disregarded [him] with an indifference worthy of God.... Once, when he was crossing a street, a truck turned the corner and, without even ruffling [his] hair, drove straight through him.
> It was as if he were a beggar or deformed, but in that case they would at least have looked away, which was some sort

of recognition.'

The echoes also exist in a world of silence, broken only when they encounter one another. Since the sole supplies of conventional food available in this sub-world are the echoes of occasional provisions transmitted to Mars, cannibalism is rife; and the majority of fresh human sub-beings are generally butchered the moment they emerge bewildered from the transmission chamber. The struggle of an army officer to survive in this shadowy environment, against a darker backdrop of impending nuclear war, is the central theme of the novel.

*****

And so to time travel itself. As a possible escape route out of prevailing states of the human predicament, it has probably been more thoroughly exploited in science fiction than any other theme. Nevertheless, the overriding message in most stories seems to be that, while it may provide the individual with temporary or permanent release, the facility of time travel is scarcely a gift we should dissipate our hours in striving to attain. We have already considered one of the most imaginative examples — and still the most finely written — in the genre of a journey into the future; but if Wells's Time Traveller was the forerunner of a host of voyagers into the unknown, the paradoxes he returned to report were those of the human future and not of the actual mechanics of time.

Among the many who have followed Wells across the time barrier, Isaac Asimov has been one of the most successful in producing a full-length novel in which the unique and uncanny qualities of the subject are fully sustained. In *The End of Eternity* (1955), he portrays the highly questionable activities of an extra-temporal organization employing what can best be described as a 'lift-shaft' extending up into the future by more than ten thousand millennia.

The 'eternals' have established themselves as the epitome of social planning agencies — whatever in the centuries ahead they regard as hazardous or otherwise undesirable undertakings for Man, they set about obliterating before the events have even begun to take shape. This they achieve by plotting with computers the minimum reality change required to redirect the course of history, and then sending in a technician to make the physical alteration. In most cases the action involved appears almost trifling: the prevention of a particular phone call at a certain point in time; the removal of an individual bottle from its usual place on the shelf. In such a way the eternals control the progress of humanity along paths they judge profitable and secure. However, for the story's central character, Harlan, who as a change technician has no say in the processes of judgement and planning, there is a multitude of centuries where he would willingly take affairs into his own hands to remodel the societies he observes:

> 'The 482nd was not a comfortable Century for him. It was not like his own austere and conformist homewhen. It was an era without ethics or principles.... It was hedonistic, materialistic, more than a little matriarchal....
> In a hundred ways Harlan thought the society sick and therefore hungered for a Reality Change. More than once it occurred to him that his own presence in the Century, as a man not of that time, could fork its history....
> Unfortunately, to do that, he would have to step outside the bounds of the spatio-temporal chart and that was unthinkable.'

In view of Harlan's originally authoritarian disposition, it is an added paradox that he is chosen as the instrument that will finally put an end to the eternals. Their downfall is wrought by a society existing some ten million years hence which has succeeded in obscuring its own era from the travellers' scrutiny. It is also a civilization which has developed its own techniques for ranging visually — in preference to travelling — through time; and it can see in the future the eclipse of man as a consequence of the unnaturally superimposed pattern of progress which he is being obliged to follow: 'In ironing out the disasters of Reality, Eternity rules out the triumphs as well... in averting the pitfalls and miseries which beset man, Eternity prevents men from finding their own bitter and better solutions, the real solutions that come from conquering difficulty, not avoiding it.'

At the close of the novel Harlan is persuaded to effect, by inaction, the reality change which destroys the eternals. It entails leaving the inventor of time travel stranded in the 1930s, so that he is unable to exist in the later age when he would have genuinely made his discovery. (Factually, the final paradox is rather more complicated than that; but in the absence of the space Asimov was able to devote to its explanation, this brief description must suffice. Those interested in a more detailed unravelling of a time-travel paradox will hopefully be content with the account of Robert Heinlein's most striking treatment of the theme at the end of this section.)

Taking an extra-temporal setting even farther into the realms of fantasy than *The End of Eternity*, Fritz Leiber wove the humorous plot of *The Big Time* (1958) around a comfort station which caters for the needs of forces waging a war throughout time as far back as the days of ancient Egypt. Again the conflict involves the changing of earlier history to render the contemporary reality anew.

On the other hand, in an effectively harrowing tale, Richard Matheson has infused the element of time travel into the type of science fiction-cum-horror story at which he is particularly adept. His 'Return' tells of an American professor, Robert Wade, who travels five hundred years into the future and accidentally crashes his time machine at its destination. Although he knows it is capable of repair, the scientists whom Wade meets in A.D. 2454 refuse to let him near it. Mystifyingly, they insist that for him there can be no return. However, the scientific advances of the day have made it possible temporarily to reconstruct beings from the past; and the professor's wife, whom he left expecting a child in 1954, is reconstituted for his benefit — although he is warned that, because of the time distance involved, her reconstruction will last for less than an hour.

During their brief meeting Wade learns to his anguish that his wife died in childbirth, having lost any will to live after his failure to return. As he attempts to comfort her, her body begins literally to fall to pieces in his arms. This appalling experience adds to his determination to recover his time machine and to regain his own era. In this he succeeds, but as he hurries towards his home through the night he is horrified to discover that his own body is disintegrating. Only then does he understand the efforts made to prevent him from travelling back — he had died on arrival in the twenty-fifth century and his present form is itself simply a reconstruction. Hopelessly, he struggles up the stairs to his wife's bedroom on 'the corroded remnants of his disappearing legs':

'*There'd be no life for me without you.*
Her remembered words tortured him. His crying was like a

gentle bubbling of lava.

Now he was almost gone. The last of him poured over the rug like a morning mist....

"Mary, Mary" — he could only think it now — "How very much I love you."

...Then the woman, smiling in her uneasy sleep, was alone in the room except for two haunted eyes which hung suspended for a moment and then were gone; like tiny worlds which flare up in birth and, in the same moment, die.'

Travel to the past is perhaps less popular in the genre than forays into times to come, although a variety of stories have been written around attempts to rescue Jesus of Nazareth from the cross, including one by Michael Moorcock on a successful ruse to impersonate Him. In *Slaughterhouse Five* the *fictional* science fiction writer, Kilgore Trout, who appears in a number of Vonnegut's works, wrote one such saga which Billy Pilgrim unearths in a New York pornographic bookstore. It tells of a time traveller who goes back to resolve once and for all the question whether Jesus *died* on the cross or was taken down alive. He is the first person up the ladder, with a stethoscope secreted beneath his robe. The Son of God proves 'as dead as a doornail'. He also manages to measure the body: 'Jesus was five feet and three and a half inches long'.

The Tralfamadorians, of course, are in a position to witness the entire passion of Jesus at a sitting. They remain unimpressed:

'On Tralfamadore, says Billy Pilgrim, there isn't much interest in Jesus Christ. The Earthling figure who is most engaging to the Tralfamadorian mind, he says, is Charles Darwin — who taught that those who die are meant to die, that corpses are improvements. So it goes.'

In preference to travelling back to encounter the historical Jesus, Wells precipitated Him forwards into an eternal dreamland in *The Happy Turning* where He was able to sound off personally to the author under the heading, 'Jesus of Nazareth discusses his Failure'.

As a *cause célèbre* for mental gymnastics it is doubtful whether time travel will ever be portrayed to better effect than it has been by Robert Heinlein in 'By His Bootstraps' (1941). (If a sign existed to indicate a warning to the more delicate who might during the dark hours doubt the reality of their own existence, the nature of 'free will', the principles of entropy and the concept of *ding an sich* — here is where it should rightfully appear.) In a boarding-house in a university town of mid-twentieth-century America, Bob Wilson struggles to complete a thesis on metaphysics. He is weary from many late nights of study and a half-empty gin bottle rests by his elbow. His work is interrupted by a stranger who emerges from a Time Gate which suddenly appears in a corner of the room. The Gate leads to a period 30,000 years ahead in the future; and the stranger endeavours to persuade Wilson to step through it into a brighter tomorrow. However, while he is still considering the offer, a second man materializes from the Gate who insists that it is the very last thing that Wilson should do. There is a curious resemblance between the two visitors which puzzles Wilson; but before he is able to question further a brawl erupts which leads to the hapless student being knocked backwards through the Time Gate in any case.

When he recovers, he finds himself in an extraordinary palace being tended by a middle-aged man named Diktor, and waited upon by a train of alarmingly generous examples of feminine pulchritude. Diktor explains that between them they can share the pleasures of a future beyond Wilson's comprehension. The palace and the Time Gate have been built by a species of extra-terrestrials who ruled humanity for twenty thousand years before departing as unexpectedly as they came. The race of men they have left behind are so utterly docile that their emotional responses to Diktor, their ruler, can be likened to those of good-natured dogs. All Wilson need do to enjoy this Arcadia for the remainder of his days is to go back through the Time Gate to his old room in 1942. There he will find a man whom he must persuade to join Diktor and himself in the future.

Wilson agrees, and he travels back to his own time. He is astonished to find that the man he is intended to fetch is *himself* who, tired by working on the thesis and half-drunk, fails to recognize his own face beneath three days' growth of beard and the bruises acquired in the fight. As Wilson attempts to persuade his earlier self to come through the Time Gate, he realizes that he is simply acting out the original scene in his room, but now from the opposite point of view. Consequently, he is only mildly surprised when another figure steps out of the Time Gate; but he is disconcerted to discover that it is a third image of himself. He is at a loss to understand why the newcomer is so insistent that the earliest Wilson should not join Diktor and that the three of them have been trapped in a time paradox. He lashes out at his third self; and the fight ensues which ends in the earliest Wilson falling through the Gate.

The newcomer is furious at the outcome of the brawl; and by this time Wilson himself is beginning to entertain doubts regarding Diktor's honesty. Resolving to learn the truth, he in turn enters the Gate, leaving his third self to expostulate on his lack of sense. Restored to the far future, Wilson confronts Diktor and demands an explanation. The older man maintains that the situation is perfectly clear: the earliest Wilson *had* to fall through the Time Gate so that he (Diktor) could send him back as the second image to collect the earliest Wilson in the first place. But:

'Wilson took a deep breath and got control of himself. Then he reached back into his academic philosophical concepts and produced the notion he had been struggling to express. "It denies all reasonable theories of causation. You would have me believe that causation can be completely circular. I went through because I came back from going through to persuade myself to go through. That's silly."
"Well, didn't you?"
Wilson did not have an answer ready for that one... .'

Had it been forthcoming, the answer should have run: '*Causation in a plenum need not be and is not limited by man's perception of duration.*'

Diktor asks Wilson to return a final time to the twentieth century to bring back a number of items which he has written down on a list. He then shows him how the controls of the Time Gate are worked. Wilson, now doubly suspicious of Diktor's motives, notices that the Gate is still set at the time of the original meeting in his room. Hoping to break the circle in which he seems paradoxically enmeshed, he plunges through before Diktor can alter the controls. Thus he arrives back in his room as the third image of himself who endeavours to prevent his second image from sending the earliest Wilson into the future. Once again the fight breaks out during which he accidentally knocks the earliest Wilson into the Gate. He remonstrates with his second image, who is now determined to have it out with Diktor and who — ignoring Wilson's warnings — departs on another journey through time.

160

Finally left alone, Wilson puts into action an alternative plan to defeat Diktor. His idea is to return to the future, but to a period some years earlier than that of his encounters with the man. He obtains the supplies on the list given him, assuming that if Diktor had need of them, then so will he. They consist of a number of books, among them Machiavelli's *The Prince* and Hitler's *Mein Kampf*, a portable gramophone and a liberal selection of records. He then steps into the Time Gate and appears once more in the palace, narrowly avoiding Diktor and the second image of himself. Hastily he resets the Gate's controls for ten years earlier and goes through for the last time.

He comes upon the palace deserted — obviously Diktor has yet to arrive on the scene. Using a handwritten dictionary he has pocketed during his second visit to Diktor, he learns to converse with the local inhabitants who are perfectly happy to accept his authority. 'Diktor', he discovers, is not a name, but simply the word for 'chief'.

Several years pass, during which Wilson learns to administer and to 'improve' this odd society with the guidance of the books he has brought from the twentieth century. Eventually his word is taken as absolute law and he has only to play the gramophone to charm his subjects into a state of quasi-worship. It is perfectly natural in the circumstances that they should address him as 'Diktor', although Wilson himself waits impatiently for the original holder of that title to make his entrance. Nevertheless, he is convinced that his own position is now sufficiently impregnable to resist any challenge from the older man.

When the full ten years have elapsed and there is still no sign of the other's appearance, Wilson becomes increasingly puzzled. Suspecting that the solution may lie in the past, he attempts with some difficulty to focus the Time Gate back to the remote area of 1942. Engrossed in the task of sharpening the image of his old boarding-house room in the scanner, he is startled to hear a thud behind him and to find the unconscious form of a young man who has evidently just fallen through the Gate. On examination, he recognizes it as his younger self — the paradoxical events of what for him was ten years earlier are about to be played again! With this realization, he at last understands that there *is* no other Diktor; the man was simply a senior version of himself, the version which he has now — in his own relative time — become. It also occurs to him that unless the chain of events is repeated exactly as it was before, the whole basis for his personal existence as Diktor will be jeopardized. The end of the story sees him taking the necessary steps which will, in effect, *guarantee his own past.*

'By His Bootstraps' is a masterly illustration of the metaphysical complications involved in the concept of time travel. We are left with the conclusion that the extraordinary series of scenes involving four separate space-time images of the same man has always been happening — and will continue to do so — throughout infinity. The Tralfamadorians, of course, would consider that a perfectly acceptable proposition.

*****

Whether we regard infinity as a continuous process of interrelated events or as an interminable sequence of individual cine stills, the Cosmic influence on time may yet have surprises in store. J.G. Ballard has ingeniously combined the mathematics of physics and the factual discovery of anti-matter to foresee, in *The Crystal World* (1966), the final annihilation of time:

> 'Where anti-particle and particle collide they not only destroy their physical identities, but their opposing time-values eliminate each other, subtracting from the Universe another quantum from its total store of time. It is random discharges of this type, set off by the creation of anti-galaxies in space, which have led to the depletion of the time-store available to the materials of our own solar system.'

The result of this time depletion is the ultimate *crystallization* of earth and all the life it supports: 'There the transfiguration of all living and inanimate forms occurs before our eyes, the gift of immortality a direct consequence of the surrender by each of us of our physical and temporal identities.' Time has ended. All that ever happened, happened yesterday — but a kind of human consciousness lives on in an appreciation of universally static crystalline beauty.

In an earlier story, 'The Voices of Time' (1960), Ballard has written movingly of this long deterioration in temporal vitality. To the individual specialists at work in an experimental research station, the awareness of decay takes different forms. For one, it is the slowing-down in the frequencies of radio signals emitted by distant stars; for another, who finds himself sleeping longer each day, it is a matter of biochemistry: 'The ribonucleic acid templates which unravel the protein chains in all living organisms are wearing out, the dies enscribing the protoplasmic signature have become blunted.' His extending periods of sleep, which could easily be taken superficially as a neurotic escape from the pressures of late twentieth-century existence, are, he argues, in keeping with a general biological decline that ranges from a continuing fall in world wheat-production to the increasing drop in birthrate which confounds the neo-Malthusian projections made during the 1960s. In the same way that the life of one particular organism is limited, so is the duration of the entire biosphere:

' "It's always been assumed that the evolutionary slope reaches for ever upwards, but in fact the peak has already been reached, and the pathway now leads downwards to the common biological grave.... Five thousand centuries from now our descendants, instead of being multi-brained star-men, will probably be naked prognathous idiots... grunting their way through the remains of this Clinic like Neolithic men caught in a macabre inversion of time.... I pity them, as I pity myself. My total failure, my absolute lack of any moral or biological right to existence, is implicit in every cell of my body...." '

Again the forbidding outlook of T.H. Huxley, which we have encountered much in this study, permeates the scene. The haunting quality of universal decay which Ballard has instilled into 'The Voices of Time', as if to ennoble the tale with an atmosphere of aesthetic sorrow, calls to mind — as few stories in the genre can — the ancient Japanese concept of *Mono no aware*. This is the philosophy of sadness brought about by perfection — the idea that beauty contains its own death and that the most beautiful thing is the beginning of decay. Therefore, by long Japanese association, everything in decline — because it is dying — is beautiful. It summons echoes of the terrible beauty found by Wells's Time Traveller in the far future, as it does — in a similar sense — of the ephemeral glory of the sparks which Kingsley Martin suggested Wells could see flying off the wheels of cause and effect as they turn.

If the inexorable grinding of those wheels is predetermined ultimately to close the temporal circle, it will only reinforce the suspicion that time has never been on humanity's side, manipulate it how we will. For those who, understandably, choose to seek consolation in an unconventional philosophy, Vonnegut's way — in spite of his character's compulsion to return again and again to the inferno of Dresden — is as good as any:

> 'If what Billy Pilgrim learned from the Tralfamadorians is true, that we all live forever, no matter how dead we may sometimes seem to be, I am not overjoyed. Still — if I am going to spend eternity visiting this moment and that, I'm grateful that so many of those moments are nice.'

11 The Teacher and The Taught

*Science is a match that man has just got alight. He thought he
was in a room — in moments of devotion a temple — and that
his light would be reflected and pillars carved with
philosophical systems wrought into harmony. It is a curious
sensation, now that the preliminary splutter is over and the
flame burns up clear, to see his hands lit and just a glimpse
of himself and the patch he stands on visible, and around him,
in place of all that human comfort and beauty he anticipated
— darkness still.*

H.G. Wells, 'The Rediscovery of the Unique'

When is an extra-terrestrial not an extra-terrestrial? The answer
is: when it thinks like a man! The mere mechanics of getting
humanity to the stars are as moondust compared to the vast
process of assimilation and adaptation which will be required
when Man first meets his match in an alien life-form. As we have
noted earlier in this study, the likelihood of human emotions
existing in an utterly nonhuman metabolism is not particularly
strong. It *is* difficult to conceive of an intelligence which functions on entirely different principles to our own; but it is a
probability which we should sensibly accept as we approach
that historic meeting. The alternative territories on which the
grand confrontation is usually acted out in science fiction are
earth and those worlds indigenous to the aliens. Certainly there
are also stories where the meeting takes place on neutral ground
— Edmund Cooper's *Transit* (1964), in which men and the inhabitants of another planet in our Galaxy are brought together
to determine who is better equipped to colonize space, is a good
example. They are, however, very much a minority.

Such is our own rate of scientific and technological advance
that, in spite of its growing acceleration, we doubtless have little
to fear in terms of colliding with extra-terrestrials of our own
accord during the immediate future. No such certainty exists
when it comes to the possibility of *them* discovering us. Man
has occupied his natural biosphere long enough to have assumed
an ingenuous sense of security from outside interference — other
than what some regard as that of a deistic order. However much
we may feel insecure about our own natures, we are arrogant

enough to conclude that it is of no other species' concern. In Wells's *The War of the Worlds* that, ironically, is precisely the case; the Martians are sufficiently unconcerned about humanity to set out cheerfully to obliterate it. Another superior intelligence to approach earth can be found in Fred Hoyle's *The Black Cloud* (1957); and its powers are so far in advance of those of Wells's Martians that it is fortunate for Man that its intentions are benign. Paradoxically, when the Cloud attempts to pass on its knowledge and understanding to the most intellectually adept of the scientists who have contacted it, the burden of incoming data is more than his brain can bear. The coming of the Cloud has taught man, chasteningly, that there is much which he is as yet *incapable* of being taught — at least at the pace the Cloud must needs impart it. Nevertheless, it was Einstein himself who maintained that there was nothing in the Universe which, given time and sufficient dedication, man could not comprehend.

On an entirely different level, Theodore Sturgeon has written in 'The World Well Lost' (1953) an entertaining account of the telling lesson which results from the unexpected arrival on earth of a pair of extra-terrestrials. Their parent planet requests their extradition because they are wanted criminals. Since the visitors appear so delicate and innocuous, and are obviously deeply in love, there is a widespread reluctance to return them to meet an undisclosed fate. In fact, the popular worldwide television service warms to the two lovers — as indeed it might:

'Their eyes were full of wonder, each at the other, and together at the world. They seemed frozen in a full-to-bursting moment of discovery; they made way for one another gravely and with courtesy, they looked about them and in the very looking gave each other gifts — the colour of the sky, the taste of the air, the pressures of things growing and meeting and changing. They never spoke. They simply *were* together.'

Not until the pair are heading outwards again into space do their disconcerted sympathisers discover that they are male homosexuals. The story, in fact, is one further plea by Sturgeon for a less hypocritical attitude towards minority groups. It is also a good illustration of just how difficult it will probably be to pass any kind of judgement on an alien race from a purely human viewpoint.

James White has provided an intriguing variation on this

166

theme in his novel, *All Judgement Fled* (1968), in which an alien spaceship plunges out of control into the solar system. When an exploratory team of astronauts is sent out to reconnoitre, they are confronted by an assortment of life-forms, only one of which is actually intelligent. The problem is — which? Since any type of communication normally used by man proves ineffective, the solution is finally reached by a tortuous process of logical deduction.

In William Tenn's 'The Liberation of Earth', the incursion of other-worlders into man's Lilliputian orbit has more ominous implications. The arrival of a huge alien starship heralds the 'friendly' occupation of the planet as a forward base for a race of giant extra-terrestrials known as the 'Dendi'. The visitors address a delegation from the United Nations Organization in a nearly prehistoric dialect of Bengali, the only language they found worth mastering during their previous touchdown on earth in the remote past. When an interpreter is eventually forthcoming, humanity learns that a galactic war is in progress between the Dendi — upholders of a multi-global federation — and the Troxxt, an evil wormlike species which is threatening the peace of the Milky Way. An appeal to earth's leaders to co-operate with the Dendi in eliminating the menace meets with a generous reception; what, they ask, can humanity do to help? Well, nothing as it happens — except to stay out of the aliens' way while they prepare their defences.

Subsequently, the Dendi erect an awesome array of armour while *Homo sapiens* looks on incredulously. Occasional directives from the enormous visitors are treated to instant compliance, regardless of intermittent misunderstandings. One such results from an admonition of 'evacuate Washington'. The American Secretary of State waits half a day in full diplomatic regalia to enquire whether it was the State of Washington the Dendi had in mind, or the city of Washington D.C. Unhappily, when the expected Troxxt attack is launched, the Dendi force proves unequal in the match. It is not without humiliation that earth learns that it has been assisting an outlying platoon commanded by the equivalent of an infantry sergeant. But worse is to come. When the victorious Troxxt ships descend, Man is lectured at inordinate length on his foolishness in believing the outrageous lies of a life-form based on silicon.

The Dendi, claim the Troxxt, are actually the tyrannical master-race of the Galactic Federation, while the Troxxt themselves are the champions of the Protoplasmic League, fighting valiantly to break the others' despotic rule. A shamefaced humanity surrenders up its leaders, who are promptly executed, and agrees to help its new 'liberators' in their glorious crusade. However, if one-tenth of earth's population perished in the first battle, that decimation bears no comparison with the carnage which accompanies the Dendi's counter-attack. Seas boil, entire steppes are burned away, and the continent of Australasia is dissolved into the Pacific. The Dendi reoccupy a tattered earth and duly harangue what remains of its population:

'How could we have been so naive, the Dendi wanted to know, as to be taken in by the chauvinistic pro-protoplasm propaganda? Surely, if physical characteristics were to be the criteria of our racial empathy, we would not orient ourselves on a narrow chemical basis? The Dendi life-plasm was based on silicon instead of carbon, true, but did not ... *appendaged* vertebrates ... such as we and the Dendi ... have infinitely more in common, in spite of a *minor* biochemical difference or two, than vertebrates and legless, armless, slime-crawling creatures who happened, quite accidentally, to possess an identical organic substance?'

Execution of the leaders appointed under the Troxxt follows as a matter of course; and when the protoplasmic warriors drive the Dendi off some eighteen months later, they are hard put to find any men willing to accept positions of responsibility in their new regime. They are hard put to find any men at all, for the latest skirmish has ripped a deep collar of matter from the northern hemisphere, leaving earth pear-shaped and with an unnerving orbital wobble. Deciding that the planet is no longer viable as a battle base, both the Dendi and the Troxxt depart. The few human survivors are left to compete with a mutated species of giant rabbits for each other's carrion, desperately sucking at a dwindling atmosphere and hanging on grimly when earth's eccentric gyrations threaten to hurl them precipitously into space. They can, as the narrator concludes, 'say with pardonable pride that we have been as thoroughly liberated as it is possible for a race and planet to be'.

New concepts of loyalty could thus be a decisive factor in our dealings with extra-terrestrials, as they are — in a maternal sense — for the women of various nationalities who find themselves impregnated with alien genes in John Wyndham's *The*

Midwich Cuckoos (1957). The fact that their children are gifted with inhuman extra-sensory powers, and are openly hostile to the institutions of Man, hampers the mothers little in cherishing their offspring and in many cases dying for them.

Wyndham's novel is a disturbing example of the kind of Fifth Column activity by which 'the Eyes that watch us' may choose to attempt a subtle invasion of Man's domain. An even more sophisticated ploy is envisaged in Philip K. Dick's 'War Game' (1961), where trading links are in the course of being established with many inhabited worlds. In the Terran Import Bureau of Standards, which is responsible for safeguarding humanity against any deleterious effects of alien goods, officials are perplexed by the most recent batch of children's toys to arrive from Ganymede, the longest moon of Jupiter. Among a number of what appear to be innocent items is a highly complicated miniature fort, complete with a set of mechanical soldiers who are programmed to storm it, penetrate its defences, and finally to reassemble on the outside in readiness to go through the performance again. The Bureau's experts are deeply suspicious of the toy, considering it far too sophisticated in concept for the relatively simple entertainment it provides. Is it, perhaps, a bomb — designed to detonate after a certain sequence in the soldiers' manoeuvres? (The Ganymedeans are known to be considering the possibility of military action to reinforce their drive for economic supremacy over the inner three populated planets of the solar system.)

After exhaustive tests during a period of weeks, the fort is eventually judged harmless, but the head of the Bureau will still not authorize its sale on the open market. A colleague unknowingly hits on the explanation when he suggests that the toy may have been designed deliberately to arouse and sustain their suspicions. While everyone's attention is directed towards it, might not some far more invidious, but innocent-seeming, game be allowed to slip through unchecked? And in fact it has been just that—an apparently innocuous variation of 'Monopoly' in which, curiously, the object is to shed one's shareholdings, rather than to increase them. The Ganymedeans are clearly content to wait a generation before they attempt their economic takeover and Dick's story can be interpreted as a futuristic vision of the subtle psychological warfare which ideologically opposed terrestrial nations, who are nevertheless currently strengthening trading links, may one day pursue:

'As he got up from the board, Joe Hauck grumbled, "I don't get it. What would anybody see in a game where the winner winds up with nothing at all?"

... As stock and money changed hands, the children became more and more animated.

... Already the two youngsters were learning the naturalness of surrendering their holdings. They gave up their stocks and money avidly, with a kind of trembling abandon.

Glancing up, her eyes bright, Lora said, "It's the best educational toy you ever brought home, Dad!" '

An even more subtle alien influence is related in Isaac Asimov's 'Breeds There a Man?' (1951), in which the research which could lead to the perfection of a force-field is hampered in a variety of ways — in particular by the leading scientist's irrational compulsion to take his own life. Convinced that he has arrived at the correct formula, he struggles to commit his ideas to paper, at the same time endeavouring to resist a fiercely compelling death-wish. His frantic scribblings are deciphered by others who are less affected by whatever external force seems determined to deny Man access to the only truly effective defence against nuclear attack. At the climax of the tale, the force-field is successfully demonstrated, producing a glittering barrier impervious to every known offensive device. In the same moment its inventor, briefly freed from the scrutiny of his doctor, finally achieves his suicidal aim. However, the wishes of an entity temporarily superior to Man have been thwarted for the time being. The conflict is adjourned *sine die*.

*****

The lessons that man may learn from extra-terrestrials on his own territory are essentially those which a weak being receives at the hands of a stronger. We have yet to contend in reality with a species which can not only devastate us physically, but also outwit us with a minimum of mental effort. In comparable conflicts in the animal kingdom, the less fitted species generally backs down, allowing the superior lifeform its dominating role in the ecological environment. Few science fiction authors imagine man doing likewise; although it could be argued that, on an ethical basis, the rational believer in progress should give way to an obviously superior race, recognizing it as the fitter.

The one exception to such abasement might just be an invasion of his planetary home, which it could be ethically contended Man is entitled to dominate, regardless of his past behaviour in brutally colonizing the territories of less fortunate members of his own race. But if humanity ought to adopt an eternally defensive position on its home ground, the situation is hardly improved when it comes to the conquest of space.

The first lesson of space must be, inevitably, the appreciation of its vastness. As we noted in our consideration of machines, the great barrier to human interstellar travel is our limitation to a speed below that of light. If that obstacle can never be overcome, Man may still go to the stars, *and* colonize other worlds, but he will not attain what could ever be called a centrally administered empire. The most urgent directives, radioed at the velocity of light, would tend to lose their significance when received after an interval of five or more years! Spaceships leaving earth to explore other star systems will indeed be travelling arks, if they are to be crewed by humans at all; for beyond the very shortest interstellar flights, no individual could hope to live long enough to see again his native planet. The first children of men to be born outside the confines of our solar system will be delivered, in all likelihood, not on *extra-terra firma* but in ships chasing outward the elusive rays of our parent sun.

Such is the situation in Edmund Cooper's *Seed of Light* (1959). However, the starship *Solarian* in the novel is a travelling ark in more respects than one. It contains all that remains of humanity after earth has been ravaged by nuclear war. As its first destination, the *Solarian* heads towards Alpha Centauri, hoping to find in that system a planet which can be naturally inhabited by Man. The five men and five women who originally crew the ship are in no position to found a new home for humanity in an overtly hostile environment. There will be no follow-up fleet to bring supplies and life-support equipment to make tolerable a markedly inhospitable world. Unless the *Solarian* can find a planet with the same basic characteristics as those of earth, human history will end in a diminutive metal mausoleum lost somewhere in the emptiness of the Cosmic night.

As it happens, there *is* no earthlike satellite circling Alpha Centauri; and so the starship plunges on, investigating system after system at a relative snail's pace across the Milky Way. Generations of children are born, grow to maturity to command the *Solarian*, and in their turn step down to accept the authority of their young. New branches of physics are explored, and the velocity and capabilities of the ship are continually improved. Ten generations on from the first crew, the early logs of the flight are beginning to assume the allegorical qualities of the original books in the Bible:

'Earth, whose history was still preserved on microfilm in the archives of the *Solarian*, was no longer imagined as a real world, a planet with a rather unusual geophysical pattern that still rotated round one of the brighter stars in the black and limitless sky. It had become an almost religious concept; and the manner in which the *Solarian* had left Europe Three invoked a supernatural element; for Earth had assumed the status of paradise, and the way in which man had been forced to leave his natural planet seemed like an expulsion of fallen angels.'

If all writers in the genre were scrupulously to observe the light barrier in their accounts of space-flight, the meeting of Man with aliens would be an unusually rare occurrence. As it is, such useful aids as the 'space-drive' and the 'space-warp' have been employed by most authors to overcome the inhibitions of our present knowledge of physics. None of them has actually explained very convincingly just how these methods of crossing the interstellar gulf conspire to work; although the familiar mobius strip enters frequently into otherwise woolly descriptions of a spacetime continuum which, not content with being curved, often ends up in the shape of a pretzel. The majority of writers are happy now to take the destruction of the light barrier for granted and to rely on 'the willing suspension of disbelief' to carry the reader with them. Granted this facility, it is perfectly possible to envisage vast galactic empires bent under the sway of man; and advocates of this unlikely future — from 'Doc' Smith onwards — have obligingly done so.

Nevertheless, few efforts in that direction have achieved the imaginative sweep of Isaac Asimov's trilogy which began with *Foundation*, to be followed by *Foundation and Empire* and *Second Foundation* (1942-49). The three books chronicle the eclipse of a human civilization consisting of no less than a million worlds centred upon the giant planet of Trantor. As this immense empire begins to disintegrate, and the outer worlds lapse into barbarism, a team of psycho-historians on Trantor predicts

172

a period of anarchy which must almost certainly endure for thirty thousand years. Against this prospect one small hope prevails — a hope that, by the establishment of a powerful foundation dedicated to the arts and to science and technology, the age of chaos may be reduced to a mere millennium. Based on the concepts of psycho-history, a science which utilizes both psychology and the study of the past to plot a critical path analysis of the future, the Foundation is duly formed. As a precaution, it is duplicated in its entirety at a secret location at the other end of the Galaxy.

As the centuries — and the conquests of the barbarians — progress, the centre of the empire is duly sustained by the Foundation's guidance — until an event occurs which could never have been predicted in the critical path. A mutant arrives on the scene who has the power to manipulate minds. Despite his physical deformities, he is able to use his gift to enslave people irrevocably to his will. It is therefore only a matter of time before he brings the warring factions of the outer worlds under his control and challenges the Foundation itself. Disastrously, the citadel of learning falls.

In his drive to weld anew the remains of Trantor's empire, the mutant searches for the last obstacle to separate him from absolute power — the mysterious Second Foundation. Secure in its hiding place for several hundred years, and shielded from the pressures which have occupied its twin, the Second Foundation has devoted its talents to the study of parapsychology. The mental powers of its members, who appear outwardly to be simple farmers, prove superior even to the mutant's — and the grand strategy of the earlier psycho-historians is thus restored.

The social message for the present in the *Foundation* trilogy is that in any age of rapid or anarchic change, human cultural achievements — one of the frequently unsung benefits of intellectual progress — must at all costs be preserved.

Whereas Asimov's accounts of colonies in space have usually depicted Man as retaining his present physical characteristics, other writers have seen him as changing, or being changed, to fit more comfortably into an alien environment. Given, for example, the advance in molecular biology of a future time, there is every possibility that human beings could be produced in any shape or form which was necessary to ensure their survival on very un-earthlike worlds. James Blish has envisaged just such a situation in his story 'Surface Tension' (1952), depicting a colony founded on a planet where the only form in which human life can begin is microscopic and aquatic. The colony is established in a dozen or so puddles, the sole clue to its ancestry being a brief account of human history engraved on microminiature metal plates deposited in each pool. The story concerns the efforts of the inhabitants of one particular puddle, who have succeeded in dominating their own environment, to indulge in what they optimistically regard as space travel. Most of the plates left with them have been lost in a battle with predators during what to them was their pre-history; and they are no longer aware of their personal littleness. They build a two-inch long, water-filled spaceship of fibre and weed which proves powerful enough to break through the ceiling of their sky — the surface tension of the water at the top of the pool! It is only then, when they see for the first time the immensity of the starry night, that they begin to appreciate their true insignificance in the Cosmos. To beings such as these, Man today — let alone what he may have become capable of achieving a thousand years hence — could seem nothing less than a god.

*****

Returning to the immediate future, it is interesting to compare the differing treatments with which Robert Heinlein and Arthur C. Clarke followed up their respective accounts of a successful landing on the moon. We have already looked at a particular aspect of Heinlein's *The Moon is a Harsh Mistress*, in which the lunar colony is finally successful in winning its independence from earth. As the story's title implies, life on the moon is hardly luxurious. The colonists, who were originally transported there as social undesirables, have a saying which they later adopt as a battle cry — 'TANSTAAFL' (There ain't no such thing as a free lunch!). They also have an unusual, but socially enlightened, system of communal living that they call the 'Line Family'. To some extent it is based on many of the ancient tribal systems of man, inasmuch as there is a head of the family and 'senior' and 'junior' wives who move up in the pecking order as their elders die. However, it is in other respects reminiscent of the loving group relationships which Michael Smith encourages in *Stranger in a Strange Land*. During a visit to earth, an emissary of the lunar colony highlights the custom's causes and advantages:

174

' "They arise, as marriage customs always do, from economic necessities of the circumstances — and our circumstances are very different from those here on Earth ... line marriage is the strongest possible device for conserving capital and insuring the welfare of children — the two basic societal functions for marriage everywhere — in an environment in which there is *no* security, neither for capital nor for children, other than that devised by individuals. Somehow human beings always cope with their environments. Line marriage is a remarkably successful invention to that end..." '

Arthur C. Clarke has complemented his *Prelude to Space* with a series of very short and intriguing stories set around the general mechanics of moon exploration; but in 'The Sentinel' (1951) he extended his horizon to take in an oceanic view. This was the tale which was to become, more than a decade later, the source of inspiration for the film *2001*. During a geological survey of the Mare Crisium (appropriately the Sea of Crises), a crystalline obelisk is discovered which, on the evidence of the dust that surrounds it, was placed on the moon before life emerged from the seas of earth. It requires twenty years of human effort eventually to crack the protective force-shield of the beacon, for that is indeed what it is — a transmitter which has patiently signalled over the millennia the fact that it has still to be found. And of the race which left this sign-manual of its passing:

'Think of such civilizations, far back in time against the fading afterglow of Creation, masters of a universe so young that life as yet had come only to a handful of worlds. Theirs would have been a loneliness we cannot imagine, the loneliness of gods looking out across infinity and finding none to share their thoughts.
... Those wanderers must have looked on Earth, circling safely in the narrow zone between fire and ice, and must have guessed that it was the favourite of the Sun's children. Here, in the distant future, would be intelligence.'

And so they left the beacon to provide a signal against the time, if ever, when the children of earth, by crossing space, would have proved their fitness to survive — a challenge of a double significance, 'for it depends in turn upon the conquest of atomic energy and the last choice between life and death.'
Taking the interplanetary progress one stage further, we find

175

in Kendall Foster Crossen's 'The Ambassadors from Venus' (1951) an admonitory lesson delivered to the first — and last — human expedition to arrive on that world. After a number of forays into areas of lush vegetation, the team who originally concluded that there was no intelligent life on the planet are persuaded to admit their mistake. Following several lively encounters with a species of giant tree, during which their spaceship is destroyed, they reluctantly accept it as a sentient lifeform. Almost immediately the trees establish telepathic communication. They have, they explain, permitted the intrusion of *animals* into their environment because they help maintain the balance of oxygen and carbon dioxide essential to vegetable existence. Nevertheless Man, as a mere animal, must realize that he is by no means top of the evolutionary scale. It is at best an accident that he has attained supremacy on his own world, for rationally plants can lay greater claim to the position — as the only form of life *which has no need to destroy*. Animals, on the other hand, are eternal *parasites*, preying either on others of their kindred species or on the pacific inhabitants of the vegetable kingdom.

Taken aback, but not entirely daunted, the men declare that they will be delighted to welcome the trees as equals and to cooperate with them fully. They have, they confess, escaped from an earth dying in the aftermath of a nuclear holocaust brought about largely by one race's assumption that it was superior to others. They have learnt their lesson. Or they think they have:

> ' "You misunderstand. It was pointed out to you that all animal life exists as a parasite upon plant life. In our case, unfortunately, we need you parasites in order to live, but that does not imply special privileges ... As your hosts — in a double sense, you might say — we do not like to make a point of your inferiority, but we are sure you will understand our present reaction if you will consider how you might have felt if the fleas which infected your bodies, the viruses in your bloodstreams, had offered you equality and cooperation." '

Still within the bounds of the solar system, the handling of extra-terrestrials becomes more complicated, and distinctly murkier, when we consider the problems of peaceful relations with the Jovians of Asimov's 'Victory Unintentional' (1942). In this, an added example of his celebrated robot stories,

Asimov has imagined — in contrast to Dick's 'War Game' — the *human* colonization of Ganymede. When radio contact is eventually made between the satellite and the natural inhabitants of Jupiter, their reaction to any kind of liaison with humanity is so ferocious as to discourage ideas of a manned descent to the surface of the planet. On the whole, this is a face-saving outcome. The conditions in the lower reaches of the Jovian atmosphere are so uncongenial that no man would sensibly wish to venture there.

Unfortunately for the native Jovians — who happen to be amorphous tentacled creatures that 'see' by a form of sonic detection in an inky blackness where the temperature is −70°C, the atmospheric pressure more than a *million* times that of earth, where hurricanes rage and the 'air' is an unpalatable mixture of liquid ammonia and hydrogen — man is desirous of a treaty with them. What worries the colonists on Ganymede, bearing in mind the vicious reception of their initial overtures to the Jovians, is the prospect of this 'murderous' species perfecting the means of space travel. The time has arrived for a show of strength; and in this instance at least, man himself can teach a salutory, if deceptive, lesson. Three robots are built with the characteristics which will enable them to function with complete freedom on the surface of Jupiter. By aesthetic standards they are more like grotesque parodies of bathyspheres than any recognisably humanoid shape. They, in their turn, 'see' by radar; the metal of their frames is impervious to any known corrosive; and their enormous weight would anchor them in the teeth of the doyen of all tornados. Since the ship in which they descend is as peppered with holes as a colander, the crushing increase in atmospheric pressure deters them not at all.

A string of comical episodes ensues, in which the Jovians attempt to demonstrate their massive superiority over what they take to be average specimens of *homo sapiens*. But anything *they* can do, the robots do infinitely better! The final disillusionment comes when they proudly display their ability to create a force-field (the very development which humans fear, because it would enable the Jovians to escape from their planet's formidable atmosphere). When the robots cheerfully reveal that, as entities, they are personally immune to extremes in atmospheric pressure, the Jovians admit defeat and agree to abandon any further attempts to rise to the challenge of space. An ironic twist is disclosed in the last lines of the tale, when it is discovered that the robots had no programme to pass themselves off as men, and that the *dénouement* is purely a result of a false assumption on the part of a susceptible alien mentality.

*****

The consequences of interfering with unfamiliar societies and cultures has bothered 'civilized' Man little in the past, probably because the victims have been, after all, only 'less developed' branches of his own species on earth. He will do well to exercise some caution when it comes to imposing the joys of his company upon extra-terrestrials. The ceremonies and rituals of a defeated race have often proved rebarbative to the *conquistadores* of human history; the victors have usually demonstrated the barbarians' unfitness to exist by slaughtering them. It is unnecessary to detail the succession of minor wars and conflicts during the past quarter century in which such crimes against intelligence have played their unlovely part. A brilliant account of the same despicable attitude translated to another world raises James Blish's *A Case of Conscience* (1958) to a place of its own in the genre. The book relates the consequences of the discovery by a United Nations exploratory ship of a planet that, by Terran standards, is an ecological paradise. The highest life-form is an intelligent reptile which, in the course of its brief individual existence, goes through the equivalent of the entire evolutionary cycle of Man. Hatched from an egg in the sea, it passes from a tadpole-like infancy to adolescence as a land-based herbivore running wild in the jungle. As such it is a target for a variety of predators; and, if it survives, what aggressive instincts it harbours are discharged during this period of its development. Finally it emerges in its adult form as an utterly peaceful being with a profound awareness of nature and an unfailing respect for the harmony of its environment.

Into this Eden blunders the rapacious spectre of Man. Finding the reptiles incapable of resisting his intention to avail himself of their valuable natural resources, he succeeds in destroying the planet as much by accident as design. *A Case of Conscience* is undoubtedly one of the major novels of modern science fiction. Both utopian and anti-utopian (on earth the same kind of underground nightmare as that envisaged in Asimov's *The Caves of Steel* is in progress), it also carries striking religious overtones which we shall consider in our final chapter.

178

Man, as the brutish intruder into an otherwise well-adjusted society, is likewise the theme of a short, but very funny story by Frederik Pohl. 'The Gentlest Unpeople' (1958) is set on Venus, where the local population display the same reverence for a game played with a boomerang as is accorded by an increasing number of humans to golf. During a particular round, a pair of Venusians happen upon the body of a third who has evidently been done to death by one of the monsters known to favour the locality. The monster, predictably, is a representative of *Homo sapiens* — a drunken prospector as much renowned for his offensive smell as his violent manner. With implacable courtesy the delicate Venusians guide the ogre into the welcoming grasp of their Justice Machine, a powerful robot designed to restrain the most athletic of transgressors. Throughout his 'trial', the monster is assured by the natives that there can be no question of his being found guilty. And when the impossibility occurs, he is told with equal conviction that the failure of his appeal would be unthinkable. (Paramount in the Venusian code of social behaviour is the abhorrence of causing mental distress to others.) When the appeal is dismissed and the monster despatched accordingly, the aboriginals congratulate each other on 'the tact and delicacy' with which they have handled the problem: 'It is well known that monsters require even more politeness and patience than our own race. It is the least we can do for them.'

In Katherine MacLean's 'Unhuman Sacrifice' (1952) another case of murder is recorded, one which results from a subtle blend of sympathy and ignorance. The human visitors to a notably earthlike world are appalled by the common practice of suspending the native adolescents from trees for days on end during the annual rain season. When this occurs they cut down one particular youngster to whom they have become attached — only to stand by impotently while he plunges into the flood and takes root as a flourishing piece of weed, the final form of his species' life-cycle. The apparently cruel act of tying the children to high branches, far from being the obscure initiation rite which the humans had supposed, is a means of perpetuating the race in the sentient stage of its development.

The acceptance by a man of an alien culture, and his complete assimilation into its ways, is the subject of Edmund Cooper's *A Far Sunset* (1967), a novel which culminates in the discovery that mankind itself is the product of a 'seeding' by an alien

179

civilization. Man's own suspicion that such may be his origin leads to an unexpected conclusion in E.L. Wallace's 'Big Ancestor' (1954). The tale relates a future in which explorers from earth have discovered the human race already *in situ* on a multitude of worlds. Inevitably, there are discrepancies in the rates of progress among these myriad families of Man, and many rivalries arise. One thing, nevertheless, is certain — those genuine extra-terrestrials of other species who inhabit the Galaxy harbour a deep-seated fear of humanity, simply because it is so widespread.

Puzzled by his seemingly spontaneous evolution throughout the Milky Way, Man decides that he is indeed the outcome of a 'seeding' by some master race which must even now be awaiting the homecoming of its far-flung stock. Having recruited the services of an alien species, whose space pilots just happen to be superior to its own, humanity starts the epic search for its true point of genesis. And so, in the fullness of years, that proudest and most ubiquitous of beings in the Galaxy solves the riddle of his beginning. He finds the answer on a deserted world from which forty-foot high invertebrates of immense intelligence have long since fled. But they have left a confession of their negligence behind them.

They were, they admit, a much-travelled species, discovering too late the awful heritage they had bequeathed unwittingly in their wake. A virulent breed of vermin, infesting the sewers of their principal cities, had found its way aboard their spaceships. Huddled for warmth against the radioactive hulls, this ghastly tyke had mutated until it proved increasingly resistant to the most sophisticated methods of extermination. It had escaped on to many of the worlds they visited where, because of its frightening adaptability, it rapidly overran the indigenous fauna. Despite intensive efforts, including the physical destruction of hundreds of planets, no long-term means of control could be perfected. Therefore, and not without reluctance, the great intelligence had departed elsewhere, and left the Galaxy to its ruin.

It is not the easiest revelation for the group of humans who unearth this truth to accept. The alien pilot, despite his hostility to the arrogance of Man, understands that what held good in the past does not automatically hold good forever. He also knows enough of the paradoxes of his employers to be aware that the kindest gesture he can make will prove to little avail:

180

' "We are all of some origin or other and it wasn't necessarily pretty. This being [the departed intelligence] was a slug of some kind — and are you now what it describes? Perhaps mentally a little, out of pride, but the pride was false ... Don't worry about me — I won't repeat it ... But I can see you will report to everyone exactly what you found. That pride you've developed — you'll need it." '

To learn one's lesson, more 'fools' than one have said, is the mark of a true man. To learn other people's lesson for them — fully and with compassion — is the mark of a true mind.

The lesson for Man in science fiction, as he reaches out in his first fragile endeavour to attain the stars, is surely this: that if the universe is indeed the spawning ground of a myriad species, then a creative entity which exists solely to concern itself with the progress of humanity is inevitably an insignificant part of the greater whole. On the other hand, if a single entity *were* to oversee the Cosmos, Man's insignificance in the total scheme of things would go almost without question, as it would in any case if we supposed there to be no overall cosmic design. It is a mystery we shall encounter again in our final chapter, reconciling as it does what is professed as a fundamental Christian dogma with the conclusions of the most hardened outriders of advancing disbelief. The Cosmic process is as capable of destroying the earth in a trice as is a god pronouncing his final judgement. The disbeliever may argue that it matters not at all in the case of a species which existed in the first place at the whim of chance; believers of many different faiths will also hold that it signifies nothing, because God will *still* be there — when Man has come and gone.

12 Mythology is One

'Master, we come to entreat you to tell us why so strange an
animal as man has been formed.'
'Why do you trouble your head about it?' said the dervish.
'Is it any business of yours?'
'But, my Reverend Father', said Candide, 'there is a horrible
deal of evil on earth.'
'What signifies it', said the dervish, 'whether there is evil or
good? When his Highness sends a ship to Egypt, does he
trouble his head whether the rats in the vessel are at their ease
or not?'

Voltaire, *Candide*

The mind reaches far. To whatever limit an individual writer
extends his imagination in search of meaning, there are others
who, echoing Flecker's pilgrims in *Hassan*, 'shall go always a
little further'. The essays into fantasy of ancient Man, which
we touched on at the beginning of this study, sum up the early
attempts of *Homo sapiens* to create out of his own head, if not
an answer to the riddle of existence, at least a palliative to
render more endurable the cruelties and injustice of his true
history. Thus, throughout time, mythology has presented a
mirror image to existence in which the puny abilities of Man
have given way to the inimitable extravagances of the gods. It
is no accident that those myths are almost universally infused
with traces of the heroic.

Out of the tribulations of cause and effect has come also a
yearning for spiritual continuity. In the absence of T.H. Huxley's
'kindly comet' which would sweep the whole abysmal mess
away, the need for a sense of permanence emphasizes the insecurity of a juvenile species still irrationally afraid of the dark.
The current propensity of a growing number of people slavishly
to follow the dictates of a host of crackpot faiths is evidence
enough that unenlightened Man needs not only the heroes of
his culture, but also his gods.

As we draw the threads together to conclude this examination
of the future states of Man, we return inevitably to the arena of
mythology where we began. Science fiction *is*, to a large extent,
a dream of life to come. It may not automatically occur to the
enthusiast that the makings of eternity could exist as much *in-*

side his head as in a Cosmos which he might regard as an external entity. The history of science is no more than a tale of quickening discovery of all that constitutes our makeshift reality. The last mystery in that quest is the nature of intelligence itself; for without a mind to comprehend it, the universe is only the cloud of muck which the Stoics would have had us believe.

In his religions, as in so many of his highest endeavours, man appears to have wrought his own peculiar alchemy of creativity, ignorance and fear. Thoughtful, he seems to err, through personal insecurity, ever on the side of thoughtlessness. That so many of the futures portrayed by intelligent writers are almost unremittingly bleak is a terrible indictment of that lack of thought. In looking at the treatment of religion and myth in science fiction, we come perhaps to the darkest prognoses of all — and, paradoxically, to a means whereby sanity may at last be saved.

Few stories in science fiction have as their central theme one of the world's great historical religions; but among those that do are included some of the outstanding works in the genre. It hardly seems a coincidence that the majority of them are devoted to aspects of the Church of Rome. In a short and memorable tale, which takes the form of a rumination by a Jesuit astrophysicist in deep space, Arthur C. Clarke has told in 'The Star' (1955) of a manned expedition to the system of a white dwarf star that has flared as a supernova in its moderately recent past. All inner planets in the system were naturally demolished in the holocaust which reduced the star itself to a fraction of its former size; but the explorers find, orbiting at a vast distance, the shrivelled shell of the outermost planet. Amazingly, this burnt-out world is still emitting intelligent radio signals. When the expedition lands, it discovers in an underground museum the records of an advanced civilization that died with the destruction of its inner-planetary home. It was a race which had mastered the technique of space-flight within its own solar system, but had never acquired the ability to travel faster than light. Knowing that there was no escape from Armageddon once their sun showed signs of instability, this people spent the remainder of their time in establishing a Herculaneum on the remotest planet in their system and leaving there a radio beacon to identify it throughout the millennia to come.

As the human team begin their return journey, the Jesuit addresses his thoughts to the portrait of St. Ignatius Loyola adorning his personal quarters and speculates on the nature of a species who, under sentence of death, were prepared to cross space again and again to bequeath to a posterity they would never know the finest examples of their culture. They were a disturbingly humanlike race, with a warmth and beauty which had probably raised their society to a level higher than Man's. But they did not fade and die like other civilizations in the galaxy, the ruins of which Man has also found. They were obliterated even as they enjoyed the full awakening of their greatness. How, asks the priest, 'could that be reconciled with the mercy of God?'

He knows well enough the answer of his fellow crew-members to that question: a hundred suns explode in the Milky Way each year, taking numerous intelligent species with them. It is of little consequence whether those races were predominantly evil or good in a universe which exists without plan.

On the other hand, the Jesuit argues, there is no reason why God should justify His actions to humanity — to suggest as much is akin to blasphemy. But the circumstances of this particular cosmic extinction have left him wavering at the limits of his faith. When the expedition arrived in the region of the white dwarf, he had no means of knowing exactly when the supernova occurred. A study of the rocks on the last remaining planet, however, has enabled him to calculate the precise date:

' "... I know in what year the light of this colossal conflagration reached our Earth. I know how brilliantly the supernova whose corpse now dwindles behind our speeding ship once shone in terrestrial skies. I know how it must have blazed low in the east before sunrise, like a beacon in that oriental dawn.

There can be no reasonable doubt: the ancient mystery is solved at last. Yet, oh God, there were so many stars you could have used. What was the need to give these people to the fire, that the symbol of their passing might shine above Bethlehem?" '

James Blish's *A Case of Conscience* is, as we noted in the preceding chapter, a novel with marked religious overtones. In one respect at least it bears a common factor with Clarke's story — a member of the United Nations survey team that happens upon an ecological paradise is also a Jesuit priest. The planet 'Lithia', some fifty light years from earth, boasts an idyllic environment which is additionally a natural repository for the most lethal radioactive mineral yet uncovered by Man. But it is the nature of the planet's highest life-form which concerns the Jesuit father. The purpose of the survey is to report to the UN on the desirability of trading with, and possibly colonizing, Lithia. The priest's final recommendation is that the planet should be sealed off from earth for ever!

In his explanation Father Ruiz-Sanchez emphasizes the fact that Lithia's reptilian civilization follows naturally, and without guidance, the highest system of ethical behaviour which has ever been conceived on earth. In fact, the Lithians are able to live with no difficulty, *and without a single deviate*, by a code which the best of humanity can only struggle to obey. The code, in the eyes of Ruiz-Sanchez, is obviously that of Christianity as interpreted by the Roman Catholic Church. But the chances of two identical systems of ethics evolving on such dissimilar worlds as earth and Lithia are, he maintains, truly astronomical. Even more extraordinary, all the evidence suggests that the Lithian concept of ethics *never has evolved*; it was simply there in the first place. The Lithians have accepted a series of propositions, such as the equality of all individuals, without having attempted a serious analysis of any of them. They are, apparently, a race without a conscience. This, and the Lithians' complete indifference to the idea of a Creator, arouse the Jesuit's profound suspicions. The whole planet and its culture can only be an immense diabolical trap. Consider the premises:

' "... *One*: Reason is always a sufficient guide. *Two*: The self-evident is always the real. *Three*: Good works are an end in themselves. *Four*: Faith is irrelevant to right action. *Five*: Right action can exist without love. *Six*: Peace need not pass understanding. *Seven*: Ethics can exist without evil alternatives. *Eight*: Morals can exist without conscience. *Nine*: Goodness can exist without God. *Ten* — but do I really need to go on? We have heard all these propositions before, and we know What proposes them." '

However, to accept that it is all a trap, one must grant the Devil the ability to be creative — a process which Ruiz-Sanchez is painfully aware amounts to the heresy of Manichaeism. In the event the UN decides to delay any recognition of Lithia pending a further investigation. Only when a young Lithian, brought to earth by the original survey ship, reaches maturity and begins to incite insurrection in Man's overpopulated underground cities, is Ruiz-Sanchez persuaded to act. Unofficially excommunicated because of his heresy, he is nevertheless told by his Pope that there is still a way open to him for salvation. This is the ancient ritual of exorcism, a practice which the Jesuit had assumed to be long discarded by his Church.

While he is agonizing over the outcome of his decision, another member of the survey team has returned to Lithia to construct a plant for the extraction of the deadly mineral. Since the process he intends to employ is derived entirely from theory, there is a real danger that it could lead to an uncontrollable chain-reaction. The starship which carries the final items of equipment he needs also brings back as a stowaway the Lithian who has precipitated widespread riots on earth. As Ruiz-Sanchez, resigned to the consequences of his choice, pronounces Pope Gregory VIII's chilling words of exorcism, the feared chain-reaction actually begins and Lithia is destroyed. It is left to the reader to speculate whether the cataclysm is as much a case of coincidence as it is of conscience.

These stories by Clarke and Blish are striking examples of how two practised science fiction writers, neither of whom is a committed Christian, have applied their skills in the handling of a religious subject within the confines of their accustomed medium. In contrast, and apparently unique in the genre, are three books by a Christian writer who elected to employ science fiction as one means by which to propagate the Christian concepts of good and evil in the twentieth century. C.S. Lewis's trilogy, *Out of the Silent Planet* (1938), *Perelandra* (1943) and *That Hideous Strength* (1945) have a curiosity value which probably exceeds their real effectiveness as examples of speculative writing. In the opening novel, two humans journey to Mars using a sphere very reminiscent of Cavor's in Wells's *The First Men in the Moon*. Mars, or 'Malacandra' as Lewis chooses to call it, is peacefully inhabited by three intelligent races who between them constitute the planet's intellectuals, its aesthetes and its artisans. They are ruled by a good spirit, 'Oyarsa', with the help of the 'eldila', a benevolent collection of lesser spirit beings. Earth, according to Oyarsa, has been in quarantine since the war in heaven expelled Satan, 'the Bent One', and imprisoned him as the evil overseer of mankind. However, by their flight to Mars, the earthmen have shattered the divinely-imposed protective barrier; all Hell is now, literally, about to break loose.

The first manifestation of the Bent One's new-found freedom

occurs on 'Perelandra' (Venus), a planet at the 'Garden of Eden' stage of its development. Satan inveigles himself into the body of one of the original human space-travellers and attempts to re-enact the scene of the Fall with the Venusian counterparts of Adam and Eve. The timely intervention of Oyarsa foils him in his genuinely fiendish intentions; and the archetypal beings of Perelandra are left with their candyfloss paradise intact.

The scenery shifts finally to earth for a grand confrontation in *That Hideous Strength* which lacks only a bout of unarmed combat on the brink of the Reichenbach Falls to complete the high drama. The forces of good elicit the assistance of a rein-carnated Arthurian knight, a lady clairvoyant, Merlin (the old wizard himself) and — for *good* measure — a bear, to bring about the downfall of the National Institute for Co-ordinated Ex-periments. This organization, run by scientists and technocrats, aims to convert humanity into a model of behavioural engi-neering and to cover the world with concrete — a familiar anti-utopian pastime. Man, as a member of the Institute sees it, must learn to take control of himself, implying that *some* men must rise to take control of the remainder. It will not, after all, require that much effort:

> ' "Quite simple and obvious things, at first — sterilization of the unfit, liquidation of backward races (we don't want any dead weights), selective breeding. Then real education, in-cluding pre-natal education. By real education I mean one that has no 'take-it-or-leave-it' nonsense. A real education makes the patient what it wants infallibly; whatever he or his parents try to do about it. Of course, it'll have to be mainly psychological 'at first. But we'll get on to bio-chemical conditioning in the end and direct manipulation of the brain..." '

That Hideous Strength is an obvious and, compared with many of the anti-utopian works we have considered in this study, a curiously naive attack on the Wellsian vision of progress. (It is also a highly personal attack on Wells himself, who appears in the guise of Horace Jules — the figurehead of the Institute — 'a very little man, whose legs were so short that he had been un-kindly compared with a duck'.) The high point of the story comes during a ceremonial dinner at the Institute when Jules lapses into a spate of the kind of nonsensical verbiage which Wells invented thirty years before to characterize the lack of

188

erudition in Mr Polly. A free-for-all ensues in which Jules and other leading lights of the Institute are killed. Virtue has triumphed again.

Although it was the antithesis of its purpose, Lewis's trilogy is an effective argument against any attempt to explain the nature of good and evil in a black-and-white Christian context. The perfect world he creates on Malacandra is, like many other fictionalized utopias, a place where the most placid specimen of *Homo sapiens* would probably die of implacable boredom. The evil men of the National Institute for Co-ordinated Experiments appear to the discerning mind as little better than a gang of cardboard refugees from a melodrama by Harriet Beecher Stowe. How different is the thoroughly convincing Satanic conflict pictured in James Blish's *Black Easter* (1967), at the end of which the Devil actually wins: although it would only be by the most tenuous reasoning that the book could be described as science fiction. Nevertheless, Lewis has, in a particular sense, performed a service to the student of human nature by highlighting the practical impossibility of a completely good or completely evil *man*. They are beings which might be imagined in outline, but they defy definition in detail. Even the perfect attributes ascribed to their respective messiahs by the followers of humanity's established religions bear but a semblance of their real nature as disclosed in the most authentic accounts of their lives.

It can also be held as a mark of failure against almost every religious writer, of any faith, that they have been unable to conceive a convincing portrait of the Creator. Admittedly, the only science fiction author seriously to venture into this forbidding region is Olaf Stapledon. In what he modestly described as 'a more remote and philosophical work than *Last and First Men*', he produced in *The Star Maker* (1937) a narrative which amounts to a comprehensive history of the universe! The 2,000 million years of human endeavour which he detailed in the former book are as an aside in the mind-stretching vistas of *The Star Maker*. In it he relates the rise and fall of interstellar empires which were to influence Asimov, among many others, in the succeeding generations of imaginative writers. But Stapledon was hardly prepared to leave it at that. As understanding lightens the fastnesses of the galaxies, the stars themselves are revealed as centres of intelligence, an intriguing speculation which Arthur C. Clarke was to appropriate for his short story 'Out of the Sun'.

189

However, in Stapledon's vision the stars are merely the offspring of parental nebulae, which in their own turn are the wraithlike children of the Cosmic progenitor, a sun of such burning magnificence as to render it unapproachable. This indeed is the eponymous Star Maker, an entity which exists purely to create. The Universe as we know it proves no more than a juvenile effort, spawned while this Leviathan was learning to exercise its power. It will, we are assured, improve in its subsequent performances. Meanwhile, the sentient stars, reconciled to planetary inhabitants whom they initially regarded as parasites, join in the formation of a cosmic mind which one would guess was the source of inspiration for Clarke's Overmind in *Childhood's End*.

Stapledon's essential message in *The Star Maker* is the expression of the relatively straightforward concept of an evolutionary process of growing intelligence which functions independently of a remote creative force. It has been a common enough conclusion among many of the rational thinkers throughout human history, and a useful indication that real intelligence is perfectly capable of assessing its own relevance in space and time. It is, of course, the outcome of *reason* in preference to *belief*; and as such it is in fundamental opposition to the conventional religious outlook which envisages a Creator who is also the fountainhead of all knowledge and thought.

*****

In a collection of essays published under the title *Fact and Faith* in 1934, J.B.S. Haldane recalled the common outbreaks of *Bacillus prodigiosus* which occurred in many parts of Europe during the Middle Ages. This humble organism was spread readily by human contact and infected bread in an interesting way, inasmuch as it produced red patches which could easily be mistaken for bloodstains. In all probability, this odd characteristic was the true culprit behind the miraculous 'bleeding host' which converted Pope Urban the Fourth to the views on transubstantiation expounded by St. Thomas Aquinas. When it confined its manifestations to consecrated bread in churches, *Bacillus prodigiosus* was piously accepted as a genuine blessing in disguise. Unfortunately, as befitted its nature, it appeared with equal regularity on loaves in people's homes. On such occasions the family concerned was usually accused of having stolen a host so that it could be pierced with daggers — an act of deicide associated with black magic. There followed the familiar extraction of confessions under torture, after which the hapless innocents were generally burned alive. The appearance of the bacillus in the right quarters also proved a useful excuse for regular pogroms of the Jews.

There are few better factual illustrations than the case of *Bacillus prodigiosus* to show how a grandiose piece of mythology can effectively be explained away by science. In a similar manner, science fiction writers have frequently taken an existing superstition, or an invented one, and illuminated it with a scientific explanation — witness Clarke's depiction of the Overlords in *Childhood's End* in the commonly-accepted image of the Devil. Richard Matheson has provided an imaginative example of the ploy in *I am Legend* (1954), describing the infection of humans by a bacillus which converts them into vampires. Among others, James Blish and Anthony Boucher have performed a comparable service on behalf of werewolves; Boucher's lycanthropic character is eventually recruited by the FBI — possibly the only organization that would have cared to accept him as a member.

In an early story, 'Nightfall' (1941), Isaac Asimov embarked on a prolific literary career by describing an extra-terrestrial race which has rarely in its history seen the stars — other than its own *two* suns. The reason for this ignorance of the night sky lies in the fact that the positions of the twin suns ensure that the planet *has no night*. Only once in a millennium are the convolutions of its system such that a complete eclipse can occur. Consequently a religion has evolved which teaches that if ever darkness descends the spirits of the gods will materialize in awful glory to plunge the world into an all-consuming madness marking the end of civilization. When scientists actually predict the imminence of an eclipse, a culture which has accepted some aspects of science and technology, but which remains uninformed of the true nature of the universe, reacts characteristically to what it thinks is the approaching end of the world. As mass hysteria mounts, the men of science attempt to hold to their rational conclusion that whatever is about to happen invites a logical explanation. But the myths of their heritage defeat them at the last. Their solar system, unlike Man's, is situated in the dense heart of a galaxy; when the stars (or spirits) do appear, their appalling brilliance and multiplicity are enough to unhinge the most resolute of inquiring minds.

Pursuing an alternative aspect of religious myth, Roger Zelazny portrayed in 'A Rose for Ecclesiastes' (1963) a Martian ecology where unusual solar storms have sterilized the entire male population. When earthmen first arrive on the planet, the disaster has already become an accepted part of Martian history; it is only because the natural inhabitants enjoy a life-span of several hundred years that there are still any Martians extant to greet the visitors. The human assigned the task of studying the planet's society and communicating with its residual members is one of earth's leading poets. Having learnt the ancient Martian language, he discovers that its principal religious script, 'the Book of Locar', is remarkably similar in spirit to Ecclesiastes. The followers of Locar have adopted the same heightened sense of pessimism which the biblical work expresses — an appropriate outlook in view of the fate about to overtake Mars.

However, when he succeeds in impregnating a Martian girl, the poet realizes that the alien race may still be partially preserved, but only if it can be persuaded to abandon its attitude of profound hopelessness. In an effort to convince the Martians that all is not lost he reads them Ecclesiastes which, he explains, was written by one of humanity's Locars. Surely they must see that mankind has gone on, despite 'one man's condemning all of life in the highest poetry...'.

 ' "...we have crossed millions of miles of nothingness. We have visited another world. And our Locar has said, 'Why bother? What is the worth of it? It is all vanity, anyhow.' "And the secret is ... he was right! It *is* vanity; it *is* pride! It is the hubris of rationalism to always attack the prophet, the mystic, the god. It is our blasphemy which has made us great, and will sustain us, and which the gods secretly admire in us..." '

The Martians, who regard the poet as a holy man, are finally convinced; and as a token of the new life granted their race he leaves them a rose which has been grown experimentally on board the spaceship. No flower has ever bloomed before on Mars.

Some myths, then, may be explained away scientifically; while others can be shown rationally to be untrue. In demonstrating the latter process, Wells aspired to a level of sustained ironical imagery in 'The Country of the Blind' (1904) which identifies it as the finest of his many short stories. It tells of the efforts of a seeing man to establish his authority in a hidden South American valley where the inhabitants have been sightless for generations. 'In the Country of the Blind', runs the old adage, 'the one-eyed Man is King.' On the contrary, Wells shows that even a two-eyed intruder into this closed environment is regarded as simply deranged:

> ' "Why did you not come when I called you?" said the blind man. "Must you be led like a child? Cannot you hear the path as you walk?"
> Nunez laughed. "I can see it", he said.
> "There is no such word as *see*", said the blind man, after a pause. "Cease this folly, and follow the sound of my feet." '

As a reflection on human nature, the reaction of the blind people to the stranger in their midst is more thoroughly dispiriting than that of the 'normal' beings to van Vogt's mutants in *Slan*. In that situation, at least, the newcomers were regarded with hostility because their superior senses were *recognized*.

*****

As we have earlier suggested, the most certain breeding ground in science fiction for the fiercest expositions of myths and religious dogma is the post-catastrophe world. In *Ape and Essence* (1946), Aldous Huxley pictured a globe suffering the aftermath of a war in which both nuclear and bacteriological devices have been used. For the most part, the remnants of humanity have reverted to a savage state. Children born with more than minor deformities are sacrificed to the Devil who, in the circumstances, has proved a more relevant supernumerary than God. Books are burnt to provide heat for cooking and — perhaps the most significant evidence of Man's relapse into his animal past — sexual relations take place exclusively during a brief mating season. In like fashion, John Wyndham developed a post-catastrophe society in *The Chrysalids* (1955 — first published as *Re-Birth*), where mutant children suffer a similar fate. Both novels, in effect, are again emphasizing the hideous aspects of a human society which elects to exist by the dictates of conformity, particularly when the more humanizing elements in the culture have been swept away. If anything, the night-

193

marish quality is heightened in Edmund Cooper's *All Fools' Day*, where bands of rapacious monks, self-styled 'Brothers of Iniquity', scour the countryside in a murderous parody of their more altruistic predecessors.

Envisaging a less common variety of catastrophe, Brian Aldiss has written in *Barefoot in the Head* (1969) an account of western civilization floundering in a state of universal hallucination. As a result of an attack by a Middle East country using hallucinogenic gases, the entire population of Europe systematically 'blows its mind'. While governments struggle to maintain some measure of control, the patterns of commercial and industrial activity change rapidly in the light of mass inconsistencies among consumers and workers; for the gas has a lasting effect, to the extent that distortions in an individual's appreciation of reality recur indefinitely. Out of this mêlée emerges a messiah of sorts — a saviour of acid-heads whose dogma is speed and whose ritual psychedelic trappings are rock music and fast cars. In his paradise of drop-outs, however, there is really no greater concern for human life than in any other post-catastrophe environment. The message is in the moving, a dedication to fast travelling which recalls Jack Kerouac's *On the Road*. Whom should it concern if only the dead on the motorways remain to record the procession's wake?

Unquestionably one of the most imaginative portrayals in the genre of a post-catastrophe world is *A Canticle for Leibowitz* (1959) by Walter M. Miller, Jnr. The novel opens some six hundred years after a global nuclear war; and it traces the history of the monks of the Albertian Order of Leibowitz. The founder of the order, a scientist at the time of 'the Flame Deluge', obtained permission from 'New Rome' to establish an abbey where any surviving records of scientific knowledge could be preserved. Shortly afterwards he was martyred in what came to be known as 'the Simplification', a period when the few remaining intellectuals and men of learning were strung up or burned by mobs who blamed them for the calamity which had overcome Man. Many of the records which Leibowitz had painstakingly gathered were also destroyed; but those which still existed were lovingly copied by generations of monks who had no idea of their meaning. Six hundred years after the Flame Deluge, a novice discovers the ruins of a fall-out shelter which appear to contain further relics of the Blessed Founder, among them a blueprint of a printed circuit that the novice transforms into a magnificently illuminated scroll. Partly as a result of the discovery, Leibowitz is subsequently canonized; and the former novice is killed by mutants on a journey back from New Rome where he has been received by the Pope. The wasted countryside is, undeniably, a hazardous place to cross; both human and animal mutants compete viciously in its wilderness for anything which might constitute food. Only in the fortified monasteries does anything resembling education prevail.

A further six hundred years on, kingdoms have arisen and warrior chiefs vie with each other for supremacy. Marauding parties make travel as dangerous as ever; but in the Order of St. Leibowitz a handful of monks have succeeded in unravelling at least one mystery from the ancient relics — they are about to re-create electric light:

'Axles creaked and groaned. The wagon-wheel dynamo began to spin, its low whir becoming a moan and then a whine as the monks strained and grunted at the drive-mill. The guardian of the dynamo watched anxiously as the spokes blurred with speed and became a film. '*Vespere occaso*', he began, then paused to lick two fingers and touch them to the contacts. A spark snapped.

...The monk on the ladder struck the arc. A sharp spffft! — and blinding light flooded the vaults with a brilliance that had not been seen in twelve centuries.'

The scene shifts forwards again, to the year AD 3781; and the result is only too familiar. The world is on the brink of its second nuclear war. But on this occasion the Church is prepared. Having fostered, and participated in, the rediscovery of science, it possesses its own spaceship which is held in constant readiness to take the Order of Leibowitz to the diminutive human colony in Alpha Centauri. As the new Flame Deluge descends, the ship thrusts heavenwards, carrying the tragic message of Man's second rise and fall to the stars.

In so brief an outline of the novel, it is impossible fully to convey the symbolic quality of Miller's achievement. Throughout the twelve hundred years covered by the narrative, for instance, the same ancient beggar constantly crosses the scene. At first he is mistaken for the Blessed Leibowitz himself; and in the final section of the work he is suspected of being Lazarus — the man raised from the dead by Jesus who must wander the earth eternally until he can identify Him at the Second Coming.

Also in the final section, where mutants are still much in evidence, a two-headed tomato seller appears. She is Mrs Grales, a curmudgeonly old lady who had a second head of youthful and innocent appearance growing out of one of her shoulders. She calls it Rachel, and frequently pesters the priests at the abbey with requests for its baptism. Since the Rachel head seems permanently asleep, the holy fathers refuse to recognize it as a separate being. However, as the horizon lights in a nuclear corona, Rachel begins to awake. At the same time the head of Mrs Grales enters its death throes, but not before suggesting that it is not only Man who should demand forgiveness:

> 'She leaned close to whisper behind her hand. "I need be giving shriv'ness to Him, as well."
> The priest recoiled slightly. "To whom? I don't understand."
> "Shriv'ness — to Him who made me as I am", she whimpered. But then a slow smile spread her mouth. "I — I never forgave Him for it."
> "Forgive God? How can you —? He is just. He is Justice, He is Love. How can you say —?"
> Her eyes pleaded with him. "Mayn't an old tumater woman forgive Him just a little for His Justice? Afor I be asking His shriv'ness on me?" '

(In a less dramatic vein Robert Frost once summed up the same, all too human reaction: 'O Lord, forgive my little jokes on Thee/And I'll forgive your one great joke on me.') As the remaining priest lies trapped and dying under the rubble of his abbey, Rachel — the unspeaking reincarnation of innocence in a dying world — administers him the last rites of his faith.

It would be an act of omission to exclude from any appraisal of the religious elements in science fiction the work of probably the most humanitarian writer in the genre — Kurt Vonnegut. His *Cat's Cradle* (1963) qualifies only partly as a post-catastrophe story, since the majority of the action occurs in advance of the ultimate disaster. Regardless of that, it ignites fuses in the imagination which place it firmly among the apocalyptic works we are considering here. To a Caribbean isle run by a Haitian-style dictator come a curious assortment of people, each with a common object. They are seeking the son of the deceased discoverer of *ice-nine* who, some time after his father's death, is reputed to have risen to the position of Minister of Science and Progress on the island.

196

Ice-nine is a form of water in which the molecular structure has been so changed as to convert it to a solid. It has one further, thoroughly alarming, property: whenever it comes into contact with normal water, regardless of quantity, it transforms the entire mass *simultaneously* into a further extension of itself. So far, the only samples of *ice-nine* held in individual hands are contained in sealed phials belonging to the inventor's three children. It is the suspicion that the eldest son may have given his specimen to the barbarous ruler of San Lorenzo which brings the visitors to the island.

Among its other curiosities, San Lorenzo enjoys a local religion answering to the name of 'Bokononism'. The fact that, as a form of worship, it has been outlawed by the dictator, who has also put a price on the head of his former friend, the prophet Bokonon, rarely deters the islanders from practising it. For a religion, Bokononism is a curiously honest deception; it is admitted at the beginning of the first *Book of Bokonon* that the whole concoction is founded on lies. Live by the *harmless untruths*, the prophet exhorts his followers, which will make a man healthy and happy, and also brave and kind. In many respects, Bokononism is a homely derivative of the harsh but realistic doctrine of 'God the Utterly Indifferent' in Vonnegut's *The Sirens of Titan*. In accordance with its Caribbean surroundings, it is frequently expounded by way of the calypso:

'Someday, someday, this crazy world will have to end,
And our God will take things back that He to us did lend.
And if, on that sad day, you want to scold our God,
Why go right ahead and scold him. He'll just smile and nod.'

At the climax of the tale the dictator of San Lorenzo, who is dying of cancer, commits suicide by touching a crystal of *ice-nine* to his tongue, immediately solidifying the water content of his body. There follows a series of macabre accidents which culminates in his rigid corpse being tipped inadvertently into the ocean. The catastrophe is all-embracing. In a spectacular chain reaction all the seas of earth turn to *ice-nine*, not to mention the rivers which flow into them, and the moist land that feeds their streams. An eternal blue-white frost descends over the home of mankind — and over most of its children. The narrator, who has begun to write a history of the cataclysm, comes upon a valley in the island strewn with thousands of bodies of the followers of Bokonon. The prophet, who is conspicuous by his absence, has left a note saying that he had been summoned by the people to explain what God now expected of them. He told them that God had clearly had enough of them, and that they 'should have the good manners to die'. This they have done, by rubbing their fingers on the frosted ground and putting them to their lips.

With his manuscript nearly completed, the narrator heads for San Lorenzo's only mountain — which has never yet been scaled — still undecided as to what he should do when he has reached its peak. On the way he encounters the banished prophet for the first, and last, time. The old man has just written the final sentence to *The Books of Bokonon*:

> 'If I were a younger man, I would write a history of human stupidity; and I would climb to the top of Mount McCabe and lie down on my back with my history for a pillow; and I would take from the ground some of the blue-white poison which makes statues of men; and I would make a statue of myself, lying on my back, grinning horribly, and thumbing my nose at You Know Who.'

*****

The main purpose of this study, as its subtitle indicates, has been to examine the social implications, whether intended or accidental, of those science fiction stories which can be deemed of serious content — and to draw what lessons we will. To that end we have covered a deal of ground — enough, it is hoped, to provide a stimulating view of a unique facet of modern writing. If it has not been entirely a comforting experience, that is a good enough reflection on the nature of the material under study. It would be a merry fellow who, having gained acquaintance with the proportionately few works we have considered here, could again regard with absolute equanimity — had he done so before — the regular pronouncements of politicians on economic growth, multi-targetted nuclear missiles, the limits of bureaucracy, the problems of racial integration, or the likelihood of at least *one* country on this miniscule globe actually meeting *to the letter* the Universal Declaration of Human Rights to which most were signatories in the United Nations assembly of 1948.

In short, we have been studying the outpourings of realists who have seen little of comfort ahead. That the majority of them are not *overwhelmingly* pessimistic could be interpreted facilely as a manifestation of one more incalculable quirk in human nature. Above reason, hope — in the last eventuality — usually prevails.

The final myths we shall consider in science fiction are, symptomatically, the *new* myths — the escape routes from a dark region into worlds of mystery and light — the creation inside Man's head of the counterbalance to despair. In another of his archetypal tales, H.G. Wells wrote in 'The Door in the Wall' (1906) of a rising politician haunted by the memory of a childhood experience, either imagined or real. He recalls seeing somewhere in Kensington a white door in a street wall through which he passed into a fantastic land of wonderment. After returning to the everyday world, he fails in all his future attempts to rediscover the door, no matter how many streets and alleys he scours. On one or two occasions during his adult life he catches glimpses of it in situations where he cannot stop to investigate. Despite — or perhaps because of — his increasing governmental responsibilities, the search for the door becomes a growing obsession. Finally he is discovered dead, having walked through a door in a hoarding above a shaft which has been sunk in the vicinity of East Kensington underground station. His friend, who has recounted the story, can only guess at the reason:

'... You may think me superstitious, if you will, and foolish; but, indeed, I am more than half convinced that he had, in truth, an abnormal gift, and a sense, something — I know not what — that in the guise of wall and door offered him an outlet, a secret and peculiar passage of escape into another and altogether more beautiful world.... We see our world fair and common, the hoarding and the pit. By our daylight standard he walked out of security into darkness, danger, and death.

But did he see like that?'

The creation of entirely mythical lands belongs more often to the realm of fantasy than to that of science fiction. J.R.R. Tolkien's trilogy, *The Fellowship of the Ring* (1954—55), preceded by *The Hobbit* (1937), is a case in point. Tolkien's immensely popular accounts of the inhabitants of 'Middle Earth', an intriguing fairytale blend of Anglo-Saxon and Nordic mythology, bear occasional Wagnerian echoes of the heroic

199

Nibelungian traumas so dear to the central myths of the Nazis. A similar element of magic obtaining to precious objects can be found in Samuel R. Delany's *The Jewels of Aptor* (1961) and, more scientifically, in Philip José Farmer's trilogy, *Maker of Universes, The Gates of Creation* and *A Private Cosmos* (1965–67). Farmer tells of an individual universe created by men who have truly acquired the appurtenances of the gods, and who are suspiciously reminiscent of the 'Thetan' spirit beings around whom the extraordinary cult of Scientology – founded by a former science fiction writer, Ron Hubbard – is based. In Farmer's cosmos, where many of the cultures of human history and mythology have been recreated to exist simultaneously in a multi-tiered flat-bottomed world, the 'men like gods' frequently behave with the same disdain for the suffering of their creations that stigmatized the odd motley of incarnations who lolled about the peak of Olympus.

In such a context it is easy to see how the most eruptive force to convulse recent human history could have readily come from the pen of a speculative writer. Although it may seem paradoxical, and predictably distasteful, Adolf Hitler could well emerge in retrospect as the most 'god-like' being of the twentieth century. That he was worshipped by a large section of the Germanic peoples, as Stalin rarely was by the Russians, identifies him as the more charismatic of the two. He also behaved with an utter contempt for human life entirely in keeping with the gods of yore; and in his fall he brought the holocaust – a familiar promise of the gods – upon his supporters and opponents alike.

Had it not happened in reality, the almost mystical, and absolutely irrational, appeal of the Nazi ideology which stimulated a substantial part of the collective human *id* – not only in Europe, but in most continents on earth – could be laughed off as a product of the wilder imaginings of Zamyatin, Aldous Huxley or Wells. The similarity becomes progressively more eerie when we consider the emphasis placed in the genre on the fight of the individual, only to find in *Mein Kampf* – most of which approximates to a piece of fifth-rate science fantasy – the following complementary views:

> 'From millions of men ... *one* man must step forward, who with apoditic force will form granite principles from the wavering idea-world of the broad masses and take up the

struggle for their sole correctness....

...At long intervals in human history it may occasionally happen that the politician is wedded to the theoretician. The more profound this fusion, the greater are the obstacles opposing the work of the politician. He no longer works for necessities which will be understood by the first good shop-keeper, but for aims which only the fewest comprehend.'

In the end, however, the heroic quality of the quest for understanding in the human future may provide an answer in itself. To journey hopefully may indeed prove infinitely better than to arrive. In John Brunner's 'Earth is but a Star' (1958) (the title is another quotation from Flecker's 'Golden Road to Samarkand'), a straggling band of characters wander in a lonely and dangerous search across a dreamlike world. The intended parallel with Flecker's pilgrims is too close to be ignored:

'We are the Pilgrims, master; we shall go
Always a little further; it may be
Beyond that last blue mountain barred with snow
Across that angry or that glimmering sea,
White on a throne or guarded in a cave
There lives a prophet who can understand
Why men were born: but surely we are brave,
Who take the Golden Road to Samarkand.'

More remotely still, Samuel R. Delany has conjured in *The Einstein Intersection* (1967) the collision in the far future of an alien galaxy with the Milky Way. As a result, a race of semi-mystical extra-terrestrials find themselves the inheritors of an earth Man has already left. Almost intuitively they attempt to act out the human myths which still lie heavy upon the deserted globe, perceiving as they go a subtle quality of change:

' "...We have taken over their abandoned world, and some-thing new is happening to the fragments, something we can't even define with mankind's leftover vocabulary. You must take its importance exactly as that: it is indefinable: you are involved in it....

"As we are able to retain more and more of our past, it takes us longer and longer to become old; ... everything changes. The labyrinth today does not follow the same path it did at Knossos fifty thousand years ago. You may be Orpheus: you may be someone else, who dares death and succeeds." '

Beyond this, and as a last reminder of the probable insignificance of mankind in the overall Cosmic design, Arthur C. Clarke has recorded in 'History Lesson' (1949) an example of what could be the final myth of man. From the future reptilian civilization of Venus come envoys who find the earth sterilized by its yet most encompassing Ice Age. During their stay they excavate a cache containing what they believe is evidence of the highest human culture attained before the curtain was lowered upon mankind. One of the finds, a reel of cine film, occupies the attention of the Venusians to the practical exclusion of all else — for it depicts the actions of an arrogantly bad-tempered biped which they take to be the typical image of man:

> 'For the rest of time it would symbolize the human race. The psychologists of Venus would analyze its actions and watch its every movement until they could reconstruct its mind. Thousands of books would be written about it. Intricate philosophies would be contrived to account for its behaviour.
> But all this labour, all this research, would be utterly in vain. Perhaps the proud and lonely figure on the screen was smiling sardonically at the scientists who were starting on their age-long fruitless quest?'

Millions of times the film will be shown, and its final words blink upon alien screens. But the Venusians, and the galactic races to follow them, will never comprehend the significance of the real translation of those hieroglyphs: 'A Walt Disney Production'. The short but agonizing passion of humanity will be judged throughout eternity by the irascible contortions of Donald Duck.

If, as many science fiction writers appear to believe, the world can only become darker, then the escapes into dreamland which they have so effectively portrayed could indeed be a mythological experience, and as therapeutic as those by which ancient Man was able to identify himself with the gods in an effort to alleviate his pain. And if to be 'god-like' is a genuine dream of human purpose, who is to deny that there is anything untoward in our seeking that experience inside our heads, rather than on the grey proscenium which the Cosmic process seems to have fashioned for us?

For those who wish to be brave in reality, there will be room in the future to pursue the struggle, even if — as much science fiction suggests — it may be a contest they can never win. Another part of the destiny of Man is to know that he will someday end — both as an individual and as a race. It is arguable whether in the limitless realm of imagined existence, as much in regard to the Tasmanians as to the Tralfamadorians, there is much importance where those respective endings lie. The illusion will finish only when the last man has ceased to dream.

THE END

Great hail! we cry to the comers
    From the dazzling unknown shore;
Bring us hither your sun and summers,
    And renew our world as of yore;
You shall teach us your song's new numbers,
    And things that we dreamed not before:
Yea, in spite of a dreamer who slumbers,
    And a singer who sings no more.

Arthur O'Shaughnessy, 'The Music Makers'

A select Bibliography of Books dealing with Science Fiction

Aldiss, B.W. *Billion Year Spree: The History of Science Fiction,* New York and London, 1973.

Amis, Kingsley *New Maps of Hell,* New York, 1960; London, 1961.

Atheling, William, Jnr. (James Blish) *The Issue at Hand: Studies in Contemporary Magazine Science Fiction,* Chicago, 1964. *More Issues at Hand: Critical Studies in Contemporary Science Fiction,* Chicago, 1970.

Bailey, J.O. *Pilgrims Through Space and Time: Trends and Patterns in Scientific and Utopian Fiction,* New York, 1947.

Bretnor, Reginald (ed.) *Modern Science Fiction: Its Meaning and its Future,* New York, 1953.

Clarke, I.F. *The Tale of the Future: From the Beginning to the Present Day: A Check-List,* London, 1961.

Davenport, Basil (ed.) *The Science Fiction Novel: Imagination and Social Criticism,* Chicago, 1964.

De Camp, L.S. *Science Fiction Handbook,* New York, 1953.

Franklin, H.B. *Future Perfect: American Science Fiction of the Nineteenth Century,* New York, 1966.

Green, R.L. *Into Other Worlds: Space Flight in Fiction, from Lucian to Lewis,* London, 1957; New York, 1958.

Hillegas, M.R. *The Future as Nightmare: H.G. Wells and the Anti-Utopians,* New York and London, 1967.

Knight, Damon *In Search of Wonder: Essays on Modern Science Fiction,* Chicago, 1956 (revised 1967).

Lundwall, S.J., Jnr. *Science Fiction: What It's All About,* New York, 1971 (first published in a shorter version in Sweden in

1969 under the title *Science Fiction — Från begynnelsen till våra dagar*).

Moskowitz, Sam *Explorers of the Infinite: Shapers of Science Fiction*, Cleveland, 1963.

Seekers of Tomorrow: Masters of Modern Science Fiction, Cleveland, 1966; New York, 1967.

Nicolson, Marjorie H. *Voyages to the Moon*, New York, 1948.

Pizor, Faith K. and Comp, T.A. *'The Man in the Moone': An anthology of antique science fiction and fantasy*, New York and London, 1971.

Rose, Lois and Stephen *The Shattered Ring: Science Fiction and the Quest for Meaning*, New York and London, 1970.

Walsh, Chad *From Utopia to Nightmare*, New York and Evanston, 1962.

Wolheim, D.A. *The Universe Makers: Science Fiction Today*, New York, 1971.

Index